Evangelism – which way now?

An evaluation of Alpha, Emmaus, Cell church
and other contemporary strategies for evangelism

CHURCH HOUSE
PUBLISHING

Mike Booker and
Mark Ireland

Church House Publishing
Church House
Great Smith Street
London SW1P 3AZ

ISBN 978 0 7151 4235 6

Published 2003 by Church House Publishing
Second edition 2005
Second impression with corrections 2010

Typeset in Rotis by Vitaset, Paddock Wood, Kent

Printed in England by CPI Antony Rowe, Chippenham, Wiltshire

We wish to dedicate this book to our respective wives, Gill Ireland and Liz Booker, with gratitude for their encouragement, support and patience in this project, and to all those faithful and dedicated evangelists around the country from whom we have learnt so much in the process of writing this book.

Contents

List of figures

Foreword

A parish seeking to think creatively about strategies for mission, evangelism and church growth can quickly become overwhelmed at the sheer variety of resources and models currently available.

The great gift of this book is that it grows out of Mike Booker's and Mark Ireland's experience of parish ministry, so is very much geared as a resource for parishes seeking to reflect on the right way forward for them, taking seriously their particular needs and contexts.

The authors provide a useful theological introduction to thinking about evangelism and Christian nurture and seek to take seriously both new insights and the richness of Christian tradition in providing guidance for the journey of Christian faith and opportunities for the celebration of decision and commitment.

The authors introduce readers to a highly considered and imaginative critique of a variety of catechetical tools that will be of enormous assistance for a parish planning any form of process evangelism. They also provide useful ideas about how to use episodic celebrations and more traditional mission-type services as part of an ongoing mission strategy in a particular locality.

Helpfully introducing ideas about Natural Church Development, cell church and models of emerging church, this book provides a number of pointers for future reading and exploration for those who are captivated by a particular model or insight.

The start of the Third Millennium has brought to many Christians in the established denominations a sense of disorientation and questioning about the right way to move forward in proclaiming the Good News of Jesus Christ. It has also brought with it enormous opportunities for a flexible re-working and re-imagining of what it means to be the Church at a time when many people are wanting to live lives which contain a greater richness and meaning. The challenge for the Church is to connect with such people that they may find the 'fullness of life' which is Christ's promise.

I very much hope that this book and the resources to which it points will assist parishes as they engage in the risky adventure of evangelism.

✠ David Ebor:
Archbishop of York
September 2003

Preface

This book is written out of our hard-won experience as priests leading local churches during the Decade of Evangelism, doing our best to make disciples for Christ and heal communities amidst all the usual pressures of maintaining buildings, paying our way and keeping the diocese happy. We also bring to this subject a wider perspective, drawing on our current roles teaching in a theological college and serving as a diocesan missioner. Reflecting on these two experiences, of parish ministry and wider church involvement, we have attempted to write a realistic book about evangelism which we hope will provide an honest and practical guide to the many strategies for evangelism on the market today.

Since the first edition in 2003, a number of key texts and resources have been published, including *Mission-shaped Church, Evangelism in a Spiritual Age*, Robert Warren's *The Healthy Churches' Handbook* and Ann Morisy's *Journeying Out*. There have also been a number of developments in the range of process evangelism courses. The second edition has been fully updated to take these into account.

The recent development of so many evangelism strategies and resources is a sign of health and vitality within the Church, and there is much we want to affirm. We realize, however, that our quest for realism may make us unpopular with some, who may not like to see their favoured resource critiqued or criticized. Nonetheless the purpose of this book is to help local churches make informed choices about which evangelism strategies may be most appropriate in their particular situation. The different resources on offer rarely refer to each other, and part of our role is to help the reader make connections, so that churches can plan their evangelism strategy in a joined-up way.

We have written not as detached observers but as people who are passionately committed to evangelism, who want to 'tell it as it is', giving a realistic picture of what works in evangelism in Britain today.

If there is one thing we have learnt from the Decade of Evangelism, it is that evangelism is a much longer process than we thought, and:

- There is no single answer. We have all read glossy flyers promoting some new evangelism course or strategy as if this is the answer we have all been waiting for. We have also seen the disappointment of people who have worked hard at a particular new strategy and seen little fruit. This can engender both guilt and despair. Yet just because a strategy proved very effective under God in one place does not mean it will prove effective in your very different context. We believe there are answers, but there is no single answer out there, and none of the answers are easy ones.

- There are some excellent tools to choose from. Although there is no single answer, the Decade of Evangelism has seen the development of many valuable evangelism resources and strategies, some of which have been heavily marketed whilst others deserve to become much better known. The key issue – which this book aims to address – is to know which tool is likely to be effective in which context, and how different tools can be adapted and used in conjunction with each other. Each of the early chapters introduces a particular strategy or course, critiques its strengths and weaknesses, suggests how and where it can be used most effectively, and suggests ways of using it in conjunction with other strategies and methods covered in this book. We conclude each chapter with some practical questions and some ways to explore the topic further.

- Small successes are worth celebrating. Dramatic testimonies are inspiring to listen to but are, in our experience, rare. More often the journey to faith is untidy, comprising a number of smaller and larger steps, backwards as well as forwards. Rather than let church members feel they've failed because they have not been party to any 'Damascus road' conversions, we need to affirm the stories of those who have taken the first steps in reaching out and building faith-sharing relationships with non-Christians.

- God is full of surprises. It is reassuring to remember that evangelism is not primarily a human activity – we serve a missionary God who is already at work in the world in all sorts of unexpected ways drawing people to himself. In our own experience our most fruitful evangelistic encounters have not come through our carefully planned strategies, but through responding to unexpected opportunities that God has placed in front of us – people who drift in through the door, particular events (good and bad) in the community, responding to what is going on in the working lives of church members. A strategy for evangelism is really useful, both in creating the climate of possibility and in equipping people to make the most of opportunities, but perhaps the most important thing churches need to do is to be prayerful – so that they recognize God's surprising opportunities when they come.

- Evangelism is worth it. There is no more worthwhile or fulfilling ministry than to see broken, empty or damaged lives transformed by the life and love of Jesus Christ, and to know that those lives are transformed not just for now but for all eternity. All Christians get discouraged at times, but when we are able to help someone we know make a significant step on the journey to faith it gives us a real lift and builds our own faith. In Jesus' parable of the sower, the farmer sows the seed with seemingly reckless generosity, on even the most unpromising terrain, knowing that many of the new shoots will not last. In the work of evangelism there will be disappointments along the way, but Jesus has encouraged us to go on sharing the good news with abandon, knowing that where it does bear fruit, the harvest will be out of all proportion to the seed sown.

'Some seed fell into good soil, and when it grew, it produced a hundredfold.'
(Luke 8.8)

Mark Ireland
Mike Booker
Feast of Mary Magdalene, 2005

1

Mission, evangelism and the Church of God

Mike Booker

> So in its totality, the Church is nothing less than the mission of God. God so loves that he sends Jesus. Jesus, in turn, so loves that he also sends the apostles in the same way as the Father had originally sent him ... The apostolic mission in all its fullness is the work of the church in every age.
>
> Michael Marshall

This book is about evangelism. It is written from a conviction that the Church of God is called to share in the mission of God, and that integral to that mission is the calling of people to follow Jesus.

The mission of God is, of course, wider than evangelism. In the fullest sense, mission is about being sent. God is already at work in mission through his Spirit in every life, every culture and every community. Christians – that is, those who follow Jesus Christ and his call to 'follow me' – must follow that call in all its dimensions. God's desire for restored human relationships, for social justice, for a right relationship between human beings and the created world, are all part of that mission. But this is not and cannot be the totality of the mission the Church is called to. There is also a call to make disciples, following the last command of Jesus to his followers as recorded in Matthew 28.19-20: 'Go therefore and make disciples of all nations, baptizing them in the name of the Father and of the Son and of the Holy Spirit, and teaching them to obey everything I have commanded you.'

This great commission from the risen Jesus Christ is not a command recorded in one Gospel alone. All the other Gospel writers, albeit in different words and different settings, stress the desire of Jesus that those who follow him should call others to follow too (Mark 16.15; Luke 24.47-49; John 20.21-23).

The mission of God is not being undertaken in all its fullness unless people are called to become disciples of Jesus Christ. Mission is not always evangelism, and some aspects of mission (responding to social injustice, for example) are very clearly not evangelism. Evangelism, then, is just one part, but an essential and indispensable part, of the mission of God. A simple pair of definitions may help in this.

Mission = God's work of reconciling the whole of creation to himself, in which we are called to participate.
Evangelism = the process by which people become disciples of Jesus Christ.

The consideration of strategies for evangelism will touch on areas that involve mission in the broader sense, but the focus will be on that specific part of mission that can truly be called evangelism. An *Alpha* group (see Chapter 2) may provide a caring welcome for a lonely person. Community development (see Chapter 7) may transform a poor person's financial future through a credit union scheme. Both of these things are good, part of God's kingdom being extended as his will is done, but neither is in itself evangelism. The focus of this book on evangelism is not in any way intended to deny or downplay the whole breadth of the Church's mission. What it seeks to do is keep thinking sharp and lead on to ask some hard questions, especially in areas where the links between wider mission and specific evangelism are unclear. Christians are good at thinking that wider aspects of mission are actually evangelism when they are not, or that approaches that might lead to evangelism are actually doing so when this is not in fact happening. Evangelism *as evangelism* is the perspective from which this study is written.

Evangelism: a quick fix for a panicking church?

There is no doubt that main-line denominations in Britain are facing multiple challenges in sustaining numerical growth, as they are across the Western world. However, when thinking about evangelism there is a need for caution before seeing it primarily as a way of boosting church attendance. There are two main reasons for this.

Firstly, if evangelism is effective in bringing increasing numbers of people to Christian faith, that may take a long time to show up in the headline figures of church membership. As clergy in our forties who find ourselves visiting quite a wide range of local congregations, our experience is still very regularly of being the youngest present in a sea of grey heads. Such is the demographic profile of the Church that there is almost certain to be a continued fall-off in attendance at many churches as a large part of the Church nationally dies of old age.

Evangelism among adults, together with the essential task of prioritizing children's and youth work, will indeed bring more people to become disciples of Jesus Christ. This is and should be the aim, but (barring a miracle, which is not unknown when God is at work!) a turnaround of overall attendance figures could take a whole generation.

Secondly, even when people do come to faith, they may never come to 'church' as currently defined by regular Sunday morning worship in a church building. New Christians will still be part of worshipping, missionary communities, but in a growing variety of new forms; new wine really does fit best in new wineskins.

Having recognized that evangelism should not, and realistically cannot, be seen as a panacea for numerical decline, it is nevertheless right to be concerned with numbers. It's easy to knock an over-concern with bums on pews, especially if they contain wallets in the back pocket! But beyond the jibe lies something far more important. Put at its simplest, unless something is very wrong then for most people where their bum goes the rest of their body and soul follows!

Church attendance as a mindless duty is very largely a thing of the past, and none of the strategies under consideration is likely to lead to its reintroduction. But real discipleship still involves meeting together. The command of Jesus with its instructions about 'teaching them to obey everything I have commanded you' must at the very least include his teaching on love and on meeting together to share bread and wine in memory of him. Evangelism is about creating a community, and if people are to grow as disciples of Jesus Christ they need to do that in the context of a community. Jesus called people to be with him before he sent them out (Mark 3.14).

The community to which Christians belong has traditionally been called 'Church', although the gathering of his followers envisaged by Jesus may have had very limited resemblance to much of the 'normal' church life we have become used to. In some of the following chapters, cell-based churches (Chapter 10), community projects which merge into shared worship (Chapter 7), the vibrant life of the Church in the two-thirds world (Chapter 6) and a whole range of other possible new ways of being Church (Chapter 11) will be studied. This will hopefully, along with many of the other approaches considered, provide a strong antidote to the idea that evangelism is just about the Church as we know it ensuring its continued dominance.

Nevertheless, the promise of Jesus to Peter that 'on this rock I will build my Church' (Matthew 16.18) still stands. As Jesus calls people to follow, so he calls them to follow *together*. Moving forward together can be easier in theory than in practice. If the local church is to move forward in evangelism, it needs a sense of the big picture, of where it is now and where it should be going.

Big-picture strategies

Acting in the light of the big picture involves thinking about strategy. This does not mean downplaying the importance of the individual contact in evangelism, of telling one's own faith story, or of small-group leadership skills. All of these are fundamental, but they relate more to the individual's small-scale responsibility, to tactics rather than to strategy. Important resources are available to help equip individuals and churches in these areas (CPAS's *Lost for Words* course is one that comes into this category). Focusing on the level of strategy, however, this book intends to identify, explain and examine some of the different larger-scale approaches to evangelism that have emerged in recent years. Many of those years were specifically designated as a Decade of Evangelism.

Learning from the Decade of Evangelism

In declaring a Decade of Evangelism during the 1990s the Churches in Britain may appear to have launched a high-profile failure, since numerical decline was not reversed during that time. This fact, however, masks other things that may be even more important in the long term. The Decade was a significant time of *learning about* evangelism. Trends and principles were identified, a number of important ventures and approaches were produced, there is now evidence that the *rate* of decline is slowing, and some dioceses are reporting growing attendances.

Drawing on interview research, John Finney's *Finding Faith Today* provided a significant starting point for some of the changes of mindset that the Decade produced.[1] Two things in particular stand out in his study, and have continued to be central elements in the developing thinking of the years that have followed. These are, firstly, the importance of the journey to faith as a *process*, and secondly, the importance of *relationships* within that process.

These two themes have become accepted within the Church in Britain with a speed and to a degree that is quite remarkable. There is a need to ponder their implications in two significant areas: the place of conversion in the light of 'process' thinking, and the nature of the Church into which the journey of faith should lead.

Conversion revisited

The idea of conversion as a process that happens over time can seem rather lukewarm compared to the stirring conversion stories that have inspired many Christians in the past. The Acts of the Apostles recount the stories of Paul's dramatic conversion on the Damascus road, the Ethiopian eunuch's conversion through one conversation with Philip, and the Philippian jailer embracing the Christian faith as the result of an earthquake. But looked at again, even those stories seem to have had a wider dimension to them. We know little of what preceded the jailer's question about how he might be saved, but the effects of an earthquake and his own possibly impending death for failing in his duty to secure his prisoners may have concentrated the mind wonderfully! Earthquakes are pretty exceptional occurrences, and perhaps this is one clear example of an on-the-spot crisis conversion. In the other two cases there clearly *was* something going on before the conversion event. Paul had been challenged for some time by the witness of believers, and in particular by Stephen's death, and the Ethiopian was a God-fearer who already knew and studied the Hebrew Scriptures. Even in what may initially appear to be dramatic, one-off events, the journey was already under way in each case: Luke's record of the stories in Acts majors on the arrival.

The journey model may actually provide a more helpful way of understanding many of the other conversion stories in the New Testament. Peter's journey to faith occupies the whole of the period of Jesus' public ministry, and if there is a conversion moment it cannot be definitely identified. Was it his first response to the call of Jesus (Mark 1.16-18), the enthusiastic expression of somewhat muddled faith on the road to Caesarea Philippi (Mark 8.29), the affirmation of his love for the risen Lord in John 21.15-19, or at some other time?

If there is a weakness in the 'journey' model of conversion, it is that it can be unclear about exactly when someone making the journey has arrived. If we are all on a journey, either towards faith or growing in faith, what difference is there between believer and non-believer? Is this even helpful terminology to use, since the shared journey of all humanity towards God leaves us all ultimately in the same state?

Missiologist Andrew Kirk helpfully provides a way forward here, by distinguishing between *conversion* and *regeneration*. Writing of the misunderstanding that an outward decision to accept Christ is the sole goal of evangelism, he states:

> Such a view, however, confuses conversion with regeneration, human activity with God's activity. Regeneration is certainly a single event in which God brings to birth a new nature within the person who trusts Jesus Christ for salvation. Conversion, however, has both a beginning and many repetitions.[2]

5

The need for regeneration remains, but the exact moment at which it happens is ultimately God's responsibility, not that of the evangelist or the evangelistic strategy. Novelist Vikram Seth, able as an Indian citizen to walk across the Himalayas from Tibet into Nepal, records his confusing journey across mountain tracks. He had left the final Chinese customs post behind and was heading, to the best of his knowledge, towards Nepal. The journey continued, but he had no idea of his exact location, only of his intended direction. Fording a stream and climbing up a small path, he was surprised by a man who appeared from behind a rock and announced himself as a Nepali customs officer. Somewhere in his journey Seth had crossed the international boundary. The location of the boundary was of limited importance to him: what mattered was the official who assured him he had arrived!

John Finney found that the public marking of faith was of enormous importance for many people.[3] Baptism or confirmation were of great help in letting them know they truly were believers. Other, less traditional, gestures, such as getting up out of one's seat to come forward at an evangelistic rally, may also be life-changing. They *may* coincide with the moment of regeneration, but what matters more is their role in marking firmly and publicly the new believer's status as one of the Christian community.

Sara Savage, a Christian psychologist, has commented on the relative impact of sudden and slower conversion experiences:

> Sudden conversions have been thought to be the precursors of greater religious commitment; hence they are sought for as the mark of being a 'real' Christian. In fact, Liu found that it is conscious commitment, not a 'sudden' conversion experience, which promotes religious devotion. Liu compared religious commitment following sudden and gradual conversions. Commitment was measured in terms of identity commitment and resource commitment (time, activity, money). His results showed there was no difference in terms of commitment between sudden and gradual converts. What does make a difference is making a conscious commitment at some point, whether that process was sudden or gradual.[4]

What matters, it would seem, is not the speed of conversion but rather the certainty of convertedness. The journey continues, but the noting that at some point a boundary has been crossed (as in Vikram Seth's meeting the Nepali customs officer in the story above) is of fundamental importance.

Church revisited

The challenges to the nature of the Church which contemporary evangelism can present have already been noted. The likelihood of people wanting to join the club will continue to decline if the club remains unwilling to change its rules for new members.

Traditionally, some churches have had tighter boundaries than others. This can be true of local congregations, and it can also reflect denominational polity. Adult baptism and signing a form may be necessary for membership of a Baptist church, for example. In this understanding of the Church, conversion and church membership may both be marked by baptism (see Figure 1.1a).[5] In contrast, the exact status of a member of the Church of England or the precise route to becoming one is nowhere clearly spelled out. Churches with fuzzy boundaries have the great advantage of being accessible to non-members because non-members have no reason to feel that is what they are!

An understanding of conversion as faith journey makes a warm and welcoming church 'fringe' essential. Those moving towards Christian faith need to be able to be present in and around the Christian community, and indeed to be a valued part of that community even before they are certain they have 'arrived' on the level of clear and explicit Christian belief. This pattern of belonging

Figure 1.1 Shapes of the Church

1a Conversion and membership

1b Church and society merge

1c A church that is distinctive but welcoming

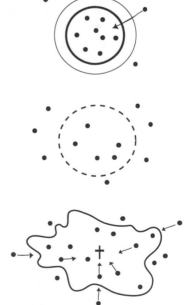

before (fully) believing* has been the experience of many over the years, and churches need to ensure sufficiently open doors to allow this to continue. Some of the new forms of church encountered while researching for this book have exemplified this in encouraging ways: they involve those who are seeking, listen to their views and let those views influence decision-making in the church.

A number of significant issues begin to arise once the implications of a welcoming, fuzzy-edged church are looked at seriously. One is the significant danger that fuzzy-edged churches (as in Figure 1.1b) will be fuzzy all the way through! At the core of what the local church is about there needs to be genuine commitment to a gospel that is worth believing. The welcoming church that has little to offer besides welcome is unlikely to provide life-changing hope for the serious searcher, and it should not be surprised when the journey of faith takes enquirers elsewhere.

A second danger is that the core of the church is rather less attractive than the fringe. Many churches have good relationships with the local community, for example through shared community action or in the welcoming pasta-and-video atmosphere of a process evangelism course. The gospel believed by the church members may indeed be life-changing, but enquirers are not keen to have their lives changed just so that they then fit in with the traditions and culture of Sunday morning church.

Belonging and believing are not the whole process in themselves: they need to be followed by becoming. In the past there was sufficient residual Christian awareness for many to accept Christian faith as a package. Believing inevitably meant belonging to the Church as it was and had been; becoming inevitably involved the acceptance of patterns of worship and behaviour that were simply part of the deal. The challenge facing Christians in evangelism today is wider but also more exciting than that. The becoming can and should involve both church members and new believers, as together they work to discover what church can and should be. Perhaps a better model is what Figure 1.1c is attempting to represent: a church where some believe and are moving more and more towards belonging, and where others belong while they work out the full meaning of belief. The edge is messy and overlapping, but what matters is the presence of God in Jesus Christ at the heart, and the movement of those around ever closer to him.

---

*British society has been described as one in which people believe without belonging – that is to say, one where they hold on to a residual religious belief even though church attendance has largely been abandoned. But both research and anecdotal evidence indicate a steady fading of any explicitly Christian content to that general belief. If people are to grasp and retain a genuine Christian faith within our pluralist and fast-changing society, they will need to be part of a community of believers, a group in which the full nature of that belief can be worked out.

Since the first edition of this book, the Church of England has encouraged radical re-thinking of what the local church might be like, through the publication of the *Mission-shaped Church* report. Chapters 10 and 11 of this book look at cell church and at planting other new forms of church. However, that is not meant to imply that other, more traditional churches are let off the hook. The challenge which faces every church, without exception, is that of being open to re-shaping and to growing in new and unexpected ways as mission is given a priority over the preservation of the patterns and structures church members may know well and find secure.

Life with Alpha

One feature of the Decade of Evangelism was the growth in the number of strategies and approaches to evangelism that became available. Some were (and are) clearly identifiable and marketed packages, others were more general movements. Firmly in the first of these categories it is not only realistic but also important to note the remarkable growth and the continuing importance of the Alpha course.

Measured both by national profile and by the number of local churches involved, Alpha is by far the most significant new component for any evangelistic strategy that has emerged in recent years. It depends upon and encourages relationships and works with the concept of conversion as a journey to faith. It contains within it the means to develop a new community of welcome outside the regular Sunday worship times, and has the potential to challenge the life of a whole church to learn from the atmosphere of an Alpha group.

It is not the intention of this book to sell the Alpha course (that is being done very effectively already!), but nor is there any intention to knock it. Alpha will be looked at more comprehensively in Chapter 2. If there is a danger with Alpha it is that the busy local church leader will receive a regular stream of messages, be they from the Alpha publicity machine or from other individuals closer to home, that the way forward for his or her church must be more Alpha courses undertaken with yet more enthusiasm. More Alpha courses may work, but they may also fail to meet the needs of the local situation. Alpha is one answer, but it may not be the best and it is certainly not the only one.

What else is going on?

Surrounded already by Alpha publicity, a church leader might have spent a couple of free afternoons (if such things exist) reading about the phenomenal growth of cell churches in Singapore, received an invitation to involve the local church in a community development project, and been encouraged by

9

a regional church officer to welcome a visiting group from a linked church in Uganda. Meanwhile, a mail shot publicizing something with a different name, which looks a bit like Alpha while proclaiming it is new and distinctive, may have dropped through the letterbox.

What is the best course to chart through all the initiatives that are out there? To say yes to everything will be a recipe for overwork among the leadership and confusion within the congregation. To stick to one well-known formula may be overlooking the very thing that could energize the local church and lead to fresh patterns of effective evangelism.

Awareness of good resources and approaches at the local church level is nowhere near as great as it should be. Under-resourced Christian organizations are sitting on valuable materials and wise insights which too many local congregations have not yet discovered. At the same time, not every resource is the right one for every situation. Some are more suited to one situation than another. Others will work best when partnered by other things in the life of the church and the surrounding community. All come from a particular theological perspective, and an understanding of that perspective will help local churches assess if this is the way forward for them. Much is useful; nothing is the universal panacea to evangelistic malaise.

By assessing a range of materials and approaches this book aims to raise awareness of what is available, primarily for churches and church leaders who realize they need to know more. In every case there is more to be said – it cannot all be covered here. If something in the following chapters challenges or excites then please investigate further – the information on web sites, organizations and suggestions for further reading provided at the end of each chapter is designed to encourage this.

The stories of those churches that have worked with the materials and approaches under consideration will provide an important part of the discussion. In some cases examples of best practice have been sought out, but more often the stories come from a range of ordinary churches, and many of the general observations reflect discussion with people in leadership in such places. If any approach is to be effective in the life of the Church in Britain it must be effective in the context of the average as well as the exceptional.

The best course through the various initiatives considered is unlikely to be based around one approach alone. Rather than either–or, the answer is more often going to be both–and, or perhaps this one followed by that one. We have been disappointed to find that there seems to be a reluctance on the part of the publishers of one resource to point enthusiastically to the value and place of others. This is understandable on the level of sales and marketing, but does little to encourage continued, healthy and sustainable strategies for evangelism. Where possible we have tried to suggest how one approach might be combined with another, how a strategy might be more effective by involving more than one tactical manoeuvre. More importantly, we hope that others will also take up this task, draw on different sources, combine, follow on, in such a way that the overall result is both more effective and more representative of the whole gospel than any single component could be.

Strategies human and divine

Even the greatest strategists slip up eventually, as Napoleon discovered at Waterloo. Were this book a summary of the strategic thinking of ourselves as authors, it would have a very limited value. Were it to contribute to the local strategy of the local church under the guidance of the Holy Spirit, that would be far more useful. God is a God of surprises, and there will be local initiatives and opportunities that will be very different from anything described here. Certainly one book can never hope to cover everything.

In writing, we have had an awareness that we are sensing something of God's evangelistic strategy for our culture and our nation. That greater strategy behind what is recorded here is the only one that ultimately matters. The trends in national life and the Church's developing understanding of the appropriate missionary response to them, the repeated experiences of individual churches and projects, all have combined to give us a sense that God is at work. The missionary task faced by the Church is ultimately the call to follow Christ. Where he leads, there he will be, going ahead of us. In observing and struggling to understand some of the ways in which her Lord is leading, the Church will find itself following not only the right strategy but Jesus himself. When that following in mission and evangelism is undertaken faithfully, so the promise of Jesus applies:

'Surely I am with you always, to the very end of the age.' (Matthew 28.20)

For further information

Visit

www.baptist.org.uk/resources/mission_evangelism_resources.asp?section=31
www.methodist.org.uk/index.cfm?fuseaction=opentoworld.content&cmid=29

Read

John Finney, *Emerging Evangelism*, Darton, Longman & Todd, 2004
Bob Jackson, *Hope for the Church*, Church House Publishing, 2002
George Lings, *Discernment in Mission: Navigation aids for mission-shaped processes*, Encounters on the Edge No.30, Church Army 2006
Dun MacLaren, *Mission Implausible*, Paternoster, 2004
Graham Tomlin, *The Provocative Church*, SPCK, 2002

2

Alpha

Mark Ireland

> Whoever you are, who desire to advance apace to the heavenly country, practise first, through Christ's help, this little Rule for beginners. And in the end, under God's protection, you will climb to those greater heights of knowledge and virtue to which the holy fathers beckon you.
>
> Rule of St Benedict

One of the most remarkable features of the evangelism scene in the UK during the last ten years has been the rise of courses like Alpha, Emmaus, Credo, Christianity Explored and Start!, all of which are designed to help enquirers explore the Christian faith over a period of weeks with opportunities to discuss the teaching in small groups. The Alpha course was first published in 1993 and since then it is claimed that 1.8 million people in Britain have done the course. It has even been featured in a television series hosted by Sir David Frost.

In the twelve years since *Questions of Life* (the book of the Alpha talks) was first published, Alpha has grown from being one church's nurture course to a worldwide movement with a high public profile. Some 7,215 churches of all denominations in the UK are registered as running Alpha, as well as 85 universities and 135 prisons. A recent MORI poll showed that more than 8 million adults across the UK (one-sixth of the population) can now identify Alpha as a Christian course and recognize its logo.[1] In addition, Alpha is running in 153 countries around the world, from Albania to Zimbabwe, and is published in 55 different languages, including Burmese and four different dialects of Chinese. Overseas, 16,000 churches are using the course, 36 per cent of them in the United States and 36 per cent in the countries of the 'Old' Commonwealth – Australia, Canada, South Africa and New Zealand. The churches in Britain owe a huge debt of gratitude to Holy Trinity Brompton (HTB), a large Anglican church in Knightsbridge, London, in the charismatic/evangelical tradition, for making the Alpha course so widely available, financed substantially by contributions from members of its own congregation as well as by the sale of resources.[2]

Like many movements, Alpha is supported by a massive publishing industry – the UK Alpha publications catalogue lists 169 different products, from books and videos to worship CDs, cookbooks, beer mats and car stickers. However, the place where you get the real feeling of being part of a mass movement is at the two-day Alpha training conferences led by Nicky Gumbel, author of the Alpha course, and Sandy Millar, formerly vicar of HTB. Some 45 such conferences were planned in 2003, nearly half of them in the USA. The conferences are the place where the huge army of local Alpha advisers receive inspiration and vision and are able to meet the leaders of the movement.

The aim of this chapter is to assess how effective Alpha is as a tool for evangelism, to identify its strengths, and to provide a positive critique of the course, addressing issues of both methodology and theology. The chapter concludes with practical questions and advice for churches thinking of using Alpha for the first time.

What is Alpha?

Alpha is defined as 'a series of about fifteen talks, given over a period of time, including a weekend or day away, with teaching based on all the material in *Questions of Life*'.[3] The original Alpha course was started in 1977 by Charles Marnham, the then curate of HTB. Marnham designed a six-session course which was held in his flat; each meeting began with a meal, followed by a talk, followed by discussion in small groups. According to Marnham, the aim was to follow up people who had recently become Christians, although from the beginning the course began to attract people who had not yet become believers. Elements were added to the course by successive curates, including the weekend away, which has become such a vital and well-known feature of the Alpha course. When Nicky Gumbel came to the church as curate in 1986 he revised the course further, particularly with non-churchgoers in mind. Following many requests to copy the course, the decision was taken to publish and market it more widely. Gumbel's book *Questions of Life*, which contains the 15 talks around which the Alpha course is based, was first published in 1993.

After phenomenal growth in the number of churches running Alpha in Britain during the 1990s, HTB expected the trend to continue in the new millennium, but in fact over the last five years the number has plateaued at around 7,000. A big promotional campaign coinciding with the ITV series in 2001 led to only about 200 more churches starting Alpha. This suggests that the potential market for Alpha in the UK is now saturated, and this has in turn led to a change in the Alpha strategy. The focus is now on producing and promoting specialist versions of Alpha – Alpha for Prisons, Alpha for Students, Youth Alpha, Alpha in the Workplace, Alpha for Forces, Senior Alpha – and on re-inspiring churches that may have run Alpha but have got discouraged.

Evidence suggests that not all the churches listed on the Alpha website are still running the course. For example, when I phoned round those listed in my home town of Walsall I found that out of the 13 courses listed, 5 of them had stopped running – 4 of them several years ago; 2 were not contactable as the phone numbers were wrong; 1 course was led by an oddball and bore no relation to Alpha; 2 had run Alpha for the first time recently, one with mixed success and one very successfully – which was a school-based Youth Alpha. That left only 3 churches that were running Alpha regularly and fruitfully, plus one other church not listed on the web site. Part of the problem may lie with the design of the website – whereas it is easy to register a course online, there is nowhere on the website for churches to remove their name. HTB is convinced that the main reason why some churches get disappointing results with Alpha is that they are not following the recipe closely enough.[4]

There is, however, another reason why the number of Alpha courses has plateaued, and that is the explosion in the number of other process evangelism courses that have been published since Alpha – including Emmaus (1996), Credo (1996), the Y Course (1998), Christianity Explored (2001), Essence (2002) and Start! (2003). The newer courses build on the achievement of Alpha in different ways and copy some of the principles and methods, but the Y Course, Essence and Start! aim to start further back, at the 'contact' stage. Emmaus and Christianity Explored have already published revised versions in 2003.

By contrast the Alpha course, which has remained substantially unchanged for twelve years, is beginning to seem a bit dated alongside some of the creative new resources on offer. The starting point of enquirers has shifted in the last twelve years, which may explain why some churches now struggle to get people to sign up for Alpha. In the 1980s, when Alpha began, people were inclined to dismiss the church as 'dull, boring and irrelevant', which is where the introductory Alpha talk begins. However today, as John Drane, a writer on evangelism and contemporary culture, has noted, an increasing number are dismissing the church because it is 'unspiritual'.[5] (Ways of engaging evangelistically with the contemporary search for spirituality are discussed in Chapter 12.) Interestingly, early in 2003 a completely rewritten and redesigned Youth Alpha was published, in a lively colour 'magazine' style, which has been warmly reviewed in *Youthwork* magazine. The question for HTB is whether the time is approaching for a similarly bold rewrite of the main Alpha course, revising not only the presentation but also the content.

Does Alpha work?

The first detailed survey of the effectiveness of Alpha was done in the Anglican Diocese of Lichfield in 1999, when all 426 parishes were asked which process evangelism courses they were using, how many people had come to faith through them, and which courses they would recommend to others. An 85 per cent response rate provided a remarkably comprehensive picture of the use of such courses in a very large and socially mixed diocese in the heart of England.

The survey showed that just six years after the publication of Alpha 61 per cent of parishes were offering one or more such courses, and another 20 per cent were planning to do so in the future. The total number of parishes in Lichfield Diocese using each course was as follows:

Course	No. of parishes	Percentage of total respondents
Alpha	148	39
Emmaus	91	24
Good News Down the Street	40	10
Credo	12	3
Own/Other	55	14*

*The percentages in this table do not add up to 100 because many parishes in the survey were using more than one course and 39% of them were using no course at all.

Emmaus had grown particularly fast, since it had only been published three years before the survey. At the same time there had been a noticeable decline in the number of parishes holding traditional missions. The speedy take-up of Alpha and Emmaus may have been influenced by the fact that perhaps the earliest process evangelism course, Good News Down the Street, was published in 1982 by an incumbent in Lichfield Diocese. (This course was the only process evangelism course John Finney was able to commend by name when he wrote *Finding Faith Today* in 1992.[6])

In the Lichfield survey parishes were asked how many people had attended their courses, and how many of these had come 'to Christian faith, commitment or confirmation' during the course. The results (from 383 parishes) showed that 6,334 lay people had attended process evangelism courses in the Diocese of Lichfield up to April 1999. Of these 1,377 (22 per cent) had, in the judgement of the priest, 'come to Christian faith, commitment or confirmation' during the course. The proportion coming to faith is significant, since at the time of the survey many of the churches were running courses for the first time, when many of those attending were usually already church members.

Two-thirds of the 6,334 people who had attended courses in the diocese had been on Alpha, and Alpha accounted for 992 out of the 1,377 who had come to faith. However, the *proportion* coming to faith on Alpha (21 per cent) was almost identical to Emmaus and Good News Down the Street and lower than the combined figure for lesser-known and home-grown courses (27 per cent). Detailed comparison of the results for the different courses is given in Figure 3.1 on page 35. The findings of the Lichfield survey were broadly confirmed by a similar survey undertaken in St Albans Diocese in 2001.

Research by Peter Brierley has produced statistical evidence that churches running Alpha are less likely to show decline in attendance, particularly if they have been running Alpha for three or more years. In March 2000 Brierley analysed all the listings in every issue of *Alpha News* of churches in England running Alpha to see how many years they had been running Alpha, and whether they had declined numerically more or less than the average between 1989 and 1998 (using data from the English Church Attendance Survey).[7]

These figures suggest that running Alpha for just one or two years has no measurable effect on the growth of a church, whereas churches that run Alpha regularly over three or more years are increasingly likely to see numerical growth.[8] *The reason for this is that where churches run Alpha for only one or two years, the vast majority of those taking part tend to be existing church members.* Churches typically see a drop in numbers after the second course; however, the significant factor in the effectiveness of Alpha is not the overall numbers attending, but the numbers of those attending who are not yet Christians. Brierley points out that courses that have been running for three or more years must be attracting outsiders or they wouldn't have lasted so long. This finding correlates with a point often made by Gumbel, that Alpha is a long-term strategy and that churches should persevere when the overall numbers attending Alpha decline after the first two or three courses, since it is the number of outsiders (rather than church members) doing Alpha that is the key to growth.[9]

Rejuvenating existing Christians?

In contrast to Brierley's very positive findings, sociologist Stephen Hunt has published a recent book, *The Alpha Enterprise*, which argues that Alpha's achievements are 'frequently overestimated'.[10] On the basis of a survey of 31 Alpha courses nationwide, he concludes that the majority of those attending the course are already churchgoers and committed Christians, and that – although Alpha does bring in those on the fringe – its main impact has been to rejuvenate those already in church through exposing them to charismatic teachings and culture.[11] Sixty-six per cent of Alpha participants surveyed by Hunt had found out about the course through their church, which indicates that they already belonged to a church; however 20 per cent said they found out about the course through friends, and 12 per cent through the media/posters/leaflets. This suggests around 32 per cent of the participants in the courses being run by local churches were not church members. Interestingly this correlates with the results of a survey undertaken by Christian Research among 1,125 churches of all denominations, which showed that 69 per cent of those attending process evangelism courses were already church members, compared to 31 per cent that were not.[12]

Hunt's argument is strong on sociological analysis but weak on theology. What his research shows is that most people have had some involvement with church before they join a 15-session Alpha course, but this does not necessarily mean that they are already committed Christians, as he perhaps assumes. Research shows that the majority of people start attending church *before* coming to faith, rather than afterwards. John Finney's research showed that 76 per cent of those converted as adults had attended church regularly at some point as a child.[13] As Finney has demonstrated, conversion is more commonly an extended process rather than a dateable event. People are likely to be some way along a journey towards faith before they choose to sign up for Alpha, but the evidence is still that Alpha is hugely effective in awakening or rekindling faith in those with some kind of Christian background.

Stephen Brian is another critic of Alpha, who argues that it 'primarily recycles existing believers', converting them not from non-believers into believers, but from one sort of Christian into another more charismatic sort.[14] Controversially, he suggests that those who thought they were Christians at the start of the course are persuaded that they were not in fact 'proper' Christians at all, so that their 'conversion' at the Holy Spirit weekend is all the more 'real'. However such an interpretation is contradicted by the Alpha training manual *Telling Others*, which strongly guides group leaders to be non-judgemental and not to criticize any church. Nonetheless, Brian's critique does point up the fact that part of the wider impact of Alpha is the disseminating and popularizing of charismatic evangelical theology among existing churchgoers of other traditions.

Why Alpha works

Alpha and all the other courses examined in this book have taken off against the background of the major shift in our understanding of how evangelism works that we looked at in Chapter 1 – namely, first, that conversion is usually a process rather than an event, and second, that belonging usually precedes believing.

A 15-session course: from event to process

The traditional evangelistic 'guest service' depends for its effectiveness on people being present who are only one sermon away from conversion. This is less and less common today – churches have to start much 'further back' in explaining the Christian faith to the increasing number of people who have no prior knowledge of it. The course gives the enquirer much more space and time to decide, providing 15 sessions of material spread over ten weeks. Although the Alpha approach feels new, it is in many ways a return to the Church of England's dominant model of communicating the faith in the centuries before Billy Graham, when catechism classes, church services, teaching at school and instruction in the home were all part of the *process* of Christian nurture.

Eating together: belonging comes before believing

John Finney's research in *Finding Faith Today* also led to a reversal of the common understanding of the sequence of conversion, whereby a person first comes to faith and then looks for a church to join. The reality he found was that the majority of people begin to attend a church before coming to faith. The diagram shown in Figure 2.1 makes Finney's point.

Figure 2.1 Belonging comes before believing [15]

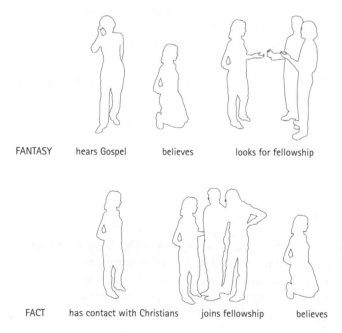

FANTASY   hears Gospel   believes   looks for fellowship

FACT   has contact with Christians   joins fellowship   believes

This principle, that belonging comes before believing, is integral to the Alpha course. Guests on the course are immediately introduced to a small group with whom they enjoy a relaxed meal at the start of each session, and after the talk the small group reconvenes for a discussion in which guests are encouraged to ask anything at all. Faith is given the opportunity to grow over a period of weeks without people being put on the spot at an early stage.[16]

There are a number of other reasons why Alpha works so effectively:

Getting everyone involved

Part of the genius of Alpha is that it enables lots of church members to get involved in evangelism, rather than leaving it to the vicar or a guest evangelist. On every Alpha course approximately one-third of the people involved are leaders and helpers, most of whom would run a mile from knocking on doors, but who are happy to do evangelism through cooking, serving, washing up, leading worship, leading small groups, putting out chairs. Charles Marnham commented to me that he had found that the releasing of lay people to take a lead in evangelism had been one of the early very important fruits of the course.

Network evangelism

Alpha courses provide a place to which church members can bring their friends to find out more about the Christian faith, as Andrew brought his brother to Jesus and Philip brought his friend Nathaniel.

The importance of friendship-based evangelism is one of the key conclusions of John Clarke's two-year research project looking at how British churches are making new disciples. Clarke concluded that three elements are usually necessary in the process of bringing someone to faith, which he together called 'The Three-Stranded Cord of Evangelism'. He identified these strands as:

- the word of God (Christian teaching)
- the friendship and personal witness of a Christian, preferably someone not too different from themselves (or the experience of Christian community)
- prayer.[17]

Building on this insight, Clarke described two primary models of church: the 'osmosis church', which people join through its institutional fringe and services, and the 'web church', which people join through the personal fringe of the network of friends and relatives of church members. Alpha works because it provides a useful tool in both situations – course members can come both from contacts made through occasional offices and evangelistic events, and from personal invitations to friends of church members.

An easy-to-follow recipe

One of the great strengths of Alpha is the high-quality training and support offered to local churches using the product. The two-day training conferences which Sandy Millar and Nicky Gumbel lead around the country provide a high degree of motivation and inspiration for evangelism, combined with thorough training in how to run a local course. The extensive network of local Alpha advisers, the publication of *Alpha News* and the many publications available give people a strong sense of being part of a national movement, and give confidence to those wanting to try running an evangelistic course for the first time.

Issues about Alpha's methodology

Issues of copyright

Those who wish to make significant changes to the Alpha course run into problems of copyright, since HTB are unwilling to agree to any significant alteration to the content of the course. Alpha resources carry a 'Copyright Statement' which states:

> Holy Trinity Brompton accepts that minor adaptations to the *Alpha* course may occasionally be desirable. These should only concern the length of the talks or the number of sessions. In each case the essential character of the course must be retained. *Alpha* is a series of about fifteen talks, given over a period of time, including a weekend or day away, with teaching based on all the material in *Questions of Life*.[18]

This was a major source of concern among clergy in Lichfield Diocese, one of whom wrote:

> We are not all into renewal of the Holy Trinity Brompton type and I understand they are not keen on adapting. The Alpha concept has been a blessing in our outreach and I would like their blessing to adapt. If not it will kill our outreach because I cannot use it as it stands in some places . . .

Some churches have stopped using Alpha because of this. However, a number of those in the Lichfield survey admitted that they adapt the course to their own needs – 'We adapt as we go along even though there is the implication we should use the material as presented.'

When I raised this issue with Nicky Gumbel himself, he replied that the Copyright Statement had been introduced because 'Friends who had been on Alpha recommended their friends to go on Alpha at their local church, but when they went they found it was not the same course . . . If I went to McDonalds in Moscow and was given a ham sandwich, I would say that's not on.' Sandy Millar, then vicar of HTB, explained that like McDonalds, Alpha aims for 'consistency', so that people can recommend the course to friends in other places with confidence. He also expressed their concern to avoid frustrations, dislike or failure being attributed improperly to Alpha when local leaders have failed to follow the recipe.

McDonaldization?

One of the strengths of Alpha – the desire to standardize the product across all countries and churches – is also in part its weakness. It is significant that when I pressed Nicky Gumbel on the need to adapt the course to local circumstances he used the illustration of McDonalds. Pete Ward, the Archbishop of Canterbury's former Adviser in Youth Ministry, wrote a critique of Alpha in 1998 which he entitled 'Alpha – the McDonaldization of Religion?'[19] Whilst keen to affirm that God is at work in Alpha, Ward argued that the factors leading to the spread of Alpha have a lot in common with what George Ritzer has called 'McDonaldization' – 'a process of rationalization ... gradually spreading across the world and into every area of life'.[20]

There is certainly a parallel between McDonalds, with its limited menu reproduced identically the world over, and what Alpha is seeking to achieve, with the same 15 talks reprinted and translated throughout the world – even with the same jokes and stories. Like McDonalds, Alpha devotes a lot of effort to publicizing the brand name, with massive poster campaigns, and to providing detailed training. However, by radically simplifying the process of evangelism and providing a carefully tested recipe and set of ingredients Alpha has enabled many churches to launch an effective process evangelism course which would otherwise have lacked the skills or the confidence to do so.

One could, of course, equally call the *Book of Common Prayer* 'the McDonaldization of liturgy and worship' in the sixteenth century. From his preface it is clear that Thomas Cranmer was seeking to lay down a uniform standard recipe for worship and establish a particular theological package across all the churches of England. It can be argued that Gumbel, as a gifted priest and author seeking to set a uniform standard in evangelism, is simply a modern Cranmer working to renew the Church in a particular direction for a new generation.

The need to contextualize

Ward points out that while Alpha is itself a contextualization of the methods of evangelism, it also hinders the necessary local contextualization that must take place if the gospel is to be heard authentically in the culture of its hearers. This is a question particularly relevant to the promotion of Alpha in non-Western countries, where the publication of books and videos containing the identical talks given in Knightsbridge, London, could be judged by future critics as a new form of Victorian missionary colonialization. The key question is whether Alpha is able to evangelize a culture or cultures from within, or only to superimpose a Western/Christian culture from without. In other words, the Alpha course may bear fruit in East Africa, but it is no substitute for the years of painstaking work by Vincent Donovan and others presenting Christ to the Masai in their own culture and context.[21]

This need to adapt one's presentation of the gospel to the local culture and context is also relevant in the UK, where the culture and social background of a great many people are a long way from those of the prosperous young professionals whom HTB are evangelizing so effectively through Alpha. Using live speakers rather than the videos of Nicky Gumbel does give local churches an obvious opportunity to contextualize the message. It is interesting that at HTB itself, where the average age of Alpha participants is about 26, Nicky Gumbel has stopped giving most of the talks himself, and has trained up younger leaders to give their own talks and illustrations (based on the Alpha manual), finding that young adults are better able to reach people of their own age group.

Alpha is a hugely valuable and effective tool in evangelism, but churches will be impoverished if they reduce evangelism and mission simply to running Alpha. As Pete Ward has commented, 'Christian mission is a much broader and probably a significantly more costly endeavour than participation in an *Alpha* course'.[22] One of the significant developments at HTB over the last few years has been a greatly increased commitment to social justice, through support of the Make Poverty History campaign, through its programme Caring for Ex-Offenders, and through The Besom, a charity which enables people who have time and money to get personally involved with helping the poor. At a recent conference at HTB, James Odgers, founder of The Besom, spoke on the theme 'From Alpha to Discipleship'. If the home of Alpha is sensing that Alpha needs to be one part of a much wider package of holistic mission, then it is important that local churches get that message, and don't think that the answer to evangelism is simply doing more Alpha. More difficult and less fashionable forms of evangelism – like, for example, the style of community ministry advocated by Ann Morisy – have a vital role in giving credibility to the church's proclamation of the love of Christ. (See Chapter 7.)

Videos versus live speakers

Gumbel encourages churches to use a live speaker to give the Alpha talks, but video recordings of him giving the talks at HTB are available as a substitute, and these are used (according to HTB) by over a third of all courses in the UK.

There is no way of knowing, without further research, how much those giving their own Alpha talks actually adapt the material in *Questions of Life* to fit their own situation or theological outlook, regardless of the copyright statement.

When the survey of courses in Lichfield Diocese asked churches to comment on the effectiveness of the Alpha course, the most frequently mentioned subject of concern was the videos – particularly the talks. These were thought to be too long and rather middle-class in style. People also commented that simply recording a live talk was an unimaginative use of a very visual medium. A local ministry adviser in the diocese suggested the course would be improved by using insights about how adults learn: 'Sitting passively for virtually an hour to watch a tape "lecture style" is far less effective for adult learning than the interactive reflective method of the Emmaus course, which is far more engaging.'

A respondent from an inner-city parish expressed great appreciation for the Alpha course but asked if Gumbel would consider how content and delivery could be geared to reaching people in more 'artisan and working-class environments', perhaps by using an equally gifted communicator videoed in a different cultural setting. A prison chaplain also made the same plea, explaining that a 50-minute video of a talking head filmed in Knightsbridge is not the best way to communicate with men with little formal education.

A shorter version of the Alpha videos – called Alpha Compact – is being released by HTB in 2005. The existing full-length videos are being edited down to 20 minutes, particularly for use by *Alpha in the Workplace*. However those who are looking for a more creative use of the visual medium than just a talking head may like to consider the *Christianity Explored* videos by Rico Tice. Rico's talks (20–25 minutes each) are filmed in a variety of locations as well as in the studio – for example, when using the illustration of the bishop in *Les Miserables*, Rico is filmed standing on the stage of the theatre. The *Start!* course published by CPAS also has an accompanying video – each of the six sessions has two 5-minute video sections, filmed in different locations around Blackpool and designed to be accessible to working-class culture. *Christianity Explored* and the *Start!* course are discussed in more detail in Chapter 4.

Questions about Alpha's theology

Among the churches that are using Alpha there are some significant concerns about the theological balance and content of the course. Following on from the initial survey in Lichfield Diocese, the bishop wrote to all the clergy using Alpha in the diocese to ask if they had any comments they wished to be passed on to the authors of the course. Among the 39 responses received were many comments of appreciation along the lines of: 'The *Alpha* course is extremely effective', 'We owe an incalculable debt to Holy Trinity Brompton for what is offered so generously', and 'Don't change a thing'. However, there were a number of areas of theological concern which churches wished to raise with Nicky Gumbel and Sandy Millar. The key issues were as follows:

- lack of teaching on the sacraments
- too much stress on substitutionary atonement and not enough on the Resurrection
- too much emphasis on speaking in tongues
- superficial approach to healing/little theology of suffering
- lack of material on social ethics.

The doctrine of the Church

The lack of sacramental teaching was the most common theological concern among the respondents. Typical comments were: 'Please include far more on the Holy Communion', 'The course seems to lack sacramental teaching', or 'Over-emphasis on "spirit" to the neglect of "sacrament"'. The Bishop of Stafford wrote:

> Obviously other process evangelism courses have different emphases, some more sacramental than others, but there is a danger 1 believe that a fairly minimalist understanding of the Eucharist in the Alpha material 1 have seen (but not used) is somewhat restrictive of one of the greatest well-springs of Christian spirituality and experience. And it was (is) *the* memorial that the Lord gave of His Passion (as St Paul says!).

Gumbel responded by explaining that the reason there is so little on the sacraments in Alpha is that this is an area of significant disagreement between the different denominations, and what he wrote about baptism and holy communion in *Questions of Life* was carefully scripted to enable it to be used by Roman Catholics, Baptists and the Salvation Army. However, the Alpha course was originally written to meet the needs of one particular London church, Holy Trinity Brompton, so the brevity of material on the sacraments may also reflect something of the charismatic evangelical theology of that church.

Whilst Alpha is only an introduction to the Christian faith, what is included in the core introduction is significant, since only two parishes out of 148 running the course in the Lichfield survey had used any of the Alpha follow-up material. It is perhaps significant that the logo on the front cover of all the Alpha materials is of *an individual* wrestling alone with a big question. There is something quite individualistic about Alpha which resonates with our culture but loses something of the corporate nature of faith – seen both in the New Testament, where whole households responded together (as in Acts 16.31-34), and in other cultures today, where turning to Christ is still a corporate decision.[23]

Figure 2.2 Comparison of the content of Alpha, Christianity Explored and Emmaus Nurture

ALPHA

1 Christianity: Boring, Untrue and Irrelevant?
2 Who Is Jesus?
3 Why Did Jesus Die?
4 How Can I Be Sure Of My Faith?
5 Why And How Should I Read The Bible?
6 Why And How Do I Pray?
7 How Does God Guide Us?

WEEKEND AWAY

8 Who Is The Holy Spirit?
9 What Does The Holy Spirit Do?
10 How Can I Be Filled With The Spirit?

11 How Can I Resist Evil?
12 Why And How Should We Tell Others?
13 Does God Heal Today?
14 What About The Church?
15 How Can I Make The Most Of The Rest Of My Life?

CHRISTIANITY EXPLORED

CHRISTIANITY IS CHRIST

1 Introduction
2 Jesus – Who Is He?
3 Jesus – Why Did He Come?
4 Jesus – His Crucifixion
5 Jesus – His Gift Of Grace
6 Jesus – His Resurrection

WEEKEND AWAY

WHAT IS CHRISTIAN LIFE LIKE?

7 You're Never Alone – The Church Family
8 You're Never Alone – The Holy Spirit
9 You're Never Alone – Prayer
10 You're Never Alone – The Bible
11 The Motivation To Keep Going

12 What Is A Christian?
13 The Devil And Assurance
14 Choices – King Herod
15 Choices – James And John

EMMAUS NURTURE

WHAT CHRISTIANS BELIEVE

1 Believing In God
2 We Need God In Our Lives
3 The Life And Ministry Of Jesus
4 The Death And Resurrection Of Jesus
5 The Holy Spirit
6 Becoming A Christian

HOW CHRISTIANS GROW

7 Learning To Pray
8 Reading The Bible
9 Belonging To The Church
10 Sharing Holy Communion

LIVING THE CHRISTIAN LIFE

11 Living God's Way
12 Serving The Lord
13 Your Money And Your Life
14 Learning To Love
15 Sharing The Faith

25

Atonement and Resurrection

The strong emphasis in Alpha on a substitutionary understanding of the atonement is a significant area of concern for some users. As one bishop put it,

> I do not believe that this explicit use of substitutionary language is justified by the Greek words translated 'for us' in the NT, and I do not believe the substitutionary theory is necessary in order to take very seriously indeed human sinfulness, our need for redemption, and the costliness of that redemption.

Responding to this concern, Gumbel commented that most criticism of Alpha comes from conservative evangelicals, who complain that it does not emphasize substitution enough. He pointed to page 46 of *Questions of Life*, which briefly sketches other models of the atonement:

> Like a beautiful diamond the cross has many facets. On the cross, the powers of evil were disarmed (Colossians 2:15). Death and demonic forces were defeated. On the cross, God revealed his love for us. He showed us that he is not a God who is aloof from suffering. He is 'the crucified God' (as the title of the book by the German theologian Jürgen Moltmann puts it). He has entered our world and knows and understands all about suffering. On the cross Jesus sets us an example of self-sacrificial love (1 Peter 2:21). Each of these facets deserves a chapter on its own, which space does not allow.

A related area of concern in the Lichfield survey was the lack of a full session on the evidence for, and significance of, the Resurrection of Jesus. The lack of teaching on this subject led one church in the diocese to create its own alternative to Alpha. Gumbel asserts that 'The physical resurrection of Jesus Christ from the dead is the cornerstone of Christianity' yet the evidence for the Resurrection is covered in just four pages at the end of the talk 'Who Is Jesus?' and its implications are sketched in under a page in another talk. This compares with a whole session on the Resurrection in Christianity Explored. Interestingly, the Emmaus nurture course used to have a whole session on the Resurrection, but the new revised version combines Jesus' death and resurrection into one session in order to give more space to Jesus' earthly ministry.

Social ethics

The lack of teaching on social ethics in Alpha is significant. It is interesting how few references there are in the 15 talks to justice issues, and how few of the stories and illustrations (which play a crucial role in the talks) are about these issues. There is not a single reference to social justice or our responsibility to the poor in the talk 'How can I resist evil?' – where the emphasis is entirely on a personal devil rather than, for example, the oppression of the poor – or in the final talk 'How can I make the most of the rest of my life?' – where the focus is on 'presenting our bodies as a living sacrifice' particularly in terms of sexual behaviour.

The space given in the Alpha training manual to power evangelism, in the style of John Wimber, suggests this is the dominant model of evangelism behind the Alpha course. Whilst the sections on 'Classical evangelism' (the proclamation of an unchanging message) and 'Holistic evangelism' (linking evangelism with social justice) are each scarcely two-thirds of a page, the section on 'Power evangelism' runs for almost four pages.[24] Wimber's theology of power evangelism reasserted biblical understandings of the person and work of the Holy Spirit, particularly in the areas of healing, of equipping ordinary Christians to minister in the power of the Spirit, and of recovering a place for intimate experience of God in the life of the believer.[25] However, his understanding of the spiritual realm tended to diminish the place of the natural in human life, seeing all sickness as the work of Satan rather than perhaps as one of the features of a fallen world in which God is working out his redemptive purpose.

As I have already noted, in recent years there are strong and welcome signs of a growing commitment to social justice issues within Holy Trinity Brompton – both in the very large numbers of members of HTB who are involved in working with the poor in London and overseas, and through the substantial ministry to ex-offenders that has come about through the large-scale use of Alpha in prisons. In 2005, besides three Alpha conferences, Holy Trinity Brompton were also hosting a conference on 'Caring for Ex-Offenders' and one entitled 'Developing a Passion for the Poor among the People of God'. In the light of all this the lack of reference within the Alpha course to the social implications of the gospel is all the more striking, and illustrates further the need to revise and update the syllabus. In the meantime, churches may want to encourage groups that have completed Alpha to use an excellent new 10-session course *Simplicity, Love and Justice*, written by James Odgers, a member of HTB and founder of The Besom, a charity which helps Christians engage with the poor and give money, time and possessions. (*Simplicity, Love and Justice* is available from Alpha Publications.)

'Join-the-dots' Christianity?

Martyn Percy, an academic who is a strong critic of the charismatic movement, draws attention to the inevitable danger that in simplifying Christianity one loses some of its essence. 'The genius of Christianity lies in its contestability. In the relentless appeal to "basics", the Alpha course obviates the implicit and explicit paradoxes in the Gospel, as well as its breadth.'[26] He points out that in Alpha the basics turn out to be a largely inerrant Bible, a homely and powerful Holy Spirit, and an evangelical atonement theory, and not the Trinity, baptism, communion or community. He points out that despite so much emphasis on the Holy Spirit, in Alpha his work is described largely in personal and therapeutic terms, rather than in terms of creation, justice, peace and reconciliation. In apt turns of phrase he describes Alpha as 'a package, not a pilgrimage', and bemoans 'salvation by copyright'.

In other areas Percy's critique is less convincing. He says that 'there is little space for people to reflect on and vent their own . . . concerns',[27] whereas small-group discussions are a key part of each evening and one of the five guiding principles of Alpha is that participants should be encouraged to 'ask anything'.[28] He also asserts that Alpha mostly 'excites and galvanises existing believers', whereas the Lichfield survey gives clear evidence of 992 people in one diocese having come to Christian faith, commitment or confirmation through the course. And Brierley's research, as we have seen, also shows that churches that have been running Alpha for three or more years are significantly more likely to see numerical growth.[29]

The doctrine of the Trinity

It is significant that within the Alpha syllabus there are two talks specifically about Jesus, three about the Holy Spirit, one about the devil, but no talk specifically about God the Father. This somewhat unbalanced presentation of the Godhead is compounded by the lack of a clear explanation of the Trinity in any of the talks. Nicky Gumbel's talk on the Trinity appears not in *Questions of Life*, but in *Searching Issues*, a book used to prime small-group leaders on the questions they are most likely to be asked. It is remarkable that such a central doctrine, which is so easily misunderstood, should be left to group leaders to explain if and when it is raised in small groups.

Suggested revisions

Taking all this into account, and acknowledging the huge contribution made by the Alpha course, I would nonetheless want to recommend to Holy Trinity Brompton, and to churches considering adopting the course, that they review the theological balance of the talks – to include more on the Trinity, the person of God the Father, the sacraments of the Church and the pursuit of social justice, and shorter, more balanced sections on the Holy Spirit and healing. Churches who wish to use Alpha as it stands may find it helpful to follow Alpha with the short Emmaus 'Growth' courses on the Church, the sacraments, the Christian hope and the kingdom of God.

Learning from the growth of Alpha

Two out of the three most popular process evangelism courses used in Lichfield Diocese – Alpha and Good News Down the Street – were each produced by a single church. How many other really effective tools in evangelism never achieve their potential impact because they originate from small churches which do not have the resources of Holy Trinity Brompton? Two of the most effective courses being used in Lichfield Diocese were written by local incumbents. This highlights the role that large churches could be encouraged to play further in helping the Church to grow, by producing new resources that could then be made available to smaller churches. Too often the only way in which larger churches are asked to help smaller churches is financially, through the 'parish share'.

The need for denominations to think strategically about how to harness the creativity and expertise of large and growing churches is highlighted in Bob Jackson's recent book *Hope for the Church*.[30] If only ways can be found to help large and small parishes share their expertise and experience in evangelism and outreach, then there will be more sense of community, rather than competitiveness or dependence, among the churches of an area. Those parishes that are financially weak may have important strengths to share in other areas. At a recent 'Evangelism Swap Shop' in Lichfield Diocese – an evening where each parish told the story of one creative evangelism initiative that had worked for them – two struggling parishes in urban priority areas told how they had developed, respectively, a thriving after-school children's worship group and a successful ecumenical millennium event in partnership with the local community.

It is fascinating to compare the low-tech 'homeliness' of the Alpha videos with the very high-tech marketing and promotion of the course. A key part in the growth of Alpha has been an extremely professional marketing strategy. HTB now employs about 140 paid staff, mostly full-time, and the Alpha offices cover an entire floor that has been specially added to the church hall. In addition, many others are employed by Alpha offices overseas.[31] *Alpha News*, edited by a news editor recruited from Fleet Street, is published three times a year. This 36-page tabloid newspaper has a circulation in Britain alone of 250,000. By comparison, the staff time allocated to the marketing of Emmaus is one half-day a fortnight.

A key question is whether Alpha have actually got it right by investing so heavily in publicity, promotion and training compared with the publishers of other courses, and whether certain other courses – like Emmaus – might be at least as effective in making disciples for Christ yet have failed to reach their potential market share through inadequate investment in marketing and training.

Talking to the Director of Communications at HTB, I found that a significant proportion of his time was taken up with finding strong personal testimonies of how God has met with people who would not have previously described themselves as Christians through the Alpha course. Every edition of *Alpha News* contains a number of these stories, and four books of Alpha testimonies have been published. The effort required to find and research these testimonies suggests that sudden, dramatic conversions from unbelief to committed discipleship are unusual rather than typical among those who attend Alpha – often it is a more untidy process.

However, testimonies clearly have a powerful impact on others searching for faith. Mainstream denominations have tended to be uncomfortable with personal testimony, except in churches with an evangelical or charismatic tradition. Yet in contemporary popular culture people absorb information through stories and personalities, as the popular newspapers demonstrate. The postmodern mindset does not begin by asking of a religion or philosophy 'Is it true?', but 'Does it work?' When people see how God has changed a person's life, then they are more inclined to take seriously the possibility of a God who is real. Parish magazines and diocesan newspapers could significantly increase their spiritual impact by actively seeking out and publishing testimonies, with photographs, of local people whose lives have been changed by Jesus Christ.

Summing up

It is only too easy to knock a course like Alpha, or to point to ways it could be improved, yet no one can take away from the fact that it was the biggest single evangelistic tool of the 1990s, and has helped many hundreds of thousands of people in the UK and around the world to come to Christian faith. The onus is on those who wish to criticize Alpha to demonstrate other, more effective methods of bringing people to faith in Christ. The story is told of a young evangelist leading a university mission who met with a group of dons from the theology faculty who criticized his presentation of the gospel. After graciously answering their questions he asked them, 'Tell me, how many people have you led to Christ?' After an embarrassed silence he responded, 'Well, I think I prefer my way of doing evangelism to your way of not doing it.'

Alpha has also performed a massive educational role in moving the churches from event-based evangelism towards process evangelism courses, which give enquirers more time to explore and discuss the Christian faith. Alpha has blazed a trail which many other courses have since followed. After twelve years on the market with minimal revision it is beginning to look a bit dated in content and style. But it is very easy to use for churches dipping their toe in the water for the first time, and the brand name still has significant pulling power that helps with recruiting enquirers. The training materials, local advisers and training conferences provide very high-quality support and expertise.

Key questions to ask about Alpha

1. Does Alpha fit the spirituality of our church?

From his vantage point as a former National Officer for Evangelism, Robert Warren has commented that the easiest way to create division in a church is through spirituality. Published courses each have their own spirituality, which may not be that of the host church. Churches across many traditions have adopted Alpha without thinking too deeply about how its spirituality differs from their own. This is of course an important issue for the many Roman Catholic churches using Alpha. Where a local church of a very different tradition is running the course, particularly if the videos are being used rather than live speakers, there is a strong possibility that those who come to faith through the course will have a very different spirituality from long-standing members of the church. This may lead to future tensions in the church and confusion for the new believer. Those wanting a process evangelism course with less of a charismatic element and more on the nature of sin (of which there is relatively little in Alpha) may want to consider Christianity Explored – discussed in Chapter 4.

2. Are we willing to use the 'package' as it is, or do we want something more flexible?

HTB are very keen to protect what they see as the integrity of the Alpha 'brand' through their copyright statement. Going with the Alpha package has clear benefits – the well-known brand name attracts people on the fringe; the course is a well-tried recipe; there is excellent training and local support; and there are lots of resources available. These must be weighed against the disadvantages, namely the lack of freedom to adapt the course to fit either the spirituality of the church or the needs of the particular group. Those wanting a more flexible tool, though with a lower profile, may want to consider Emmaus (see Chapter 3).

3. Are we willing to persevere with Alpha for several years?

Alpha is a long-term strategy. Running it only begins to lead to numerical growth when it has been going regularly for three or more years. Many churches, as we have seen, are tempted to give up after the second year as they see the numbers attending drop sharply after the first few courses. However, the size of an Alpha course is unimportant – the key thing is the number of non-Christians attending.

4. What happens after Alpha?

At Holy Trinity Brompton Alpha forms just the first part of a process of Christian initiation. Those who complete Alpha are steered into pastorate groups or into one of the following courses: *A Life Worth Living* (on Philippians), *Searching Issues* (on questions most frequently asked at Alpha), *Challenging Lifestyle* (on the Sermon on the Mount) and *The Heart of Revival* (on Isaiah 40 – 66).[32] Yet most parishes offering Alpha do not offer any of these follow-up courses – only two parishes in the whole of Lichfield Diocese mentioned using any of these courses.[33] This suggests that many parishes find the follow-up materials much less satisfactory than the Alpha course itself. In contrast, many parishes in the Lichfield survey were using Emmaus 'Growth' modules to follow on from Alpha. As well as a 15-session nurture course, Emmaus includes four books of 'growth modules' or short courses on different aspects of the faith, designed to be used flexibly according to the needs of the group.

Where to start

- **Ask around:** Talk to other churches in your area that have run Alpha – what tips have they got about making Alpha work in their context? They may also have copies of the videos you could borrow if you want to use them.

- **Read the books:** There is an ever-growing list of Alpha resources, but you really need only three books to get you started: *Questions of Life* – the book of Nicky Gumbel's 15 talks; *Telling Others* – 'How to run an Alpha course' – the book of the training conference; and *Searching Issues* – how to handle the difficult questions that come up in the small groups – each small-group leader needs a copy.

- **Go on a conference:** This is the best way to train your leaders, catch the vision and feel part of the 'movement'. As Gumbel comments, 'Running Alpha without going on a conference is like driving a car without taking lessons.' For details of forthcoming conferences see *Alpha News*, visit www. alphacourse.org or ring the Alpha office on 0845 644 7544.

For further reading

W. Archer and M. Finch, *Diocese of St Albans: Adult Nurture Survey*, A. W. Archer, 2001

Charles Freebury, *Alpha or Emmaus?* (2005, 103 pp.). Available without charge on CD-ROM from the author, tel. 01460 78501 or email charles. freebury@tesco.net

Michael Green, *After Alpha?*, Kingsway, 1998; new edn, 2001

Nicky Gumbel, *Questions of Life*, Kingsway, 1993; new edn, 2003

Nicky Gumbel, *Searching Issues*, Kingsway, 1994; new edn, 2002

Nicky Gumbel, *Telling Others*, Kingsway, 1994; new edn, 2001

James Heard, *Inside Alpha*, Paternoster, 2010

Stephen Hunt, *The Alpha Enterprise*, Ashgate, 2004

Maximising the Potential of Your Alpha Course (contact the Alpha office)

3

Emmaus – a 'journey' approach

Mark Ireland

> It must be realised that usually, after conversion, the soul is spiritually nurtured and fondled by God as a little child is by its devoted mother, who warms it close to her breast ... But as the child grows up the mother gradually ceases her caresses, sets the child down and makes it walk on its own feet.
>
> St John of the Cross

Emmaus is one of the Church's best-kept secrets. Although it is the second most widely used process evangelism course in Britain after Alpha, the majority of church members have probably never heard of it, let alone people outside the churches. The authors of Emmaus take some pride in the rather haphazard way that the course has grown and spread around the country, by word of mouth rather than by marketing strategy. First published in 1996, three years after Alpha, the course books have to date sold 65,000 copies. Although still small in comparison with Alpha, Emmaus continues to grow, and is beginning to get known abroad. If Alpha's strength lies in helping interested enquirers over the line, to commit their lives to Christ, then Emmaus aims to start further back, at the first contact stage, and to continue much further on, fully initiating new believers into the life of the Church.

The aims of this chapter are:

- to introduce Emmaus and the concepts behind it to a wider audience;

- to explore the strengths and weaknesses of the Emmaus material in comparison with other courses available;

- to help churches consider ways in which Emmaus might fit together with other courses and resources described in this book as part of a local church's strategy for evangelism.

What is Emmaus?

Emmaus: The Way of Faith is described as 'a course designed to welcome people into the Christian faith and the life of the Church'. This course was written by five authors who worked together in the so-called 'missionary diocese' of Wakefield – Stephen Cottrell, Steven Croft, John Finney, Felicity Lawson and Robert Warren. Emmaus has three stages:

1. Contact – a simple guide to help churches make contacts with their communities and build relationships;
2. Nurture – a 15-session course for evangelism and nurture, similar to Alpha but with less material on the Holy Spirit and healing, and more on the Resurrection, holy communion, money and relationships;
3. Growth – four books of Growth material, including 15 short courses for groups concerning different aspects of the Christian faith; these are designed for those wanting to grow in Christian discipleship after baptism or confirmation.

Emmaus groups do not usually have a meal together or a weekend away. Teaching is done by a leader rather than a speaker, and a wide variety of learning methods are used, including exercises, buzz groups, Bible study and plenary discussion.

Emmaus deserves a far larger share of the market than it currently has. The investment in marketing has been negligible compared with Alpha – there have been no national advertising campaigns, no 'Emmaus initiatives' and no equivalent publication to *Alpha News*. Emmaus is marketed by an executive at Church House Publishing who devotes half a day a fortnight to it, whereas the Alpha office employs 100 paid staff in London alone. As a result there is very little training and support for those who want to run Emmaus courses for the first time – just a helpful website, an occasional day conference and a handful of honorary regional consultants. Emmaus' penetration of the international market is also modest: so far the course has been translated into only four languages (compared to 55 for Alpha) – German, Welsh, Dutch and Chinese – though discussions are under way about several other versions.

Whilst investment in training and marketing has been small, considerable effort has been devoted to developing and revising the course in the light of experience. Even though the course was only published in 1996, production of the second edition is nearly complete: the revised *Introduction* appeared in 2001, and the revised *Stage 1: Contact* and *Stage 2: Nurture* were published in 2003, and new editions of the three *Stage 3: Growth* books will have appeared by the end of 2005.

Emmaus's subtitle, 'The Way of Faith', is significant. Using the picture of Jesus talking with the disciples on the road to Emmaus, the whole course is built around the idea of seeing faith as a journey of discovery and growth. This is hardly a new idea – Christianity was called 'the Way' before it was called anything else, and Christians were called 'followers of the Way' before they were called Christians. However, using journey as a model broadens the focus of evangelism from simply the period immediately before and after commitment (however long that takes) to a much longer-term process of discipleship. This helps to explain the significant difference between Alpha and Emmaus mentioned at the beginning of this chapter. Alpha is hugely effective at helping people who are already interested in exploring Christianity to cross the threshold of belief, whereas Emmaus aims to start further back, at the first contact stage, and to take the new believer through a much longer period of initiation – the Growth modules contain enough material to last for four years. This has led to many churches using Emmaus Growth modules as the natural follow-on for those who have completed the Alpha course.

Is it effective?

Given that Emmaus has a broader approach to conversion than Alpha, with less emphasis on the moment of decision, some might expect a lower percentage of participants to come to faith during its 15-session Nurture course. This is not, however, the case. One of the striking results of the Lichfield diocesan survey was that the most widely used published courses all showed almost the same proportion of course members coming to faith during the course, and that clergy using their own material or other, lesser-known courses seemed to encounter the highest proportion of course members coming to Christian faith, commitment or confirmation. The findings are set out in Figure 3.1.

Figure 3.1 Percentage of course members coming to faith, Lichfield diocesan survey, 1999

Name of course	Parishes	Attendance	New Christians	Percentage of those attending
Alpha	148	4,687	992	21%
Emmaus	91	527	101	19%
Good News Down the Street	40	320	63	20%
Credo	12	198	59	30%
Other (Christian Basics, Bishop's Certificate, Saints Alive, Welcome Course, York Course, or locally written courses)	55	602	162	27%
Totals	232*	6,334	1,377	22%

*This figure is the number of parishes using any course. The reason that this figure is not the sum of the figures in the column above is that 114 parishes were using more than one course.

Although the percentage of new believers from Alpha was slightly higher than from Good News Down the Street (20 per cent) and Emmaus (19 per cent), the percentage of such on these three courses is remarkably similar, and too close to draw any reliable conclusions – especially as the figures for Alpha include returns from 25 parishes that were using Alpha and Emmaus together. What is significant is that the figure for Emmaus is so close to that for Alpha and Good News Down the Street, given that the latter two courses are specifically evangelistic in design, whereas a 15-session evangelistic nurture course is only one part of the Emmaus material. The majority of the Emmaus modules are concerned with Christian growth rather than with initial nurture, and as a result many parishes are using Emmaus as a follow-up for those who have completed the Alpha course. This difference in emphasis and use would lead one to expect that the overall percentage of people coming to faith on Emmaus would be less than that on the other two courses.[1]

Recent research undertaken for the Salvation Army into the use of process evangelism courses showed a similar overall percentage of people coming to faith (one-sixth of those attending) to the Lichfield and St Albans surveys but a much wider variation in the percentage of people coming to faith through the different published courses.[2] The results are set out in Figure 3.2, based on a survey of 1,152 churches across the denominations.

Figure 3.2 Percentage of course members making a faith commitment, Christian Research survey, 2003

	Alpha	Emmaus	Y Course	Good News	Christianity Explored
Churchgoers	17%	38%	18%	24%	22%
Non-churchgoers	45%	50%	38%	50%	27%

These findings are interesting because they show Emmaus not only performing well among non-churchgoers, but also performing significantly better than any other published course in helping churchgoers to make a commitment of faith. This suggests that there may be something about the learning style and broader theological approach that is more accessible to those who already attend church than the 'speaker/video' style and/or distinctively evangelical theology of Alpha, Christianity Explored and the Y Course.

Return to early Church catechesis

Emmaus is deeply influenced by the rediscovery of the adult catechumenate. The catechumenate (literally, 'teaching pattern') was an extended period of careful preparation for new believers prior to baptism and admission to the

Eucharist which developed in the first centuries of the Church before the conversion of Constantine. This period often lasted three years. The rediscovery of the catechumenate began among French mission priests in Africa, and was restored to the wider Roman Catholic Church by the Second Vatican Council – leading to the development of the Rite of Christian Initiation of Adults. Peter Ball's two books played a key role in making the catechumenate accessible within the Church of England,[3] and the catechumenate approach was a central feature of the House of Bishops' report on Initiation, *On the Way*.[4]

Emmaus draws on a variety of features of the early catechumenate, including rituals of response, stages on the journey, and enough material to last a group for four years – a period similar in length to the longest early Church catechumenate. The four principles underlying the course are as follows:

1. Entry into faith is a process of discovery.
2. This process is best practised as an accompanied journey.
3. It is a process that affects the whole of our lives.
4. Effective initiation affects the life of the whole church.

Although the catechumenate is an attractive model for the Church in an increasingly non-Christian society, a long, slow process of formation is not the only route to Christian faith. There is no hint of catechumenate in the stories of the Ethiopian eunuch or the Philippian jailer, and in John Finney's research (in *Finding Faith Today*) 31 per cent of respondents said their conversion was sudden enough to be datable. On the other hand, even those with a sudden conversion need careful discipling and follow-up, and Emmaus has been found to be very valuable in Lichfield and elsewhere in helping new believers to deepen their faith.

The methodology of Emmaus

Having discussed something of the structure, philosophy and effectiveness of Emmaus, I now want to examine the three parts of the course material in more detail, which are *Stage 1: Contact, Stage 2: Nurture* and *Stage 3: Growth*.

Stage 1: Contact

The *Stage 1* booklet starts much further back than Alpha, helping churches to identify the people they have contact with in the community, and making suggestions as to how to enlarge this fringe. The style is very accessible, with simple text and pictures. The content might strike some as a bit obvious, but the key question is clear – how can we turn the many points of contact a church has with non-churchgoers (through baptisms, schools, funerals, etc.) into stepping stones on the way to faith?

The booklet does not, however, really address the key question of how to actually go about inviting those contacts to come on an Emmaus course. The section on 'The contact has been made. How do we get them there?' occupies under one page of text, despite the fact that this is precisely the point at which most churches struggle. Many churches already have a large fringe of people who have had a positive encounter with church, but who do not seem to be attracted to join a process evangelism course. The *Contact* booklet doesn't really engage with this problem and basically suggests publicity and prayer. As one commentator has put it, 'The gap is left unbridged between having the contacts and getting the people to come.'[5]

The Roman Catholic Rite of Christian Initiation of Adults envisages a clear distinction between the first two stages of the catechumenate. The first stage, a period of initial enquiry, is a 'no strings attached' experience in which Christians make themselves available, often to a group of people who have expressed some interest in the Christian way. This leads into the second stage, in which more formal instruction takes place and the candidates are expected to attend worship. Emmaus Nurture seems to belong in the second stage rather than the first, which means that churches may need to run some kind of open-ended group working through enquirers' questions before they are ready to join Emmaus Nurture. One possible model for handling such a group is given later in this book, at the end of Chapter 4.

One important group of potential contacts not mentioned in *Stage 1: Contact* is lapsed church members. Richter and Francis, in *Gone But Not Forgotten*, argue that 40 per cent of the population of England used to attend church at least six times a year (excluding Christmas and Easter), and that half of these are open to the possibility of returning to church at some time in the future.[6] If their estimates are correct, this is a massive pool of people (10 million in England alone) who might respond to some sensitively worded invitations to specific events.

Stage 2: Nurture

The 15-session Nurture course closely parallels Alpha, with the same purpose of helping enquirers to discover what Christians believe, come to a personal faith and begin to grow spiritually. Although many of the topics covered are the same, a comparison of the outline of the two courses shows some significant differences of theological emphasis – see Figure 2.2 on page 25.

Interestingly, there is a stronger trinitarian balance in the Emmaus syllabus than in Alpha. Emmaus starts with two sessions on God as Creator and Father, whereas Alpha has three sessions on the Holy Spirit and one on the devil, but none specifically about God the Father. Emmaus Nurture has only one session on the Holy Spirit; however, there is a four-session course on the Holy Spirit in the follow-on Growth material, and part of this could be grafted into Nurture by those who feel that otherwise Emmaus is too light on the Holy Spirit. Alpha and Emmaus both give two sessions to Jesus, but Alpha places more emphasis on the cross, whereas Emmaus used to give more space to the Resurrection. Significantly, the revised Emmaus syllabus combines the cross and Resurrection into one session in order to give more space to Jesus' earthly ministry. Emmaus has a session on holy communion and one on giving and lifestyle, in place of Alpha's sessions on healing and spiritual warfare.

The theological balance of the Emmaus Nurture course is much broader and should appeal to those churches that do not sit comfortably with the charismatic evangelical theology of Holy Trinity Brompton. The use of five authors of different traditions (though all of them Anglican) helps to give Emmaus a broader feel than courses by a single author, but it may lack the coherence of a single underlying world view that comes from a single author. Emmaus should also prove attractive to the many respondents in the Lichfield survey who felt that Alpha has too much on the Holy Spirit (especially glossolalia) and not enough on the first person of the Trinity, the Resurrection, the sacraments, the social dimension of the gospel, and the issue of steward-ship. However, by starting straight in with God the Father rather than addressing people's common presuppositions about Christianity (as in the first Alpha talk, 'Boring, Untrue and Irrelevant?'), Emmaus presupposes a greater degree of initial interest in the Christian faith. Since, for most churches, recruiting people to join a nurture course is the most difficult part, getting people to go on Emmaus may be even harder than getting them to do Alpha – especially given its much lower public profile.

Leading an Emmaus group also requires much more preparation by the group leader than is required for running an Alpha course. Whereas with Alpha the leader can simply play the video and ask the questions set out in the book, with Emmaus there are handouts to explain (although these are optional), no course video to fall back on, and fewer discussion questions are provided. There are some suggestions in the Nurture course about possible video or multimedia resources to supplement the course, but getting hold of these would again take some time and effort. However, as I shall discuss in the next chapter, research shows that the more thought and work a leader puts into preparing a course, the more fruitful that course is likely to be.

Both Alpha and Emmaus have a strong didactic content that starts with the Church's agenda rather than the agenda of those who are beginning to ask big questions about the meaning of life. Starting with the Church's agenda is understandable in a religion based on revelation, but it may not make it easy to attract onto the course those seeking answers to questions about why a relative has been struck down with cancer or whether all religions lead to God. The questions most asked by non-Christians – about suffering and about other faiths – are scarcely addressed in Emmaus. This appears to be deliberate: as the introductory manual says, 'We believe that the appropriate point for letting the enquirer set the agenda completely is first contact.' However, there is no guidance given in the first book, *Stage 1: Contact*, as to how to address these most sensitive issues prior to the Nurture course, either in a group or on a one-to-one basis. As Charles Freebury has commented in his comparison of Alpha and Emmaus, 'It is surprising that Emmaus, which otherwise offers such a wealth of material, seems to leave leaders to set off unaided in a territory as hazardous as suffering and human sexuality.'[7]

Churches wanting to run the Emmaus Nurture course need much more help engaging with the questions that non-Christians are asking than is offered in the Emmaus material. The Alpha booklet *Searching Issues* may be a helpful resource for Emmaus group leaders, though some will not be comfortable with the conservative line taken. Interestingly, some churches using Emmaus with enquirers have found better results by starting with one of the Growth courses, on personal identity or spirituality, before tackling the Nurture course. In a postmodern context many enquirers are more interested in experience than in doctrine, therefore short courses on prayer or personal wholeness may be a better starting point than apologetics.

Changes made in the second edition of the Nurture course include the use of inclusive language and a standard Bible version (the NRSV) throughout, with more of the biblical material taken from the Gospel of Luke. Liturgical material has been harmonized with *Common Worship*. There are also more suggestions about possible video clips to use to help illustrate the teaching. This is helpful since Emmaus is now the only one of the five main process evangelism courses (see Figure 4.1 on page 49) that does not come with a video. A CD-ROM is also provided, but this contains copies of the handouts, liturgical material and some useful publicity material for introducing the idea of Emmaus to churches, rather than any audio material to use in the teaching sessions.

Significant changes have also been made to the content of some of the sessions of the Nurture course, with increased emphasis on the way that sin and redemption affect the whole of creation, not just individual lives, and on the Incarnation and the proclamation of the kingdom. In addition there is more about baptism in the sessions on 'Becoming a Christian' and 'Serving the Lord', and a greater place is given to teaching (or 'handing over') the four key texts identified in the Church of England report *On the Way* as being important to Christian initiation – the Lord's Prayer, the Apostles' Creed, the Summary of the Law and the Beatitudes. This receiving, or learning by heart, of a few key texts is a welcome return to an element of Christian initiation that has been somewhat lost in recent years.

Stage 3: Growth

A ten-week course is not sufficient to initiate people into the Christian faith – it can give people an initial encounter with God, which it may do extremely well, but still leave the job of Christian initiation only partly done. Robert Warren, the Church of England's former National Officer for Evangelism, has, on the basis of extensive research into initiation, said: 'Properly to initiate people into a new world view and new lifestyle takes anything from eighteen months to two years, to allow the faith to percolate a person's whole mindset. Otherwise you have what I call a bolt-on spirituality, which is just added on top of a secular world-view.' This is precisely where the Emmaus Growth modules come into their own.

The three books of Growth modules, designed to follow on from the Nurture course, are perhaps the strongest and most valuable feature of Emmaus. There are a wide variety of nurture courses on the market, but only Emmaus offers the breadth and quality of follow-up material for discipling new Christians on towards maturity of faith. The three books contain a total of 13 short courses for group use, as summarized below:

Knowing God
- Living the gospel
- Knowing the Father
- Knowing Jesus
- Come, Holy Spirit

Growing as a Christian
- Growing in prayer
- Growing in the Scriptures
- Being church
- Growing in worship – understanding the sacraments
- Life, death and Christian hope

Christian Lifestyle
- Living images
- Overcoming evil
- Personal identity
- Called into life

Because most of these are quite short courses, of four or five sessions, they provide a very flexible resource for the leader, acting as a menu from which to choose according to the specific needs of the local group. They are written by the same authors and in the same style as the Nurture course. There are useful photocopiable handouts for each session. The flexibility and attractiveness of the materials is one reason why many churches that run Alpha now use Emmaus Growth modules for their follow-up rather than the Alpha follow-up material.

Emmaus Growth modules can also be used to provide excellent and inexpensive resources for ongoing housegroups. Housegroups could all be encouraged to use the same short courses, perhaps linked to a preaching series in church, or each group could be left free to choose which short course it would like to do next. Second editions of all the Growth books – *Christian Lifestyle, Growing as a Christian* and *Knowing God* are now available. The changes made are fairly modest, but include updating to Common Worship and the NRSV version of the Bible, together with shorter handouts and an accompanying CD-ROM containing the handouts and some supplementary material. *Your Kingdom Come* is out of print, but the material on the Beatitudes from this book was recently released as a Lent course under the title *Life Attitudes.*

Four Emmaus Bible Resources have been added to the Emmaus collection. These are Bible study guides for individual and small-group use. The books cover Luke 24 (*The Lord is Risen!* By Steven Croft), Acts 13-20 (*Missionary Journeys, Missionary Church* by Steven Croft), Jonah (*A Rebellious Prophet* by Joy Tetley) and Colossians (*Christ our Life* by David Day). Against the background of the long-standing decline in Bible reading among church members, these attractive books could be a valuable tool to help new believers develop a habit of regular Bible reading at a key stage in their spiritual development.

Youth Emmaus

Youth Emmaus, a 15-session nurture course, was published in spring 2003. It is designed for youth groups and as a confirmation course and is pitched at the 11–16 age group in particular. The syllabus for Youth Emmaus is essentially the same as the adult Nurture course, but the material is presented in a much more visual, interactive and lively way to appeal to a younger age group. Although trailed as having more on sex and less on money than the adult Nurture course, there is remarkably little in Youth Emmaus about boy–girl relationships, despite this being a major interest to those in the target age group. This is a real pity, as love, sex and marriage are areas where young adults desperately need help to develop a Christian 'mind', rooted in values of commitment, faithfulness, respect and self-sacrifice.

One of the strengths of Youth Emmaus is its very creative material for use in worship with young people, including celebrations to mark stages on the faith journey of group members. The material suggesting different ways of leading prayer in a participative and interactive way would be very helpful in any youth or CYFA group, where persuading teenagers to take part in prayers usually has a huge embarrassment factor. Ideas suggested include devising text messages to God, painting stones, giving each other strands of wool, moulding plasticine whilst asking God to transform people or situations, and making 'holding crosses' out of papier mâché.*

One distinctive and very valuable feature of Youth Emmaus is an optional extra session on 'hot potatoes'. This focuses on three issues, two of which are often the biggest stumbling blocks for enquirers of all ages: 'Why does God allow suffering?' and 'Don't all religions lead to God?' The third hot potato is entitled 'Heaven and Hell – what happens when we die?' The material in this session on suffering and world religions could be a very useful resource for any group working with adult enquirers at the Contact stage before they are ready to join the Nurture course.

A new follow-on course for those who have completed Youth Emmaus is due to be published in 2006. This will follow the *Stage 3: Growth* model and examine the themes of worship and Christian discipleship.

Strengths of Emmaus

One of the great strengths of Emmaus is its flexibility. Unlike Alpha, with its carefully worded copyright statement, Emmaus positively encourages adaptation of its material. Doing this rather than using the material off the shelf harnesses the expertise of the local leader, who knows the individual needs of each person in his or her group. Adaptation means spending more time in preparation, but this also means that the leader has more invested in the group, and is likely to be more confident in using the material. It has been said that 10 per cent of people are inventors, 30 per cent are adapters, and 60 per cent are adopters, using things as they are. Encouraging more clergy and church leaders to be adapters rather than adopters could be one of the significant long-term benefits of Emmaus.

*A holding cross is usually made of wood, and is designed to be held in the palm of the hand while praying.

One of the distinctive features of Emmaus is the willingness of the authors to revise their material extensively in the light of experience and feedback received. The publication in 2003 of new editions of Stages 1 and 2 shows a strong commitment to listening and responding to those who use the course. In a fast-changing culture this may well mean that Emmaus has a longer-term future than Alpha. Whilst there have been minor amendments to *Questions of Life* and a remake of the videos, the Alpha course is substantially unchanged from when it was first published twelve years ago.

Another strength of Emmaus is the variety of learning styles it employs. People learn in different ways: 'activists' like small buzz groups and workshops; 'reflectors' prefer larger group discussions and video; 'theorists' like lectures; and 'pragmatists' like meeting the experts. Whilst the 45-minute length and didactic style of the Alpha talks appeal mostly to theorists, an Emmaus session has quite a different feel and appeals more to activists. The talks are much shorter, there is more Bible study and a variety of other activities, and handouts give more detail than the equivalent Alpha manual.

One of the distinctive strengths of Emmaus is the provision of special services to involve the whole congregation in marking stages on the enquirer's journey of faith. These 'celebrations along the way' derive from the practice of the early Church, and can be included as part of Sunday worship, involving the whole Christian community in celebrating, praying for and supporting candidates along their journey of faith. Since faith is understood as an *accompanied* journey, Emmaus also encourages church members to become involved as sponsors for those on the course, praying for them and perhaps attending the course with them.

Emmaus is also much cheaper to run than Alpha or Christianity Explored, with no meals to cook and no weekend away to organize. With no videos and few training conferences or manuals there is also less to spend on resources and training. Each Emmaus session includes photocopiable (or downloadable) handouts for each course member – these are a real plus, and save the cost of buying a manual for each course member which is needed with Alpha and Christianity Explored. The handouts on the revised Nurture course have been reduced to two pages per session, which is a further saving, and means less time at the photocopier.

Issues when using Emmaus

Emmaus has a much lower public profile than Alpha, which may make it harder to attract enquirers to join a group. A person's decision to join Emmaus will depend much more on the credibility of the local church and on the quality of their relationship with the person who has invited them to join. This lack of a national 'brand name' is partly due to the lack of investment in advertising, but partly also a consequence of Emmaus's policy of encouraging local churches to adapt the material to suit their local situation and to choose their own name for the group. Churches choosing to run Emmaus also have to manage with very little back-up beyond the resources themselves – occasional one-day taster courses are held, but there is nothing to match Alpha's support network with its two-day training conferences, *Alpha News* mailings and local Alpha advisers.

The Emmaus web site was significantly expanded in 2004 and moved to a new location – www.e-mmaus.org.uk. It now provides quite a lot of useful material for those thinking of running the course, including the handouts and Powerpoint presentations used at their occasional training days. All the current resources are profiled, along with the nine honorary regional consultants who are now available to give help and advice. Part of the new site is a directory of local courses, though this was not yet operative at time of writing. Much less has been written about Emmaus than about Alpha, but Charles Freebury's privately published report (see end of chapter) provides a very helpful detailed comparison and critical evaluation of the two courses.

The lack of a weekend away makes the 15-session Nurture course last much longer than Alpha or Christianity Explored, both of which also have 15 sessions but tend to last only ten weeks because several sessions are covered on the weekend away. On Alpha three sessions and a Communion service are fitted into the weekend, and the first talk is often given at an intro-ductory social event before the course. Signing up for a 15-week course is a lot to ask of the kind of tentative enquirer who might show interest after a carol service or a baptism interview. One solution is to break the Nurture course up into three short courses. A better way may be to offer some kind of exploratory pre-Emmaus group in the Contact phase to deal with enquirers' issues and questions and then feed them into the Nurture course when they are ready. Churches that find that signing up for Emmaus Nurture is too big a step for their potential enquirers may like to offer a short six-week course like Start! (see Chapter 4) or Essence (see Chapter 12) as a pre-Emmaus course.

The lack of a meal at the start of each session and a weekend away (which are features of both Alpha and Christianity Explored) also means that there is less opportunity for relaxed fellowship and friendships to develop. The omission of a meal was surprising in the first edition of Emmaus Nurture, since one of John Finney's important insights on evangelism is that belonging comes before believing. However, the revised Nurture course includes suggestions about having a simple bring-and-share meal three times during the course, and also encourages churches to consider the possibility of adapting the course to include a weekend away. One of the issues about providing a meal at each session (apart from the cost and the work involved) is that in urban priority areas – such as the one where Steven Croft pioneered the course – people often prefer to eat at home rather than in groups. One compromise tried with success in various places is to start sessions with a dessert rather than a full meal.

Conclusion

Emmaus is an outstanding and comprehensive resource that deserves to be much better known than it is. The *Stage 2: Nurture* course parallels Alpha and Christianity Explored but with a broader theological outlook and a wider variety of learning styles. The absence of a meal and the weekend away makes the course cheap and easy to run, but provides less opportunity for belonging to precede believing. Because the Nurture course lasts longer than Alpha, and does not have the pull of a strong brand name, churches need to do a lot more work at the *Stage 1: Contact* stage to attract enquirers and get them ready to start the course. Some of the materials examined in the next chapter – like Start!, or a home-made enquirers' course – may help bridge the gap between meeting non-Christians and their being ready to enrol on a 15-week course. *Stage 3: Growth* is a unique resource among process evangelism courses, providing 15 short courses that churches can use flexibly in the vital work of helping move new Christians on to maturity of faith and full initiation within the body of Christ. The Growth courses are also very suitable for post-Alpha use and for ongoing housegroups.

Key questions to consider when using Emmaus

- Having made contacts with non-Christians, how will I attract them to come onto the Nurture course?

- Does the Nurture course start far enough back for the people I am in contact with, or do I need some kind of pre-Emmaus group to address the questions they are wrestling with?

- If I am planning to use the Nurture course, should I follow the Alpha model and include some meals together and/or a weekend away?

- If I am using an alternative nurture course, could I use the Emmaus Growth modules to follow on from Alpha, or with existing housegroups?

How do I get started?

- Visit the web site – www.e-mmaus.org.uk
- **Ask around:** There are approximately four Emmaus conferences a year. Email the head office emmaus@c-of-e.org.uk. Ask around local churches to find who has used the course and what advice they would give about making it fit your local situation. Diocesan missioners or other local advisers in evangelism may be able to put you in touch with churches in your area using Emmaus.
- **Buy the resources:** *Nurture* may be used as a stand-alone course, but to get the most out of it you will probably benefit from some of the supporting resources. The *Introduction* gives some basic background to Emmaus and has tips on running groups. *Contact* is of use if your problem is getting a group together for a *Nurture* course. *Leading an Emmaus Group* has practical tips on running groups. *Travelling Well* by Stephen Cottrell and Steven Croft makes a good handbook for members of the Nurture course, as its chapters parallel sessions 6–15 of the Nurture course.

For further reading

Stephen Cottrell et al., *Emmaus: The Way of Faith*, National Society/Church House Publishing, 1996

Charles Freebury, *Alpha or Emmaus?* (2005, 103 pp.). Available without charge on CD-ROM from the author, tel. 01460 78501 or email charles.freebury@tesco.net

House of Bishops, *On the Way – Towards an Integrated Approach to Christian Initiation*, Church House Publishing, 1995

4

Other courses – or write your own?

Mark Ireland

> I found myself more and more interested in spirituality and religion,
> but I never thought of going near a church.
>
> John Cleese

The main problem at the moment appears not to be the lack of evangelism courses, but the lack of people to go on them, which suggests that churches need to do significant preparatory work in which enquirers set their own agenda and raise their own questions before many of them are ready to work through somebody else's agenda in a published course.

One of the most surprising findings of the Lichfield survey into the effectiveness of process evangelism courses was the discovery that a higher proportion of attenders came to Christian faith, commitment or confirmation through lesser-known or home-made courses than through either Alpha or Emmaus. At the same time we found that clergy were much more diffident about recommending their own material than about recommending Alpha and Emmaus. The reasons for this are discussed below. One of the most heartening things about researching for this book has been the discovery of just how much creative energy is going into writing evangelistic and catechetical materials, most of which is never seen beyond the parish for which it is written.

Since the publication of Alpha and Emmaus, there has been an explosion in the number of new process evangelism courses on the market. Some of them have been widely publicized, but the majority have been circulated on a fairly small scale. This chapter aims to introduce the reader to some other widely available courses, offer some critique of them, and encourage local churches to seriously consider producing their own material, either adapted from other sources or written to fit the needs of their own particular situation. Figure 4.1 summarizes the pros and cons of the main published courses discussed in this book.

Figure 4.1 Strengths and weaknesses of the five main process evangelism courses

	Pros	Cons
ALPHA Starts with Jesus *15 sessions*	Strong brand name and national publicity helps attract people Easy-to-use resources National training conferences Network of local advisers Blends doctrine and experience Meal – belonging before believing Weekend away – importance of journey or pilgrimage	Lack of flexibility – no permission to adapt Thin on sacraments Thin on social ethics Are 3 sessions on the Holy Spirit too many? Weak follow-up materials
EMMAUS NURTURE Starts with God *15 sessions*	Theological breadth – 5 authors of differing traditions Flexibility – adaptation encouraged Starts at 'contact' stage Uses greater variety of learning styles 'Growth' modules provide excellent follow-up to 'Nurture' course or Alpha	Unfamiliar name, less well known Length – 15 weeks is a big commitment No videos Needs more preparation by leader Lack of training and support Lack of 'belonging' – no meal or weekend away
CHRISTIANITY EXPLORED Starts with the Bible *15 sessions*	Strong on grace Based on Mark's Gospel Teaching people to handle the Bible Illustrations from contemporary films and novels Meal and weekend away – belonging before believing Talks shorter than Alpha	Can feel heavy on sin and judgement Only 1 session on Holy Spirit 'Masculine' feel – lots of rugby stories
START! COURSE Starts with the enquirer *6 sessions*	Starts at the 'contact' rather than nurture stage – pre-Alpha Learning style accessible to non-book culture Short – only six sessions Very creative use of video More inclusive presentation – black/white, male/female	Moves fast – from contact to decision in six weeks Slightly naff graphics Few answers given on difficult issues like suffering and other religions Only a starter – needs follow-up
Y COURSE Starts with a question *8 sessions*	Starts further back – pre-Alpha More inclusive – female and black presenters Tackles issues of suffering and world religions	Quite intellectual – videos are in lecture format Lack of material on Christian lifestyle Only a starter – needs follow-up Rather stilted videos

Christianity Explored

The course most similar in style to Alpha and Emmaus Nurture is Christianity Explored, which was published in 2001. This course also has 15 sessions, which are spread over ten weeks, with a weekend away after week 6. Christianity Explored is written by a New Zealander, Rico Tice, who is curate of All Souls, Langham Place, London. The course was originally called 'Christianity Explained', but the title has been changed – not, as I first thought, as a move away from 'explanation' to a more postmodern exploration model, but to distinguish it from an Australian course called Christianity Explained. Christianity Explored is consciously modelled on Alpha, and each evening begins with a meal and has a meaty (but shorter) talk followed by discussion in small groups. (A comparison of the 15 topics covered by Christianity Explored, Alpha and Emmaus is given in Figure 2.2 on page 25.) The first session begins by listening to people where they are, using as an ice-breaker the question 'If God were here and you could ask him one question, and you knew that he would answer it, what would it be?' Enquirers are then pointed to Jesus as the one who can satisfy their deepest needs, and to the Gospel of Mark as the place to find out about and encounter Jesus Christ.

The strength of Christianity Explored is its strong engagement with both the Bible and contemporary culture. A lot of Tice's illustrations of biblical themes are drawn from contemporary films and novels, many of which would be familiar to his audience. This opens up possibilities for creative use of video clips as part of some of the talks, now that the Christian Copyright Licensing Scheme has been extended to offer cover for the use of films in church. The rest of Tice's illustrations seem to come from the world of rugby (he used to captain his university team), which does make them feel quite masculine and hearty; however, local churches are encouraged to adapt the material and to use their own speakers, rather than the cassette tapes or videos, providing scope for a more inclusive reworking of the teaching material.

What makes Christianity Explored different from Alpha is primarily the difference in theological position between All Souls Langham Place (where John Stott used to be rector) and Holy Trinity Brompton. Both are large and influential evangelical Anglican churches, but All Souls does not share the charismatic emphasis of HTB, and stresses the centrality of biblical exposition rather than personal experience of the gifts of the Holy Spirit. Thus there is only one talk on the Holy Spirit (compared to three in Alpha), and the first five weeks are all Bible studies on the person of Jesus as recorded in Mark's Gospel. The Christianity Explored web site suggests that the course can be used as a pre-Alpha course, since it examines in more depth the material covered in the first three Alpha talks. However, the difference in theological emphasis between the two courses could be quite confusing for an enquirer who was invited to do both courses in succession.

Alongside its emphasis on Bible study, Christianity Explored has a very strong emphasis on sin and grace. As the handbook explains, 'A firm and counter-cultural emphasis on sin makes *Christianity Explored* a disturbing experience . . . Grace is only amazing when sin is seen clearly.'[1] One of the constant refrains of Rico's talks is, 'We're more wicked than we ever realised but more loved than we ever dreamed.'

Such an emphasis on sin and judgement is certainly counter-cultural; the question evangelistically is whether it is also counter-productive. Telling people that they are more wicked than they ever realized may work among the kind of confident young professionals whom All Souls Langham Place is reaching very effectively. Many people who are searching for faith today, however, including those who come from a deprived background, struggle with issues of self-worth and low self-esteem, have low academic attainment, have suffered from overbearing parents or have been the subject of abuse. Although Christianity Explored emphasizes grace as well as sin, such people may indeed find the course 'a disturbing experience', but one that makes it harder for them actually to hear the good news that they are more loved than they ever dreamed. Although Jesus began his ministry with a clear call to repentance (Mark 1.15), he also modelled a radically inclusive approach to the outcasts and sinners whom the religious leaders had marginalized – see for example Matthew 9.10-13.

A thoroughly revised second edition of the course was published in 2003, only three years after the course first appeared. The main change is the addition of a set of videos (as with Alpha) to enable people who are unable to deliver the talks 'live' to run their own course. The videos will be reissued in DVD format in 2005, with English subtitles for the hard of hearing. Unlike Alpha, parts of the videos are shot on location around the UK rather than in church, which makes for a much more dynamic presentation. There are also tie-ins with the web site to enable users to download free resources to help promote and run their course. There are also signs of a more proactive marketing strategy, with Rico Tice leading training days on Mark's Gospel in Australia, New Zealand, Singapore and South Africa as well as in the UK.

Take up of Christianity Explored seems to have been quite slow in England – there are only 44 courses listed on the website, though there are another 40 in Scotland, 7 in Wales and 25 in Ireland. However there are many courses running that have not registered, and the number of courses running worldwide is estimated to be several thousand. A number of translations of the course are in process, and an 'English Made Easy' version has been published, for the use of international students and those with low levels of literacy. To help new Christians, a new Discipleship Explored course designed to follow on from Christianity Explored has been piloted and is being prepared for publication – it comprises eight sessions and is based on Philippians (as is the 9-session Alpha follow-on course *A Life Worth Living*).

For more information, visit www.christianityexplored.com or contact the UK distributors, The Good Book Company, 37 Elm Road, New Malden, Surrey KT3 3HB www.thegoodbook.co.uk.

Start!

Published in 2003, Start! was described in its initial flyer as 'more "Yeah" than "Ya!"; more football than rugby; more beer than wine; more B&Q than Laura Ashley; more mug of tea than cappuccino . . .' Start! is a bold attempt by the Church Pastoral Aid Society (CPAS) to plug a clear gap in the market for a contemporary video-based presentation of the Christian faith that is shorter, more creative visually and more accessible to working-class culture than any of the existing process evangelism courses. The video is presented by two people (one northern white male, the other southern black female) in a lively magazine format shot in a variety of locations (including Blackpool beach, pier, shopping centre and amusement arcade). The video consists of short segments designed to lead into a Bible passage or an activity, or to open up a subject for discussion in the group. This format makes the video clips a very flexible resource that local leaders can adapt and use imaginatively in a variety of contexts, for example in youth work or prison. The six sessions cover:

1. Life is for living (Issues of meaning, purpose, identity)
2. Oh my God! (Is there a God and how on earth could we know?)
3. Jesus who? (Summary of Jesus' life, historical and scientific back-up)
4. What's gone wrong? (Issues of evil, sin and reality)
5. Dying to save us (What God has done – cross and resurrection)
6. Into the arms of love (How do I respond?)

The accompanying course book includes creative use of pictures as part of the teaching, which is valuable for those from a non-book culture. For example, in session 1 there is a large picture of a busy railway station with people doing lots of different things, and members are asked to choose one they identify with – 'If beginning with God is like setting out on a train journey, where are you?' In session 3 a range of very different pictures of Jesus is spread on the floor and members are invited to pick out one picture that says something to them about Jesus, and to say why they chose that picture. In session 4 the issue of what is wrong with the world is opened up by asking members to choose a newspaper headline from a selection of cuttings spread out on the floor. Alongside this very effective visual material there is quite a bit of Bible study, mostly based on Luke's Gospel.

The high level of demand for Start!, not only in urban priority areas but also in leafy surburbia, has surprised CPAS. Whilst some middle-class clergy may be put off by Robin Gamble's 'in your face' presentation and by the slightly childish graphics in the handouts, the course is proving very popular with lay people who find courses like Alpha, Emmaus or Christianity Explored either too long or too highbrow. However, the course can feel a bit hurried – moving as it does right from first contact to a clear challenge to commitment by the sixth week. The need for follow-up groups is even more important because of the brevity of Start!, and churches may find that the Emmaus Nurture course provides a natural follow-on. Indeed, churches running Emmaus Nurture but struggling to recruit people for it may wish to use Start! in the contact stage as a kind of pre-Emmaus course. Session 2 provides a good opportunity for enquirers to talk about what makes it hard for them to believe in God, but doesn't give many clues as to how to deal with the issues that might be raised, such as suffering or world religions.

For further information, visit www.cpas.org.uk, or contact: Church Pastoral Aid Society, Athena Drive, Tachbrook Park, Warwick CV34 6NG. Tel. 01926 458458.

The Y Course

The Y Course is an eight-week enquirers' course published in 1999 by Agape, the people behind the Jesus Video Project. The style is similar to Alpha, with eight worthy 30-minute talks available on video, followed by discussion in small groups. The videos are simply produced, with a talking head speaking to a rather artificial audience. The course aims to start further back than Alpha, and to address the questions that non-Christians are asking:

1. Is there more to life than this?
2. Can anyone know what God is like?
3. Are we expected to believe what happened so long ago?
4. If Jesus was so good, why was he executed?
5. Why so much suffering and so many religions?
6. Is there really life after death?
7. Can God make a difference in my life?
8. Who wants to be stuck with a bunch of boring old rules?

This is a very worthwhile aim, but the key question is whether these eight questions really are the ones that non-Christian enquirers are asking. Some of them – particularly on suffering and world religions – really engage with their agenda and provide stimulating answers, whereas others – question 3, for example – seem more like a question devised by Christians on which to hang important teaching input, in this case the historical evidence for Jesus.

This illustrates the tension implicit in all courses aimed at first-contact enquirers – how far to let them set the agenda and how far to structure the course around a balanced presentation of the Christian revelation. Experience shows that enquirers are much more likely to be attracted to courses that start with the questions they are actually asking, rather than with the questions that evangelists wish they were asking!

The book of the talks, *Beyond Belief,* could be a useful resource to draw on for those devising their own enquirers' courses or setting up a more open-ended group in which enquirers set more of the agenda.

CaFE (Catholic Faith Exploration)

CaFE is a new four module video- (or DVD-) based course produced by Catholic Evangelisation Services, whose director is David Payne, formerly of Catholic Alpha. Something like 450 Roman Catholic parishes have tried Alpha, but the majority of these have not continued with it. Payne has sought to learn from the difficulties experienced in trying to introduce Alpha to a Roman Catholic context, where there is little experience of small groups, where evangelism is rarely talked about at local level, and where there is still an implicit suspicion of courses of 'protestant' origin. The result has been to produce something which looks and feels Catholic, and which has been very well received by the hierarchy. Cardinal Cormac Murphy O'Connor opens the introductory video by commending the course as a response to the need for 'a new evangelization' so often referred to by Pope John Paul II.

Module 1 – Knowing God Better
Module 2 – Exploring the Catholic Church
Module 3 – Catholics Making a Difference
Module 4 – Outward Faith Sharing

CaFE starts much further back than Alpha, and aims to introduce evangelization as simply one natural part among many of being a Catholic. The initial module – Knowing God Better – aims simply to get Catholics meeting in small groups in the parish to think about and deepen their faith. Much of this material could also be used in an Anglo-Catholic context. The second module explores more distinctively Catholic teaching about the Church, sacraments, Mary and the saints. The third module uses the examples of Lord Alton, LIFE and CAFOD to talk about applying one's faith in daily life, working on behalf of the vulnerable and poor, and then to bearing witness to one's faith. Only in the fourth module are members encouraged to invite others to join them for a short evangelistic course, and here various alternatives are offered, including the Alpha course.

For further details contact: Catholic Evangelisation Services, PO Box 333, St Albans, Herts AL2 1EL. Tel. 01727 822837 or visit www.catholicevangel.org.

Foundations of Faith

Published in 2003 by Church Union, Foundations of Faith is a series of six books which gradually work through the Nicene Creed. The titles of the three books published so far are: *God, Revelation and Creation, Our Lord Jesus Christ* and *Sin and Reconciliation.* They are written by a group of Anglican clergy of a distinctively Catholic tradition convened by John Broadhurst, Bishop of Fulham, and are clearly influenced by the Emmaus approach. Each book contains five sessions, as signing up for five weeks at a time is felt to be less daunting than the 15-week Emmaus Nurture course. A youth version is also planned. The course is designed to be studied on one of two levels, either at the introductory level for confirmation candidates, or at the more advanced level for existing church members.

For further information, visit www.faithhousebookshop.co.uk, or contact: The Church Union, Faith House, 7 Tufton Street, London SW1P 3QN. Tel. 020 7222 6952.

Writing your own course: opportunities and pitfalls

In the Lichfield survey we found that many churches were running courses that had been produced internally, often written by the clergy themselves. Such authors tended to be very diffident about recommending their material to others, yet the returns showed a significantly higher proportion of people coming to faith than where a church was using one of the popular published courses (see Figure 3.1 on p. 35). All the parishes using process evangelism courses were asked whether they would recommend them to others either as an aid to evangelism or for teaching the faithful. The results are set out in Figure 4.2.

Figure 4.2 Percentage of parishes recommending different process evangelism courses in the Diocese of Lichfield, 1999

Name of course	Aid to evangelism	Teaching faithful	No. of parishes using the course
Alpha	115 (78%)	115 (78%)	148
Emmaus	52 (57%)	65 (71%)	91
Good News Down the Street	27 (66%)	18 (45%)	40
Credo	8 (67%)	10 (83%)	12
Own/Other	16 (29%)	33 (60%)	55

What is striking is that, whereas only 29 per cent of those using 'other' process evangelism courses would recommend them as an aid for evangelism (compared with 78 per cent of those using Alpha), a significantly higher percentage of those on the lesser-known or home-produced courses actually came to faith in Christ than on either Alpha or Emmaus (see Figure 4.3).

Figure 4.3 Percentage coming to faith through lesser-known or home-produced courses in the Diocese of Lichfield, 1999

Name of course	Percentage coming to faith
Alpha	21%
Emmaus	19%
Lesser-known and home-produced courses	27%
Average for all courses	22%

What this appears to show is that when clergy take time and effort to devise their own course, related to the particular culture and people they are working with, they are likely to find this more effective than using a pre-packaged course 'off the shelf'. Writing an 'in-house' course takes a great deal more time but may yield more fruit than using a published course with less preparation. This research also shows that there are some very gifted church leaders around who have produced excellent and effective courses for their own use which could perhaps be made available more widely.

Using your own expertise

What locally produced or adapted courses benefit from is the expertise of the local church leadership. Although the authors of published courses have a great deal of knowledge about how people in general come to faith, and are very gifted in explaining the Christian faith to a wide audience, another crucial centre of expertise is located in the clergy and lay leadership of the local church. They are the ones who are expert in the culture, the faith background and the particular spiritual journeys of those whom they have invited to join a particular course.

The strength of courses like Alpha is that they provide an easy-to-follow recipe for those lacking confidence or skills in evangelism. The weakness, however, of prescriptive courses which discourage local adaptation is that they do not harness the equally important expertise of the local leadership, who often know what particular course members need to help them on the next step of their faith journey.

That said, those thinking of producing their own courses would be well advised to become familiar with one or more of the published courses, so that they can build on the research and development that have gone into them, and so that they do not omit any of the key ingredients, such as:

- Is there a warm, welcoming environment, perhaps with a meal, so that belonging can come before believing?
- Are we willing to let the enquirers set part of the agenda, particularly at the beginning, so that the course connects with where they are at?
- Is the teaching of high quality, biblically based, and in harmony with the doctrinal standpoint of our church?
- How will we enable small-group discussion, sensitively led, which enables people to feel secure enough to ask anything at all?

Locally produced courses naturally provide a perfect fit with the spirituality of the church running them. From his vantage point as former National Officer for Evangelism, Robert Warren has commented that the easiest way to create division in a church is through spirituality.[2] As we have already noted, the published courses each have their own spirituality, which may not be that of the host church. Where a local church of a very different tradition is running the course, particularly if videos are being used rather than live speakers, there is a strong possibility that those who come to faith through the course will have a very different spirituality from long-standing members of the church. This may lead to future tensions in the church and confusion for the new believer.

An alternative approach: starting where people are

In my previous parish, having used Saints Alive and Alpha at different times, I eventually stumbled on an approach which I found very effective – something I called an 'Enquirers' Group' which followed no published course as such. I recruited for the group by gradually noting down names of interested enquirers or positive contacts through baptism, school contacts, pastoral visits, and so on. When I had at least half a dozen I would then invite them to come round to the vicarage for an opportunity to ask questions and find out more about the possibility of believing in God. I made clear that I hoped this would be the first of a series of meetings, but I also explained that how long the group lasted and how we approached the subject would be up to those who came along. I then advertised the group in church in a low-key way, hoping that two or three Christians – but no more than that – would come along so that enquirers would be in the majority and feel at ease.

At the first meeting I would get people to introduce themselves to each other and say why they had come. Then I would get out two big sheets of flipchart paper and begin by saying that we were here to explore the possibility of believing in God. I would then ask, 'What makes you think on a good day that there might be a God?' and write down their responses – the birth of a child, a beautiful sunset, or whatever – and discuss these with the group as a way of opening up the possibility of belief. Then on the second sheet I would write down answers to my second question, 'What makes you think on a bad day that there can't be a God?' I would then discuss the second sheet with the group and we would decide what was the biggest issue for people in the group and start there the following week. Right from the first session we would read the Bible together, and begin to see how the Bible could speak to the issues we were discussing.

I have found such an approach to be very relational, and much more nerve-racking than following a set course, but I also find that God steps in again and again when leaders are prepared to be vulnerable. The group was not quite as open-ended as this sounds, as I had a clear picture of the kerygma, the gospel truth, that I wanted to cover, and had a variety of resources to help me over the coming weeks, culled from a number of different courses. However, by starting where the group were at, rather than where a published course thought they ought to be at, I found a much greater degree of engagement from the start. I also found it helpful having a few church members in the group with me, as I was able to bounce questions off them and lead a discussion, rather than being expected to have all the answers.

A question-based approach such as the one described above demands much more of the leader than leading a conventional course, but it is potentially far more sensitive to where people are. As with so many evangelism strategies, there is a trade-off between using packages 'off the shelf', which is much easier but may not be as effective in the particular context, and developing one's own materials, which may well be more effective and more satisfying for the leader but takes a lot more time. The fact that clergy prefer to use published courses rather than their own suggests that they may feel more confident with a well-known brand of course, despite the fact that, as we have seen, home-produced courses tailored to the local situation have been shown to have the highest percentage of people coming to faith.

Dealing with difficult issues

Those who agree to come on an evangelistic course are often asking big questions about life, but published courses tend to focus on their own agenda rather than address the most frequently asked questions of course members. Nicky Gumbel identifies the seven issues most often raised by enquirers (in descending order of frequency) as suffering, other religions, sex before marriage, the New Age, homosexuality, science and Christianity, and the Trinity. Stephen Hunt, author of a recent critique of Alpha, has produced an almost identical list, with suffering (50 per cent) and other religions (15 per cent) predominating, confirming Gumbel's experience that these two are 'overwhelmingly the most common objections to the Christian faith'. Gumbel has written a helpful apologetic book, *Searching Issues*, which covers all these issues, yet none of them is addressed in the main Alpha talks themselves. *Searching Issues* is designed to help small-group leaders answer these big questions when raised by members during Alpha. Likewise, the top questions of suffering and other faiths are not addressed directly in any of the Emmaus Nurture or Growth material. The authors decided after much discussion that such apologetic material would lengthen the course still further – although an optional extra session on these two 'hot potatoes' has been inserted in Youth Emmaus (see p. 42).

Charles Freebury, author of an in-depth comparison of Alpha and Emmaus, makes the important point that this failure to address the questions people are asking may help to explain the struggle that many churches have in getting non-churchgoers to sign up for their evangelistic courses, and also why many people who start a course fail to complete it – a proportion which Holy Trinity Brompton estimates is as high as 30 per cent.[3]

One of the great advantages of preparing your own course is that you have the freedom to start where the members of your group are, and to address the particular questions which have led them to sign up for the course. Suffering and other religions are both complex and sensitive issues, but Youth Emmaus and the Y Course each have a session covering these two issues which leaders might find helpful – the talks of the Y Course are published in *Beyond Belief*.[4] Charles Freebury has prepared Emmaus-type sessions on suffering and world religions which he is willing to circulate. Gumbel's book *Searching Issues* gives a helpful introduction to all seven of these 'hot potatoes', although many leaders may want to offer a different answer from the conservative evangelical line given.

Drawbacks to running any type of process evangelism course

Those with no one to invite them

Process evangelism courses tend to work well where there is a fringe or network to recruit from – either the church fringe or the network of friends of church members. However, those on the fringes of church life today probably account for only 10 per cent of the population, and many people, perhaps the majority, have no Christian friends who are able and/or willing to give them a personal invitation to join a course. Alpha invests heavily in an annual advertising campaign, but calculates that less than 10 per cent of those joining a course do so as a result of seeing an advertisement; the rest do so through personal invitation.

Friendship evangelism, however, has obvious limitations. Churches that want to develop an effective evangelism strategy need to consider ways of making contact with unchurched people who live in their area. One approach that could be worth considering is the Jesus Video Project, where church members visit homes to offer a free copy of the Jesus video, and pay a follow-up visit later to see if the video has aroused interest. Another approach is to 'prayer-visit' particular streets in a parish or area, letting the residents know that their street is to be prayed for in church the following Sunday and asking if there are any particular issues people would value prayer for.

People who don't like small groups

Whilst many people warm to the idea of a small group where they can belong and ask questions in a safe environment, there are others who may be searching for God but who would run a mile from having to join a small group or discuss their innermost thoughts about God with people they know. This may be especially true of men and teenagers, as seen by the profile of those who respond to advertisements placed by the Christian Enquiry Agency.

One new resource which may particularly help churches in reaching those who want to explore faith whilst retaining anonymity is the rejesus web site, www.rejesus.co.uk. This is a site dedicated to providing reliable information about Jesus Christ, and was launched in June 2002 with the support of the Christian Enquiry Agency. There are over 900 pages with pictures, articles, bulletin boards and so on. The simple step of putting this web address on all church publicity – for example, Christmas cards and harvest invitation leaflets – could open the way for a number of people who might not be ready to be seen at their local church to find out more about the Christian faith in the anonymity of their own home. Likewise, putting the web address on every church noticeboard would also mean that the curious could find out a bit more about Jesus Christ before taking the big step of going to a church service for the first time. Often church noticeboards give the impression that the only way to find out more information is to ring the minister, which is a daunting step for many. Displaying such information about web sites would also communicate to passers-by that the church is interested in helping them on their spiritual journey.

One church that wanted to reach beyond the network of people who had some contact with church members decided to give away a present to every home in the area. They bought a large supply of bars of 'Divine' fairly traded chocolate, wrapped them up attractively and put one through the door of every house. Inside each package was a small slip of paper containing nothing on it but a web address. Recipients who chose to visit the web site found a simple notice that this chocolate was a gift with love from such-and-such a church. This was a very low-key approach, with no direct invitation to attend a service, yet the church received more positive response to that initiative than to any other evangelistic activity they had undertaken.

Conclusion

There is now a wealth of good process evangelism courses on the market to choose from, and churches should not be shy of adapting them to their own situation or producing their own material, since home-produced courses seem to have the highest proportion of people coming to faith. The main problem that many local churches face is finding enough enquirers to go on the course that they wish to run. This is often because the published courses begin with the agenda of the evangelist – the good news as revealed in Jesus Christ – rather than with the agenda of the tentative enquirer, who is beginning to ask big questions about the meaning of life but may have all sorts of hang-ups about Christianity, including particularly the questions of why God allows suffering and why there are so many different religions.

There is an important difference between the pre-catechumenate stage, when seekers and enquirers need to be able to set the agenda, and the catechumenate stage, when people are ready to be instructed in the Christian faith through courses like Alpha, Emmaus and Christianity Explored. Newer courses like Essence and Start! are clearly attempting to begin in the pre-catechumenate stage and are already beginning to help many to faith. However, the best answer of all for the point of first contact with seekers or enquirers may be to invite them to meet, either in a group or one-to-one, on their territory in an open-ended, informal way where they can help set the agenda and pose the difficult questions that hold them back from exploring Christianity further. Such an open-ended group demands a lot of the leaders but is a vital step before many of today's religious seekers will be ready to embark on a more formal process evangelism course.

For further information

Visit

www.rejesus.co.uk

Read

Charles Freebury, *Alpha or Emmaus?* (2005, 103 pp.). Available without charge on CD-ROM from the author, tel. 01460 78501 or email charles. freebury@tesco.net
Nicky Gumbel, *Searching Issues*, Kingsway, 2001
House of Bishops, *On the Way – Towards an Integrated Approach to Christian Initiation*, Church House Publishing, 1995
P. Meadows and J. Steinberg, *Beyond Belief,* Word Publishing, 1999
R. Tice and B. Cooper, *Christianity Explored*, Paternoster, 2002

To explore the 'contact' stage, and to create an atmosphere in which process evangelism courses are likely to flourish, a valuable new resource is:

Bob Jackson and George Fisher, *Everybody Welcome*, CHP 2009. The course consists of a DVD, Leaders' Manual and Members' Manual

5

Missions and evangelists – a crisis within the process?

Mike Booker

Through the Holy Spirit, who distributes His charismatic gifts as He wills for the common good (1 Corinthians 12.11), Christ inspires the missionary vocation in the hearts of individuals.

Documents on Vatican II

Parish missions: out of date?

As we have seen, the Decade of Evangelism was in many ways a decade of learning about evangelism. Certain things stand out in that learning process. Central to this is the recognition that for most people the discovery of faith is a process, a journey. This is reflected both in the shorter journeys represented by process evangelism courses, and also in longer journeys which may take many years. Fundamental too has been a deepening understanding of the relationship between believing and belonging. People not only need time to hear the message of the gospel; that hearing needs to be lived as well as spoken.

Christian teaching in schools, the tradition of Sunday school attendance, even a generally accepted assumption that we live in a Christian society – all show signs of increasing decline. As people start further away from a position of Christian believing, so the journey to faith is likely to take longer. As people know less of the Christian message, so the need for its authenticity to be borne out through relationship will if anything increase, the postmodern question being not 'Is this true?' but, more often, 'Does this work, does this feel genuine?'

In the light of the pattern described above, it is not surprising that the Decade of Evangelism was also a decade in which a number of evangelists went out of business. The focus of thinking during the Decade moved from missions (as separate, one-off events) to mission (as an ongoing focus of church life). One piece of advice given at the start of the Decade was: 'Don't invite an evangelist'. Maybe a statement that strong was needed to challenge the existing mindset. If running a special mission event with a special evangelist was the sum total of a local response, there would never have been the transformed status of evangelism in the local church that the Decade aimed to create. But there is nevertheless a long tradition of special mission events and of special evangelistic people, and they can and should still have a significant place in the evangelistic work of the Church.

A historical perspective

The role of the travelling evangelist leading special mission events can be traced back to Paul and his companions in the New Testament. Where there was no local church, pioneer evangelism was clearly the way in which the gospel could reach new places, but even once local churches had been established, Paul and his companions returned to the locations they had visited on their earlier missionary travels. The stated purpose, interestingly, was to encourage the believers (Acts 15.36; see also Paul's stated desires in his epistles: Romans 1.11f.; Philippians 1.8), but such was Paul's evangelistic instinct that it is unlikely that his return visits did not also produce fresh converts, as Romans 1.13 implies. Visits from Paul and other travelling evangelists seem to have been a continuing experience for the Pauline churches.

The line of travelling evangelistic ministry can be traced through Church history, with the travelling prophets mentioned alongside local leadership in the *Didache*, Celtic missionaries, medieval preaching friars, and (in a more clearly continuous tradition with the present day) Wesley, Whitefield and the other preachers of the eighteenth-century evangelical revival.

John Wesley's visits to the corners of the British Isles were clearly not pioneering mission: the Church had been established there for centuries. There was a basic awareness of Christian belief, and people could be called back to it. Wesley sought to preach the unchanging gospel. What was different about Wesley's approach was that he realized that he needed to do so in ways that seemed brash and vulgar both to himself and to his critics, but which were necessary to reach those not touched by the local church. As a high-church Anglican himself, Wesley recoiled from the idea of open-air preaching, but ultimately recognized it as essential for mission. Such was the dedicated nature of his missionary pragmatism that he even got up at 5.00 a.m. so that he could preach to agricultural workers on their way to the fields. From Wesley and Whitefield onwards, a continuous tradition of open-air preaching and travelling evangelism can be traced up to the late twentieth century. It is a tradition that can be found on both sides of the Atlantic, and it is from across the Atlantic that the most significant recent figure has come.

The Billy Graham effect

The ministry of one man, Billy Graham, has had such an impact on the life of the Church in Britain that his work needs special mention. Like Wesley before him, Billy Graham called many back to faith. Seen as a brash young American in the eyes of a conservative British church when he arrived, publicly criticized by church leaders from the Archbishop of Canterbury downwards, Billy Graham (and especially his earliest missions) changed the face of post-war British church life.

Interestingly, the response to Billy Graham in terms of enquirers 'getting up out of their seats' was less marked in the early Harringay crusades than in his later visits. Of the estimated 1,872,000 who heard Billy Graham speak at Harringay and in other meetings during his 1954 visit, a total of 36,431 came forward for counselling after making a commitment or re-commitment.[1] This gives a response rate of just under 2 per cent. Of these, half were under the age of 19 and two-thirds were female. Frank Colquhoun, writing soon after the event, commented: 'It is known that a proportion of those who entered the Counselling Room proved to be a disappointment.'[2]

It may come as something of a surprise to note that the response to Billy Graham's appeals shows a distinct pattern of growth with each succeeding visit. By the 1960s there was a detectable increase in the proportion of his hearers making a commitment, and by Mission England in 1984 the figure had grown yet again. Each of the regional centres that hosted an evangelistic mission week with Billy Graham in 1984 recorded a response rate many times that of the 1954 figure, with an average overall of 9.4 per cent of Graham's hearers coming forward during the whole Mission England campaign.[3]

So what was going on? If the statistics of the three main Billy Graham visits to England reveal a growing response rate, are we actually right in identifying a shift from crisis to process in the way most people now come to faith? Is the answer to our evangelistic needs actually a continuation of big-event evangelism and big-name evangelists?

One person especially well qualified to comment on these questions is Gavin Reid. Actively involved in evangelism through the second half of the twentieth century as a parish priest, travelling consultant and latterly a bishop, Gavin chaired Billy Graham's 1984 Mission England visit. He is also the originator of the term 'process evangelism' and identified in advance of John Finney's ground-breaking research the primary importance of personal relationships between Christian believers and their non-Christian family and friends in the journey to faith.

Commenting on Billy Graham's 1984 visit, Reid described it as 'a last gasp for big preaching evangelists'.[4] By the 1980s, Billy Graham was the last of these. By then, his reputation was established even outside the Christian community: it was high profile and untarnished by the scandal associated with some other evangelists from across the Atlantic. If anyone could still fill a stadium it was Billy Graham. More than that, the churches now trusted him. Nationally, preparation was far better organized in the light of the experiences gained through earlier visits, and individual Christians had the confidence to invite their friends to hear him. Perhaps no other figure could have had the impact Billy Graham did in 1984. Certainly, no obvious candidate was waiting in the wings to succeed him.

Why special events can go wrong

The Billy Graham formula cannot be repeated. An evangelistic mission, in the great bulk of British towns and neighbourhoods, simply cannot expect to work in the same way as the early Billy Graham crusades. The residual faith that enabled one single, eloquent appeal to make such an impact is generally no longer present. Even where a genuine leap of faith is made by the hearer, the habit of going to church weekly is so unfamiliar that follow-up based around an invitation to church membership will be unlikely to succeed. The expectations of some clergy and church members may still be coloured by their own experiences of crusade evangelism in earlier life (the impact of the early Billy Graham missions on vocations to ordained ministry was considerable), but this is not adequate reason in itself to emulate the approach today.

There may well still be many important ways in which parish missions and travelling evangelists can fit into local church evangelistic strategies today, but it is only honest first to face up to some of the disappointments generated by special mission events.

A lack of local ownership

If the energy and initiative to stage a mission come from an outside evangelist, or originate in a wider local church grouping with one or two key figures making the running, others will respond with far less enthusiasm. There is a lack of ownership, with church members possibly being encouraged, cajoled or even bullied into taking part. Events may be well-publicized and planned, but the numbers attending are still disappointing. Many church members are deeply uneasy about inviting their friends and neighbours to things that they have not chosen, or where they fear the 'cringe factor' may simply be too much to stomach.

An inward-looking focus

An alternative scenario may be equally unpalatable. Perhaps a well-known speaker or worship leader has been invited. They may draw the faithful in large numbers, but the whole occasion is too deeply embedded in church culture to make sense to many who are outside the worshipping community. Meetings are packed with the eager ranks of the faithful, but non-church friends are few and far between.

A bolt-on activity

A one-off event can deflect attention from the more pressing need to view the whole of church life as a missionary activity. A parish mission can too easily become a bolt-on part of church life, run and owned by those who 'like that sort of thing'. Again, the cultural gulf between church and society is likely to mean that events are sparsely attended, since those with the energy and commitment are occupied in making the mission happen while others feel little ownership. Any converts will be unlikely to survive as church members. Having made just one significant step in a long journey, they will need support and nurture, but the limited evangelistic energy within the church will have been exhausted by the one-off event, which is not integrated into a whole church strategy. At its worst this can then further deepen the resistance to evangelism in general on the part of church members. The 'we tried it several years ago and it didn't work here' attitude does little to encourage new evangelistic ventures in the future.

Evangelists and the local church

Working with travelling evangelists is not always straightforward. Brash revivalism, the 'lone ranger' mindset which makes relationships with local Christians uneasy, the pastoral repercussions of the evangelist's instinctive desire to clinch the deal, have all left questions in the minds of many about the appropriateness of professional evangelists in the current cultural climate.

Yet it would be wrong and unfair to write off the work of gifted individuals because of prejudice and third-hand anecdotes. Perhaps more dangerous is the temptation to leave evangelism to the experts. The feeling then is that inviting an evangelist means the local congregation can tick the 'evangelism' box and view that part of their mission as covered. Evangelism is too important to be left to outside evangelists alone. It must be a shared enterprise, the work of the whole people of God. However, just as churches need clergy, musicians, children's and youth workers and a whole range of others with particular callings, so there remains a need to draw on the gifts of evangelists. As a good worship leader or choir mistress will lead others in the worship of God, so a good evangelist will lead others in their shared work of evangelism.

The Church of England has begun to make significant moves towards recognizing that evangelists are needed. In setting up a College of Evangelists, national accreditation is now available to evangelists from a range of backgrounds. In researching for this book it has been fascinating to encounter a large number of people who quite clearly have gifting as evangelists. They have a hunger and enthusiasm which stand out, even when they are not discussing overtly evangelistic topics.

The Church needs evangelists. Their gifts can touch the parts other church members cannot (so easily) reach. They can also touch the parts the vicar cannot reach. Until recently at least, clergy selection and formation have majored heavily on gifts related to pastoring and teaching. There has been less encouragement to ordinands with a primary gift of evangelism. This is understandable: evangelists do not always fit easily into church structures, and pastoral disasters caused by over-enthusiastic or insensitive clergy can cost the Church dearly in terms of bad publicity. The tendency to play safe in selecting candidates for ordination is understandable, but if the church is to reach *outside* the structures it needs to take the risk of involving evangelists in its leadership. Some evangelists will have a wider Church ministry, but many others, lay and ordained, need to exercise their ministry in the context of the local church.

Evangelists *in* the local church

Most people come to faith through long-term relationships with church members, but that should not lead us to conclude that this is the only way to faith, or even that it is the best way. It is usually unwise to attempt to get an 'ought' from an 'is'. More practically, the journey to faith that starts with relationships is likely to be one fewer people take, as nationally the Church's fringe shrinks in size. Churches themselves are more culturally distanced from the wider community as they strive to maintain Christian standards and identity in a deChristianized world. Those churches that do thrive may be those with a distinctive character and less cultural overlap with the world around. The shrinkage of the Christian community means that there are fewer and smaller congregations to have contact with the surrounding world anyway. The local church certainly needs the help and the gifts of the right people if it is to reach outwards.

The Church of England report *Good News People* represents a significant recognition of the place of local evangelists within the local church's life. In any given congregation there will be those whose gifts and instincts are evangelistic. They are part of the shared ministry of the church, but their desire will also naturally be that of someone 'who goes where the church is not'.[5] While most members of the congregation may feel happiest in a Christian setting, the evangelist's instinct will be to seek out non-Christian company.

Evangelists and the point of decision

Coming to faith may be a journey, but the evangelist's instinct will be to clinch the deal. Whether it be to clarify the nature of faith and to give confidence in Christian believing, or to challenge the hearers to take a first step, the evangelist is the person who can make something happen. Evangelists are supremely gifted in kick-starting journeys that have not yet begun, getting people out of comfortable ruts or turning them back from dead-end diversions. Spiritual journeys can sometimes seem confusingly unmapped, without signs to help us chart our progress. Whether visiting or local, the evangelist can be the person who helps people to see that a major leg of that journey can be, or has been, accomplished.

Why special events are still important: missions as part of the process

The growing recognition over the last 20 years or so that the journey to faith is a process may in part be detecting a change in society, the growing gulf between secular (or postmodern, pluralist) society and the Christian gospel. It may also be a recognition of something that has always been going on. Evangelist Bryan Green commented shrewdly at the time of Billy Graham's first Harringay crusade:

> Thousands on the fringe of the Christian Church, young and old, who are linked with some religious activity or organisation but are not yet practising Christians, will be brought to Harringay Arena. Prayer and persuasion will get them, for they are already partially in contact with the Christian Church.
>
> I hope, too, that the large scale of the effort will attract some of those right outside. Remember, if out of the total audience only ten per cent are in this category that will make nearly a thousand a night. Some conversions may occur amongst these people, but even if they are not yet ready for this we believe that their interest may be aroused, and that they may continue to seek until God finds them.[6]

The journey to faith is a process, but within that process one or more crisis points and major steps forward may be of fundamental importance. A mission event, be it for a week or more, a shorter mission weekend or a one-off special, can provide a break from normal routine and normal relationships, and thus help people to take significant steps forward in their journey of faith.

David Banbury, an evangelist working with the Church Pastoral Aid Society, has identified the following advantages of mission events:[7]

For people inside the church, a mission

- builds up and deepens congregational faith;
- creates greater confidence in personal evangelism amongst the congregation;
- builds up a sense of unity in the body (a sense of working together and building relationships);
- helps to keep mission and evangelism as a key element of church life.

For people outside the church, a mission gives people the chance to move on in the Christian journey, including . . .

- becoming interested in spiritual things;
- being interested in finding out more and being drawn onto process evangelism courses;
- making decisions to follow Christ.

A realistic assessment of the aims of a mission event needs to give full weight to each of David Banbury's points, and more. For a member of the congregation, inviting a friend to a mission event may in itself be a major step of faith. Seeing that friend come, and seeing the friend discover that there is more to Christianity than they previously thought, may be a significant step forward for both the church member and their friend. Confidence in their own ability to play a small part in evangelistic activity, and in the Christian message itself, will have grown. Belief that prayer actually makes a difference will have been strengthened. Working alongside church members will have given a new sense of partnership in the gospel. The place of mission events in building faith for believers should never be underestimated. The involvement of young people as counsellors working with those who came forward at the Harringay crusades led to a measurable increase in the number offering themselves for ordination. Having experienced the excitement of seeing somebody take a step of faith, a significant number of people chose to go on to a lifetime of ordained ministry.

If an invitation to a mission event can have that impact on a church member, what of the friend who was invited? Just possibly they may have taken the step of personal commitment and found the mission marks the start of a lifetime of living faith and discipleship. Probably they will not. But an assessment that the mission is therefore a failure, in the case of this person at least, is wide of the mark. If all has gone well there has been a powerful presentation of the Christian message. Old certainties may have been challenged, while the Christian message and the Christian community now look altogether more plausible than had previously been the case. The evangelistic challenge that seemed to draw no response may actually continue to resonate in the memory, and may fall into place in the context of a different event or another conversation some time in the future.

For both parties, a new element will have been introduced into their relationship. The church member may have struggled to articulate his or her faith in the context of this friendship, but now another person or event has done it for them. There is a new content to the friendship. A future invitation to join Alpha or another process evangelism course may receive a positive answer which would never have been forthcoming without the mission event.

Planning an effective parish mission

Building ownership

Parish missions need to be owned by local Christians. That means that special mission events should happen only if local Christians are ready to welcome them. Enthusiastic church leaders and eager travelling evangelists cannot make the decision alone. This may often mean that big-scale missions have less impact than local ones, since it is at the local level that genuine support can be assured. It is rather less often that the whole Christian community in a city will be enthusiastically behind a mission proposal.

Ownership can be built, especially if the views of local people are taken into account, if their way of doing things is listened to. One practical step is to major on events which local people feel happy with. A wise starting point may be to get the whole parish together before a mission and ask members to dream up the kinds of meeting they would find it easiest to invite their friends to. What would the meetings look and feel like? Where would they happen? The 'dream' factor can be of profound significance in building ownership of a mission.

Ownership of a mission can sometimes be hampered rather than helped by over-enthusiastic clergy leadership. Fan the Flame weeks, originating in the Anglican diocese of Chichester but now accessible to churches across Britain, aim to encourage fresh faith and commitment within and around the fringes of churches, mainly within a broadly catholic tradition. One of the strengths of the approach is the insistence that the parish's co-ordinating team is lay-led. The parish priest needs to be supportive, but nothing will happen unless the church council is prepared to initiate the contact and members of the congregation are ready to take responsibility for the organization of the local church's relationship with the visiting mission task force.

This needs to apply to the whole shape of a mission, but the nature of events needs to be owned too. An illustration from a recent mission experience makes the point well.

If there was one place I did not want to be it was at a women's craft evening a few years ago. Several female mission team members had been encouraged to go, all claiming a lack of any craft abilities, and as team leader I stayed at the back to observe. The tent in the park down by the riverbank was packed. The craft, quite frankly, was breathtaking at times. This was a high-quality event, and local church members were confident to bring their friends. In a positive and buzzing atmosphere, two people told the messy but real stories of how God had taken hold of them and woven something beautiful out of their lives. The craft evening was the idea of the local people, not of the visiting team. I thought it would be outdated and embarrassing, and I was completely wrong. Not only was the event high quality, it was *owned*, and people had confidence in the event because it was their idea and their event.

Building relationships

Some of the most important preparation for a parish mission will take place long before the mission or even its preliminary planning begin. It has to do with who people are, and how they live.

On another mission, driving up the hillside, I was uncertain how many people would be there. The usual excuses had been offered, perhaps previous commitments or a lack of baby-sitters. It was only once I tried to find a parking space outside the house that I realized this supper party was going to be bigger than most. Even in a big house, almost every space was occupied. People moved around confidently because they knew the home, and clearly knew the reputation of the hostess's cooking! One of the mission team, a retired soldier, spoke simply and powerfully of how God had called him to surrender and put his faith in Christ. The audience listened to every word, and then (over puddings which made it even more attractive to do so) stayed and talked long into the night. Conversation was clearly a natural thing in that home. The presence of mission team members simply changed the subject matter, put God on the agenda in a fresh way.

Parish missions depend on relationships, and cannot in themselves be the time when most relationships begin. Relationships take time, and genuine love. If those are offered, and offered out of conviction, long before any mission event begins, the channels are open. Mission events can change the subject of conversation, and visiting outsiders can challenge in a way that old friends may be less able to do, but hospitality and relationships need to have deep roots. An invitation from cold to a barbecue at which an evangelist will speak is unlikely to elicit an enthusiastic response; an invitation to a barbecue just for the sake of friendship will.

Growing local evangelists

At the most local level, a searching out and recognition of gifts in evangelism may be one of the most important steps that a church can take. Peter Wagner suggests that approximately 10 per cent of Christians have the gift of evangelism.[8] While this may be impossible to verify (and the percentage will grow or shrink depending upon the criteria we employ to identify the gift), it is certainly true that most congregations contain a large number of people who feel uneasy about the whole idea of evangelism, and downright terrified when a preacher exhorts them to 'get out there and do it'! At the same time, others sitting in the pews may be longing to share their faith. Natural extroverts, conversationalists and bridge-builders, their only desire is to be released from other responsibilities so that they can be free to share their faith with others in the area. These instinctive evangelists within the body of the local church can play a major role in bridge-building and community projects, in inviting friends, colleagues and neighbours to process evangelism courses, and by working in many other ways to implement strategies for evangelism.

Freeing local evangelists

Evangelists from within the congregation at a church planning meeting can be vital in helping a congregation to look outwards, and may be the ones who encourage a whole church towards taking on a mission. They are the people who can help move a conversation on at the end of a mission event, shifting naturally from polite chat to genuine discussion of what the speaker has been saying. They are the people who will stop a church from thinking a mission is over when the events have finished, and will keep up the momentum through an ongoing desire to see interest on the part of others turn into active faith.

73

Mission events need local evangelists sprinkled liberally through them! Too many natural evangelists are tied up on committees or rotas which do not give them time to exercise their gifting. Spotting and giving time to the evangelists within the local church may make the difference between a mission being a damp squib and a mission that sparks into life.

Multiple aims, multiple events

At an inner-city church in Bradford, a mission under the name of 'Moving On' deliberately aimed to help each church member move on in faith. The aim was also to help each Christian see how others for whom they cared could also move on in their journey towards full Christian commitment. Some steps were small, but nevertheless significant.

A men's five-a-side tournament and curry night did no more than build relationships, but for some women in the church those relationships were deeply significant. For a number of husbands and boyfriends these were the first 'church' events they had ever come to, and the first time they had spent time with a group of Christians. There were no spectacular conversions, but relationships had been built, and a group of men now knew that church and Christians were a lot more interesting than they had previously realized.

Elsewhere, an older church member opened up her home for the first ever time to host a church meeting. A visiting team member talked over tea and cakes about his faith, and a little group of church members and women from around the street crammed into the front parlour. A front door was opened and God was publicly named in the home in a way that had not happened before. Whatever the impact on her friends, an old lady's faith grew that afternoon.

At the end of the mission week a multi-media event proclaimed the message of Good Friday and Easter. Video, music, mime and a brief but clear address drew together the gifts of visiting team members and local church people. For two people the evening was life-changing, as they made a personal faith commitment.

In and around every church there will be people at every stage of the journey of faith. An effective parish mission needs to have something to offer to each of those stages.

This particular mission week could be evaluated in a number of ways. On one level there were 'only' three converts by the end of the week, and it could therefore be adjudged to have been relatively unsuccessful. On another level, as the stories above show, a very large number of people had moved on in their faith in many different ways. The range of events (and there were many more than those described above), the different ways in which people responded to God in new ways, were all noted and affirmed by the vicar. In looking back at the mission, each person who had taken part could see just how much had been achieved. They themselves had moved on in faith, and the steps others took, small as well as large, were noted and celebrated.

Going on a mission

My friend Brian supplies fire extinguishers. He is also an instinctive evangelist: not a professional one, but one of those people with a special gift to bring to the local church. The number of people across the Midlands who have heard about Jesus while having their business's fire safety checked out must be quite considerable by now!

Brian's ministry as an evangelist was important, but it was also lonely and one not often recognized by his local church. When the opportunity came to respond to an invitation from a nearby parish, Brian joined a small mission team for a one-off visit. Doing what he already did so well, Brian spoke naturally and powerfully of God's love and of the reality of God at work in his life. People heard the gospel, but at least as important was the fact that Brian grew, and the team grew as we saw Brian's gifts put to such effective use.

Missions need not only be about welcoming outsiders. One of the most challenging and formative experiences can be taking part in an evangelistic event elsewhere. Speaking openly about our faith on home ground can be scary, and even Jesus found that a prophet might not be honoured in his own country. It may actually be easier to take the risk of looking a fool for Christ outside the familiar environment!

One of the best-developed approaches to reaching far beyond the fringe of church life is Through Faith Missions and their 'Walks of 1000 Men'. Teams of men are involved in walks across an area of the UK, speaking in pubs and in any other available venue as they make their way through the country. The impact on the areas visited has been remarkable in some cases, but the impact on the team members may be at least as significant. Those who have seen

God work through them outside the home environment may be the ones who begin to have the courage to believe that God can use them and others *within* that home setting too.

Following on

Parish missions in the past may have seen 'follow-up' purely as a process in which church members followed up new converts, encouraging them to join churches and grow in faith. There may still be a need for this, but more often those who came to the mission have reached a different point in their journey. Many who come to a point of clear commitment during a mission will already have a church link; their believing is catching up with their belonging. Follow-up for them means being ready to welcome them, and to help them in their own following on in faith. A service during which baptismal vows are reaffirmed may be helpful in strengthening their decision to do this.

For others, the mission events may have sparked interest and a desire to keep searching. If the implication given by a mission is that this is a 'now or never' opportunity, then some of those who are most drawn by the message will have nowhere to continue their interest. Experience of leading missions over a number of years suggests that by far the most likely outcome of a mission is a small number of converts but a much larger number of enquirers, people who are not at a point of decision but who do wish to keep on doing some serious exploration. The destination for most still lies ahead, but the journey has been commenced. The task of the local church is to keep those enquirers following on in that journey.

Parish missions in the mix

Special mission events need to remain as part of the mix in local church evangelism. Standing alone, as the only expression of evangelism in local church life, their day is almost certainly past; woven in with a range of other strategies, parish missions and the special gifts of evangelists (both travelling and local) have a vital part to play. So how might a mission weave in with some of the other strategies for evangelism?

Missions and process evangelism courses

The journey to faith today, as we have stated, is likely to take longer than was the case in previous generations. Progress from having no contact with the Church to a living personal faith during the course of a short mission is relatively rare. Very often what the mission will do is play a major part in raising questions and arousing interest. The curiosity aroused may be one of the main means through which people begin enquirers' courses, but they will come very definitely as enquirers, not as converts. Given the difficulty we have seen in helping church members invite people to join Alpha, Emmaus and other process evangelism courses, a mission event may be of great importance in this. An outside evangelist may increasingly need to function as a 'salesman' for Alpha, Emmaus, or one of the other process evangelism courses available, explaining the opportunity and challenging people to find out more.

Missions and community ministry

The gospel needs to be seen in action as well as heard in words. A mission event that involves community action can speak with greater authority than one that relies on words alone. The challenge that a mission provides can and should be for believers as well as outsiders. The evangelist whose call to commitment brings a whole new group of people onto the team for the local soup kitchen may in turn be creating a great range of new relationships from which fresh mission will flow in the future.

Missions and church health

In the quest to produce healthier churches, the struggle is often less in diagnosing the problem, more in making the change. Robert Warren's *The Healthy Churches' Handbook* notes that healthy congregations (amongst other things) (i) are energized by faith and (ii) have an outward-looking focus.[9] A parish mission may be of crucial importance in challenging a church to look outwards. If it works well, and if there is the level of ownership that draws people into passionate prayer, the church may be energized by faith in a way that was unknown before the event.

Missions and new ways of being church

A parish mission may lead to a large number of enquirers being contacted all at once. Whereas individuals can be socialized and gently encouraged to become 'more like us', a special mission event may leave the local church facing the 'problem' of how to assimilate a sizeable group of new people all at once. This may provide the incentive to think afresh about what we really mean by 'church'. Will the journey towards Christian faith for this group mean a journey towards church as we currently express it, or is the church ready to move towards them? This should certainly not be the only occasion on which this question is asked, but the sudden emergence of a group of enquirers after a mission event may pose it so directly that it cannot easily be avoided.

Conclusion

There is still a fundamental need to give opportunities for points of decision and moments of commitment. Our culture is changing, and the gulf between the Church and the world around it has widened. In the past the point of crisis may more often have been a moment of conversion. Today the crisis may come earlier in the journey, and the role of a mission or of an evangelist may be to challenge people to begin taking that journey seriously. Following up is more likely to be a question of following on, with process evangelism courses giving an ongoing opportunity to investigate further.

Parish missions are most effective when a church is already looking outwards, but they can also have a major impact in encouraging that move towards being outward-looking. Often the church fringe will grow, many more people around recognizing that Christianity has much more to offer than they had previously realized. Within the congregation, the spiritual temperature can be raised and changes can begin which have a long-term impact. As one vicar in a now-thriving church commented recently about a parish mission five years before: 'That was when it all began, really.'

For further information

Visit

http://www.churcharmy.org.uk/
www.t-f-m.org.uk/Index.asp?MainID=1898
www.cpas.org.uk

Contact

Fan the Flame Missions, Bishop Lindsay Urwin, Bishop's House, 21 Guildford
    Road, Horsham RH12 1LU. Tel 01403 211139

Read

Michael Green, *Evangelism Through the Local Church*, Hodder and Stoughton,
    1990 (See especially chapter 13)
Lawrence Singlehurst, *Sowing, Reaping and Keeping*, Crossway, 1995
Paul Weston, *Planning a Church Mission*, CPAS 1993

6

Learning from the world Church

Mark Ireland

> For Africans, turning to God is a completely normal thing; indeed life
> would be unimaginable if we did not have the possibility of turning
> to God for help and protection.
>
> Bishop Sebastian Bakare, Zimbabwe

This chapter does not evaluate a particular course or strategy, but rather opens up a major resource for evangelism that many churches in Britain have yet to utilize fully. World mission has something of an image problem. If you mention a 'missionary' event in a local church people tend to have a picture in their minds of a worthy but dull slideshow in a draughty church hall followed by lukewarm tea while listening to some formidable missionary recently returned from preaching to the 'heathen' in Africa. Such stereotypes are so out of date as to be laughable, and the reality is completely different. Africa has now become a majority Christian continent where the Church is continuing to grow apace, in stark contrast with Europe where the Church is generally struggling with long-term decline in numbers. The direction of world mission has changed – instead of from north to south and from west to east, mission is now (in the words of Michael Nazir-Ali, the Pakistan-born Bishop of Rochester) 'from everywhere to everywhere'. The language of world mission has also changed to reflect the new realities, with missionaries being replaced by 'partners in mission' and missionary societies becoming 'mission agencies'.

Massive growth

Compared to the hard slog that evangelism is in Britain, the rapid numerical growth of the Church worldwide is heart-warming and inspiring. There are now many more Anglicans in Nigeria than in Europe and North America combined. Uganda is now 80 per cent Christian and a net exporter of missionaries. The West now accounts for less than 30 per cent of missionaries worldwide. In China the Church has flourished despite great hardships and is now estimated to number more than 110 million. The churches of Malaysia and Singapore are seeing rapid growth, particularly among tribal peoples. Church growth in Cambodia has been rapid since the end of the militantly atheistic Khmer Rouge in 1990 – since then 1,000 churches have been planted and church membership is estimated at 100,000. In Nepal, despite laws preventing change of religion (only recently repealed), the Church has grown from a few hundred in the 1970s to over well over 150,000 today. The contrasting trends of church membership in Asia and Europe are shown in Figure 6.1.

The graphs in Figure 6.1 show clearly that churches in Europe need help in evangelism, and that churches in Asia (as well as those in Africa and South America) may have very valuable lessons to teach us from their own experience. For too long we in Britain have thought of world mission as 'what we can do for them', whereas we now need to recognize that our own country has become a mission field and that we need others to come and help us in mission. Churches in Britain are very good at raising money and sending resources to help less affluent churches in poorer countries. However, we have been less good at recognizing the strengths of the world Church in areas where we are weak and having the humility to learn from them. One such area is evangelism.

Many churches in this country – both local and national – have direct links with churches in other parts of the world, but how far are we actually using these links to help us in our evangelism?

In this chapter I want to explore ways in which the older and sometimes tired churches in Britain can learn from and engage with the energetic younger churches (which they of course helped to plant) in other parts of the world:

- Visits from mission partners from growing churches overseas can envision churches for evangelism and help them to develop a strategic approach;

- Involvement in short mission visits abroad can fire up the faith of church members and give them confidence in sharing their faith;

- Sharing in mission abroad can have a powerful renewing impact on tired or burnt-out church leaders;

- The presence of mission partners from overseas can greatly raise the profile of a parish mission and open doors;

- Churches with active exchange links with the world Church are more likely to attract new members from ethnic minorities in their local communities;

- Helping with the cost of an air fare can turn a gap year into a life-changing experience for young Christian leaders.

Figure 6.1 The Christian community by denominational groups, Asia and Europe

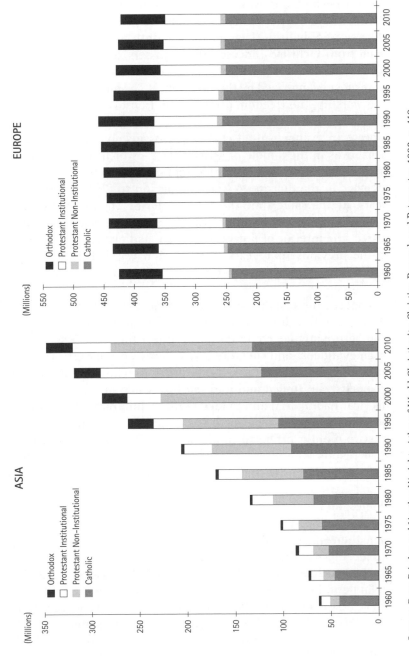

Source: Peter Brierley and Heather Wraight, *Atlas of World Christianity*, Christian Research and Paternoster, 1998, p. 110

Envisioning for evangelism

When I became a diocesan missioner Michael Sheard, who was World Mission Officer in the same diocese, wisely sent me to the Diocese of Sabah in Malaysia for a month as part of a mission team from Lichfield Diocese. Although sent as a 'mission team' we found (like so many missionaries) that we were the ones who were most evangelized by the experience. The quality of the praise and worship, the freedom given to children to use their spiritual gifts and minister to adults, and the strong lead given by the diocese in evangelism all challenged us deeply. The Diocese of Sabah was in the middle of Mission 113 – which was a challenge from Bishop (now Archbishop) Yong Ping Chung to every church member in the diocese to lead one person to Christ every three years. At the same time the Sabah Interior Mission, which was evangelizing the communities that lie along the eight rivers that dissect the interior of northern Borneo, had planted 64 churches in the previous four years. This mission was led by just eight national clergy, with 64 full-time evangelists and 400 lay leaders.

I wondered for a while what might be the secret of such a fruitful strategy, until I discovered that the policy in Sabah Diocese was that before anyone could train as a priest they had first to train as an evangelist and spend two years proving their effectiveness in evangelism. When I asked one priest how he had become an evangelist, he smiled and told me that when he was a teenager his vicar had invited him to take part in a programme for a group of school leavers in his church – a programme designed to fill in the two months off between taking their final exams and getting their results. The vicar brought the group together, gave them one week's intensive training, taught them how to deliver two simple sermons, gave them each a bag of rice and a few clean clothes, and then dropped them off in the middle of the bush to evangelize. Those who proved themselves in this testing situation were then encouraged to go on to further training. I couldn't help wondering whether I would ever have made it to ordination if I had had such an exacting apprenticeship! Obviously the situation in England is very different, but a month in Malaysia gave me a whole new realization of how much the tired institutional churches in Britain can be refreshed and learn through companionship links with young, vibrant churches in other parts of the worldwide body of Christ.

Formation of companionship links

Most Anglican dioceses already have some form of companionship link with at least one overseas diocese, but most have not yet realized the full potential of these links for two-way mission. The earliest diocesan link was formed exactly 40 years ago, between the Diocese of Sodor and Man and the Diocese of North Mbale in Uganda. Since then, the development of such links has been rapid if rather haphazard – sometimes they arise simply from chance conversations at Lambeth conferences! The advent of companionship links marked a significant change in relationships between the Church of England and Anglican churches overseas – whereas previously these were handled through the Anglican mission agencies, as the Communion matured into a partnership of independent provinces, their bishops and archbishops naturally expected direct contact with their peers in other parts of the Communion. Although this is a very positive development, one disadvantage of the formation of direct companionship links between dioceses has been that the mission agencies have sometimes felt left out in the cold. However, these agencies are now finding new roles in resourcing the world Church and providing specialist expertise to British churches in handling relationships with dioceses overseas.

All new relationships take time for trust to develop between the parties, so it is natural that the early stages of a relationship with a companion diocese will involve a lot of getting-to-know-you and friendship-building visits. Many diocesan links are still at this stage of encounter and sharing resources, whereas a true companionship of equals must involve sharing together in the common mission that Christ has entrusted to his Church. Many overseas churches are seeing large numbers of people coming to faith in Christ, often in areas where Christian witness is restricted, such as Malaysia, and in situations of persecution and suffering, such as southern Sudan and northern Nigeria. A healthy and mature companionship link is one where the sharing of expertise and resources is truly two-way, and where exchange visits have moved on from entertaining friends to sharing in cross-cultural mission and evangelism together.

Within the New Testament itself we see examples of churches in different places being enriched and encouraged by contacts from churches some distance away. In the days before the development of postal services, the New Testament letters were all carried by Christians moving from one church to another, who were made welcome by and then spent time with the members of the other church. Paul's letters also show how he challenged the church in Corinth and encouraged the church in Rome by the example of the generosity of the churches of Macedonia (2 Corinthians 9.1-5; Romans 15.26-27). The many references in the New Testament to the ministry of Priscilla and Aquila show that they exercised a much-valued itinerant ministry, using their home as a base for hospitality and ministry in Corinth, Ephesus and Rome (Acts 18.3, 26; Romans 16.3; 1 Corinthians 16.19).

No one part of the worldwide Church is or can be entirely self-sufficient: God has not arranged the body in that way. 'The eye cannot say to the hand, "I do not need you"'. The church that shuts itself off from what God is doing in other parts of the body quickly becomes sterile. We are also accountable to one another for how we use the gifts entrusted to us. For God has arranged things 'so that there should be no division within the body, but that its parts should have equal concern for each other. If one part suffers, every part suffers with it; if one part is honoured, every part rejoices with it' (1 Corinthians 12.25-26). Surely this is what truly being 'in Christ' is all about? As Michael Sheard has pointed out in a recent paper, the Church is created by and for mission – God's mission – to every community, ethnic group and nation across the world. Responsibility for this mission is shared. Even though mission in any one place is primarily the responsibility of the church in that place, we are all part of God's family. We each have different gifts to bring to the banquet.[1]

It must, therefore, be the responsibility of churches across the world to both help and challenge each other about how each is fulfilling God's mission. From his or her vantage point outside the situation the visitor from overseas can often help a church see itself more clearly and question the underlying values and assumptions of its society. For example, in the Diocese of Lichfield we need to hear the challenge of our partners in Malaysia about the priority of developing an effective strategy for evangelism. Interestingly, at the same time we need to be free to challenge them about the place they give to issues of justice and care and the social dimension of the kingdom of God.

A willingness to help and challenge each other about how we are fulfilling God's common mission must also in time lead to a greater openness and mutual accountability in matters of finance. Christians overseas may have some difficult but important questions for churches in England as to how far our lifestyle and budgets have really adapted to the missionary situation in which the Church in the West now finds itself. We may also be surprised and challenged by some of their budget priorities. For example, aid agencies working to provide the most basic facilities among refugees from the genocide in Rwanda were taken aback when they discovered that the refugees wanted them to build a church in the camp before they built a clinic.

Benefits of overseas links

A mission trip to an overseas diocese can have a huge impact on the spiritual development of those who take part, as I have seen in so many people who have spent time in our link dioceses in Malaysia. Such visits enable people to take a huge step of faith, and at the same time be challenged by the love and joy of Christians who have so little materially. They also find themselves in situations where they have no choice but to 'give a reason for the hope that is within them' – often without warning! Such experiences bring the Acts of the Apostles alive in a way that a hundred Bible studies never can, and give people a confidence in God and in the power of prayer that has a significant impact on their home churches when they get back.

Sharing in mission abroad can also have a powerful renewing impact on tired or burnt-out church leaders, who find the unresponsive spiritual climate in Britain saps their energy and makes them question their calling. Before I spent a sabbatical in Africa I used to wonder what churches were doing wrong in Britain, because they saw so much less fruit in terms of new believers than in Africa. However, when I got to Africa and got stuck into preaching in a variety of contexts, I found a level of response far greater than I had at home. The result was that I came back to Britain refreshed, with a renewed confidence in my own calling and gifting, and a deeper insight into the harder spiritual climate of western Europe. I realized that it was not so much that what I had been doing was wrong, but that evangelism in Britain is hard work at present.

Active involvement in world mission also makes it easier for local churches to attract members from a variety of ethnic backgrounds. Bob Jackson's research in *Hope for the Church* shows that a church with a mixture of ethnic backgrounds is more likely to be growing numerically than a church composed of just one ethnic group.[2] Churches may see a sudden increase in numbers through the arrival of families moving to Britain who were regular churchgoers in their country of origin – this is transfer growth. However, a church that is actively involved in world mission and is used to welcoming mission partners from overseas is likely to be much more successful in attracting the many people of other cultures and nationalities who now live and work – or who are seeking asylum – in Britain.

Another reason for Jackson's findings is that the presence of a variety of cultures in a congregation is an indication that the church is generally outward-looking and inclusive, rather than inward-looking. Church members who have been offered hospitality in homes abroad will be much more understanding of how to welcome the overseas student or the black or Asian family that moves into their street or turns up at their local church one day. We are not good at hospitality in the West, and we can learn much from churches in Africa and Asia in this regard. We can also learn from their freedom in naming the name of Christ in everyday conversation, which is something that British Christians also find difficult. The relative fall in the cost of air travel makes it much more affordable for some church members in Britain to visit churches and mission partners in Africa, and more affordable to fly church leaders from Africa to Britain for mission visits. If Kenya is now a regular holiday destination from Britain, why not encourage church members to consider using their summer holiday to visit mission partners working there?

What kinds of links are possible?

A diocesan example

In 2001 the Diocese of Lichfield undertook an ambitious month of mission – HarvestTime – for which they were joined by 117 Christians from their companion dioceses in Malaysia, Canada, South Africa and Germany. These mission partners – mostly lay people – came largely at their own expense, not for a familiar 'exchange visit' but actually to share in mission weekends in parishes all over the diocese. Altogether 160 churches were involved in hosting overseas mission teams. They used their overseas mission partners in a whole variety of ways – to speak at Alpha suppers, to do open-air street evangelism or 'Any Questions?' evenings in local pubs, to visit prisons and hospitals, or speak at harvest suppers and guest services.

Having a group of Malaysians or South Africans staying in the parish raised the profile of the church in the local community and opened many doors, giving rise to photo opportunities for local papers and interviews on local radio. Some of the best opportunities to break new ground came in invitations from local schools, who gladly seized the offer of help with the multicultural part of their curriculum. Sometimes headteachers found themselves put on the spot as African or Asian visitors asked them about their own faith and commitment! Often people from other cultures can get away with a directness of approach that would not be possible for British people.

Many church members in the diocese also found their own faith refreshed and renewed by hosting and meeting their visitors. Many wrote afterwards that their Sunday worship had been transformed, and that learning to worship with their bodies as well as their lips had been 'a foretaste of heaven'. They were challenged by their visitors' freedom in talking about their faith, and their willingness to pray at every occasion – 'Why do you in England not give thanks before you eat?'

Mission partners themselves were changed by the experience. Women from Malaysia were allowed to lead worship and administer the chalice in England, having never had that opportunity at home. A lady from Canada wrote (after a previous visit): 'Before I came to England I had never dared to speak in public about my faith. When I got to Lichfield I found I could, and now

I am back in Canada I still can!' Malaysians were struck by the care for the elderly they found in English churches.

What lessons were learnt from this experience?

- Advance preparation is crucial – for both the visitors and the host parishes. Springboard held a Travelling School in Evangelism in the diocese in Lent, and this played a key role in envisioning parishes for outreach and teaching them practical skills. Representatives from overseas came over for this event and met people from the host parishes.

- Training and orientation of mission teams takes time. When the main teams arrived in September, they were given three days' residential training, along with members of host churches, before going to their first parish. Those parishes that failed to send people to the opening training conference, and to the evaluation conference at the end of HarvestTime, lost out on the spiritual impact of the mission week.

- Host churches need careful training in how to put on a mission weekend, so that they use the spiritual gifts of their visitors, rather than simply entertain them. They also need to pace the programme carefully so that they allow their mission partners genuine free time, as well as team time for prayer and preparation. Some very tired people were put back on the plane at the end!

- Cross-cultural mission is neither simple nor cheap. Mission agencies are keen to help with advice and sometimes with a top-up grant. Lichfield Diocese was very fortunate that USPG helped to sponsor the programme as a way of marking its tercentenary year.

Gap-year programmes

Gap years are becoming much more common at a variety of stages in life, not just before or after university. Much the most enriching part of my own priestly formation was the year I spent after university in a small village in the foothills of the Himalayas, teaching at a Christian school in Pakistan. This was completely beyond anything I had experienced before – I was way out of my comfort zone, thrown in at the deep end culturally and educationally. However, the support of a vibrant Christian community within that very different culture gave me a confidence in God and a desire to share my faith that has stayed with me ever since. This is not as unrealistic financially as it may sound. A few hundred pounds to help with the cost of the airfare is a very cost-effective way of investing in the spiritual development of young leaders who will go on to positions of leadership in the Church.

A number of dioceses and mission agencies now have schemes which enable young adults to spend a short-term placement with a church overseas. For example, in Lichfield Diocese the bishop and the dean decided to mark the millennium year by establishing the St Chad's Trust, named after the missionary bishop who founded the diocese in the seventh century. The trust provides bursaries to enable young adults, especially from the more deprived parts of the diocese, to spend six months to a year working in mission situations with one of the diocese's companion links in Malaysia. The trust also enables young adults from churches in Malaysia to come and spend a similar period doing mission in parishes in Lichfield Diocese.

A number of mission agencies offer gap-year and summer placement opportunities. These include USPG, Christians Abroad, Interserve and Quaker Voluntary Action – addresses are given at the end of the chapter. One example of what is available is the Experience Exchange Programme run jointly by the Methodist Church and the USPG. This programme gives volunteers over the age of 18 the opportunity to spend 6–12 months working in a different culture and environment and experiencing the Church in another part of the world. Volunteers have taught in schools, worked on agricultural, health and build-ing projects and helped with children's and youth work. No special skills are necessary and volunteers are self-funded, though substantial grants are available.

A local church example

One creative example of how a local church formed a link with a young African evangelist which lasted for ten years and proved immensely valuable to both parties took place in a Lancashire parish where I used to be vicar. The link started almost by accident, when a letter came from Anglican Renewal Ministries asking if any church could find the cost of an airfare for a young Kenyan evangelist to attend their annual conference – in return he was offering to spend a month working in their parish. The church council agreed to the idea, and I offered to provide accommodation at the vicarage. Even though Gilbert had never been outside Kenya, and I had not then been to Africa, we quickly found that we had a deep bond in Christ, and we became close friends.

Although Gilbert arrived with no luggage to speak of, he came with many gifts, in music, in teaching, in prayer and in children's work. His presence with us helped many children and adults to take significant steps forward in their Christian faith. As an African Christian Gilbert's simple trust that things would happen when he prayed challenged many of our own rationalist assumptions and gave people a new appetite for prayer, even inspiring several all-night prayer meetings. Interestingly, when Gilbert returned to Kenya, his vicar wrote to say how much he had grown in confidence and in his 'spiritual gifts' through his time in Britain.

Contacts continued, especially through our church school, and two years later I was able to spend a week in Nairobi working with Gilbert's team. A further visit by Gilbert to the parish took place the following year, during which I was able to discuss with him whether God was leading him towards ordination. He shared his deep desire to train for ordination, and also the fact that it would not be possible because he had no means of paying the college fees required. After the church had prayed about and reflected on this, they decided to sponsor him through theological college in Kenya. The church was very tempted to invite him to study in Britain, so that they could see more of him, but felt strongly that they did not want to take him out of his culture, and that training in Africa would be much more relevant to ministry in Africa than an English college course.

I was particularly keen for Gilbert to train in Africa as I had seen several examples of gifted young African clergy who had been invited to train in Britain and who had found the experience of learning a Western critical approach to Scripture very difficult. African and Western models of study are very different, and those who are highly competent at working in one may find it very hard to learn another way and then transfer back afterwards. I have also seen others who, having learnt to study in a Western context, enjoyed it so much that they never returned to Africa. In both cases the result is that the African church loses some of its most gifted leaders. In Gilbert's case contact was maintained by correspondence and by a further visit from the parish to Nairobi, and in 2001 came the joyful news of Gilbert's ordination in All Saints Cathedral, Nairobi. This in some ways marked the conclusion of the link, but the Lancashire parish felt deep joy that whilst they had received so much spiritually from the Church in Kenya they had also had the privilege of giving to that Church the gift of a fully trained priest with a heart for world mission.

Possible pitfalls

Not every personal link with a church leader from the two-thirds world is as mutually beneficial and problem-free as the one with Gilbert described above. One of the main pitfalls to be aware of is the potential for cultural misunderstandings about money. Many cultures are much less embarrassed about money than British people tend to be, and may not be shy of soliciting donations for their ministries or their families, especially from fellow believers who have much more than they do and yet seem strangely reluctant to share what they have with their brothers and sisters in Christ. If churches are on the receiving end of requests for financial support to which they do not feel able to respond, they should not feel under pressure, as those who are not embarrassed to ask are generally not embarrassed by a polite refusal. As in all things, giving to the world Church should be done wisely and be a response of gratitude, not guilt. There are, of course, occasional conmen who send unsolicited emails or begging letters, but advice from the mission agencies is that these should always be disregarded.

The other main danger, as we have just seen, is that the seductive appeal of Western affluence can deprive some overseas churches of their best young leaders. I remember one priest from Uganda who stayed with me on a diocesan youth exchange and spent all his spare time scouring the *Church Times* and sending off applications for almost every job listed! Just as a sudden win on the lottery does not tend to make people wise or altruistic in their use of money, so a sudden exposure to the much more affluent lifestyle of Christians in the West can sometimes put temptations in people's way, and make a return to ministry in their home country seem unattractive. The best safeguard is to consult widely before establishing any links, and to work through people or agencies in whom you have confidence. The main mission agencies or societies (CMS, USPG, etc.) have a great deal of wisdom and advice to offer in this area.

World Church in the mix

Planting new forms of church

Christians exploring planting new forms of church to evangelize unchurched cultural groups in the UK can learn much from the experience of cross-cultural missionaries overseas in the twentieth century. Vincent Donovan's *Christianity Explored* is an instructive place to start for those wanting insights into the process of identifying with a particular culture and inculturating the gospel into that culture.

Parish missions

Churches planning a parish mission find that if they are able to include Christians from overseas as part of the mission team it greatly helps to raise the profile of the mission in the local community and makes it easier for church members to invite their friends to local events – 'Come and meet our visitors from Malaysia . . .' An overseas dimension also provides good opportunities for photographs in the local press and interviews on local radio. Overseas visitors from another culture can open doors into local county schools glad for help in broadening the cultural development of their pupils.

Cell church

Churches exploring cell church may be helped and encouraged by contact with churches overseas that have years of experience of the cell approach and may be able to testify to the blessings they have received, in terms of both numerical growth and spiritual life. This could be very inspiring for churches considering taking the plunge, as long as they remember that stories of massive numbers of new Christians are unlikely to be replicated in the very different context of the UK.

Community ministry

Churches engaged in community ministry may be able to learn valuable lessons from the experience of Christian development work overseas – David Evans and Mike Fearon's book *From Strangers to Neighbours* describes a number of neighbourhood transformation projects undertaken by churches in Britain which have benefited from insights from Tear Fund's development work in other countries.

Conclusion

Our experience is that direct contact with the vibrant, growing churches of Asia and Africa can be enormously beneficial in refreshing tired churches in Britain and in giving them a new confidence in talking about Jesus Christ and doing evangelism in their communities. Now that many holiday-makers and gap-year students can afford to visit Africa, new opportunities have opened up for church members in Britain to gain first-hand experience of mission overseas and to develop friendships that can be long-term and of mutual benefit. In an increasingly multicultural and multi-faith society, the insights of black and Asian Christians from overseas with long experience of witness among people of other faiths will be increasingly important. Local churches with strong African and Asian links will find it much easier to attract people from the ethnic minorities within their communities. In developing world Church links there is a world of experience to draw on through diocesan and denominational world mission officers and through the mission agencies, some of which are listed below.

For further information

Contact

Any of the main mission agencies will be glad to give help and advice in developing partnerships in mission. Some useful contacts are:

Christians Abroad, www.cabroad.org.uk Tel. 020 7346 5950.
Church Mission Society, www.cms-uk.org Tel. 020 7928 8681
Interserve, www.interserveonline.org.uk/shortterm Tel. 020 7735 8227
Partnership for World Mission, Partnership House, 157 Waterloo Road, London SE1 8XA; www.pwm-web.org.uk Tel. 0207 803 3200
Quaker Voluntary Action, www.quakervolaction.charitydays.co.uk Tel. 0161 819 1634
SOMA (Sharing of Ministries Abroad), www.somauk.org Tel. 01525 237953
United Society for the Propagation of the Gospel (USPG), www.uspg.org.uk Tel. 020 7928 8681

Read

Peter Brierley and Heather Wraight, *Atlas of World Christianity*, Christian Research and Paternoster, 1998
David Evans and Mike Fearon, *From Strangers to Neighbours*, Hodder & Stoughton, 1998
Guidelines and Principles for Mission and Evangelism, Anglican Consultative Council, 1999
Living Links – How To Make Your Companion Link Even Better, Partnership for World Mission – downloadable from www.pwm-web.org.uk
Michael Sheard, *The Next Step!*, Diocese of Lichfield, 1999 – available from the World Mission Office, 68 Sneyd Lane, Essington, Wolverhampton WV11 2DX
Andrew Walker, *Voices from Africa*, Church House Publishing, 2002 – an anthology of inspiring stories from growing churches in Africa

7

Going beyond the Good Samaritan: community ministry and evangelism

Mike Booker

> Poor, talkative Christianity.
>
> E. M. Forster

> It is no use walking anywhere to preach unless our walking is our preaching.
>
> St Francis of Assisi

The Church has often been criticized for being long on words but short on action. Verbal proclamation has always been a major part of Christian evangelism. The claims made by traditional, orthodox Christianity are certainly bold and all-encompassing. Quite simply, Christians really do believe that in the gospel they have the meaning to life, the universe and everything. In a world suspicious of big claims, we make the biggest there could possibly be! Yet those claims sound hollow if they are not partnered by action. There needs to be a visible demonstration that the truth proclaimed can also be lived out. This chapter will grapple with the less than easy questions of how evangelism and social action can best fit together.

Words and actions: a long tradition

Jesus proclaimed the Good News, but he did so in action as well as in words. Luke records the doubts of John the Baptist, imprisoned and uncertain whether Jesus truly was God's Messiah. Jesus replies to John's messengers: 'Go and tell John what you have seen and heard: the blind receive their sight, the lame walk, the lepers are cleansed, the deaf hear, the dead are raised, the poor have good news brought to them. And blessed is anyone who takes no offence at me' (Luke 7.22-23). The ministry of Jesus included healing and miracles, rightly described by John as 'signs' (for example, John 4.54; 6.14) but certainly far more than just visual aids. The miracles of Jesus were not eye-catching gimmicks, but rather the expression of the love of God in desiring wholeness for all people and for the whole of creation.

Christians through history have tried to follow the example of Jesus in caring for the whole person. Medieval monasteries, Victorian medical missionaries and the Salvation Army, among many others, have provided stirring examples of Christian caring, of living as well as proclaiming the gospel. At the same time it is only honest to pause and to note the failure of much of the Church of God to practise what it preaches. For some people, a lack of social action is the result of theological conviction, the certainty that saving souls is the primary task of the Church, and that spending time on physical needs is a distraction from our central calling. Few churches would hold openly to this view, however. The laws of the Old Testament, the actions and teaching of Jesus, the belief in the resurrection of the body and not just of the soul – all these truths lead Christians to believe that the meeting of material needs and challenging injustice are very much part of the Christian task. It is in practice, in the pressure of time and the busyness of reality, that this holistic vision so often unravels. When everything we might like to do in a day simply cannot fit into the hours available, our priorities will be exposed by what is done and what is dropped.

One example among many possible stories sums up the either/or choices that end up being made when theoretical mission commitments meet reality:

The churches of a large town in the south of England reached a very wide consensus that they should hold a week of mission. The mission was to have two strands, one focusing on direct evangelism and the other on encouraging and publicizing the many ways in which the churches were already involved in community action. The aim was noble: to ensure that the message of Good News in Jesus Christ was communicated both in word and in deed. The reality was less convincing. A number of churches had a deep unease about overt evangelism. They were happy to be involved in community action but did not sign up to support the other 'strand' of the mission. Many other churches formally embraced both aspects of the mission, but in practice the energy of their planning groups and the content of their publicity majored upon the direct proclamation of the Christian message. For some, direct evangelism had the potential for undermining the good work that was being done through active Christian caring. For others, the good intention of marrying words and deeds was sidelined as time pressures revealed a theology that prioritized words.

Stories such as this need not always be repeated. Christians are involved in an enormous array of important activities within our society. Many 'secular' voluntary organizations would quite simply cease to function if Christian volunteers were removed. Many churches host community or drop-in centres, parent and toddler and self-help groups, provide the base for open youth work and soup runs or involve themselves in campaigns for local and international justice. National initiatives such as the Church Urban Fund and Faithworks do an excellent job in encouraging and resourcing a huge range of projects. What seldom emerges, though, is a clear and coherent partnership between evangelism and social action. This may be mirrored at the regional level, with some Anglican dioceses, for example, having a mission group and a board of social responsibility but no articulated strategy that brings the two together.

Searching for a holistic theology of mission

We have defined mission as: 'God's work of reconciling the whole of creation to himself, in which we are called to participate'. Practical caring for those in need, and working to transform the unjust structures that hold back the weakest in society, are very much part of this mission, and need to be recognized and affirmed as such: many church members involved in social action feel they and their work are undervalued by church leaders, whom they in turn see as concerned primarily with overtly church-centred work and the maintenance of church structures. A theology of mission that sees all movement towards greater wholeness and flourishing as God's work will inspire and encourage undervalued Christians. They need an awareness that they are indeed doing the work of the kingdom.

But action in the community can and should take the whole mission of the Church further than this. Ann Morisy, in her significant book *Beyond the Good Samaritan*, sees community ministry as a strategy for mission which:

- enables people to act like Christians;
- feeds people's imagination so that the significance of the gospel can be sensed;
- can be a force for positive change in society.[1]

The first and third of these points sum up powerfully the two-way impact of community ministry. Both Church and world have the potential to be transformed. But Ann Morisy goes on to stress that the other side of a holistic view of mission must also be addressed. If community ministry is only about practical caring and nothing else, the motivation that lies at the root of Christian engagement is left unacknowledged. It is the second statement of the three above which provides the link to evangelism. Those who participate and those who are reached gain a sense of the nature of God and his work in our world, and it is not right that this should be downplayed or unstated. Those who are at the heart of community ministry are there because God has first grasped their imaginations, because he is at work in their own hearts. As Ann Morisy writes:

> If we experience faith as being a positive gain in our lives, we cannot put brackets round this as if it is insignificant, and at the same time boast of 'openness' as a criterion for our relationship with people. The linking of community action with purposeful mission may be troublesome for those who feel it is wrong to use the Church's involvement in community and social action as a method of sharing the faith. The inclination is often to view community involvement as an unconditional gift to groups and communities under stress, and therefore passive in relation to mission. It is sufficient that the Church is seen by local people as concerned about and relevant to their lives.[2]

The logic of the statements above seems hard to fault, but as the town-wide mission story described earlier in this chapter shows, the task of holding together such a holistic vision in practice is challenging to say the least. There is a deep-rooted hesitancy about overt evangelism, often rooted in first- or second-hand experience of the insensitive and possibly exploitative evangelization of the vulnerable. In an understandable concern to distance themselves from this, Christian organizations may seem to bend over backwards to make it clear that this is not what they are about. Thus the Faithworks Charter commits participants 'Never to impose our Christian faith or belief on others'.[3] In practice this may not be too difficult to observe, since there are not many ways in which religious beliefs really can be imposed in the context of a liberal, democratic society. The anxiety is there nevertheless. The Faithworks Charter certainly is not intended to discourage evangelism, but churches may feel that the safest thing is to rule out anything that might look even a little like it.

Community ministry, worship and faith

The evangelistic strength of community ministry lies in its ability to draw others alongside in the work of Christian discipleship. If the authenticity of what is going on is sensed, partnership in action may be the starting point. As people share with Christians in the work of the gospel, so the journey of discipleship is begun even before faith is owned. Where the difficulty arises is in attempting to move on beyond this. How are Christians to enable those who share in the work of discipleship to own and to know the one whose disciples Christians are?

Figure 7.1 The 'Beckham effect'

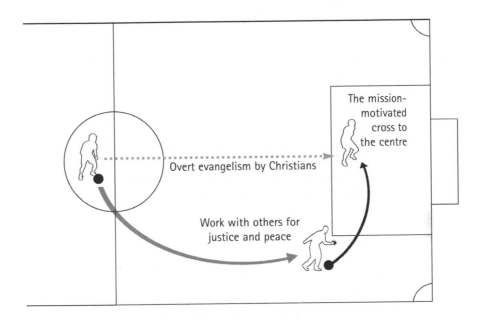

In a footballing analogy, Ann Morisy has compared the situation to free-flowing, attacking play from the wings.

A simple run from the centre of the pitch towards goal is too obvious, and unlikely to be effective. Community ministry is best compared to the movements down the wing. It is here that others will be drawn into partnership, here that the gospel may look most attractive. The drawback is that this will only take us as far as the corner flag! What is needed in addition is the 'Beckham effect', the well-placed cross to the centre which allows movement down the wing to turn into effective progress towards goal. (This last analogy is my own. Ann liked the concept, but as a Liverpool supporter she could not bring herself to use the (then) Manchester United player to support it!)

If there is a weakness in the above analogy, it is that the process in reality will be far more complex. As Ann explains in *Journeying Out*, most community ministry will be operating in what she calls the 'foundational domain'. It will be raising the possibility of God rather than bringing people to immediate and explicit faith. Then again, England's scoring rate may make the footballing imagery even more close to reality.

How, then, can churches enable this process? There are a number of key elements which can help to develop it.

1. Creating structures of participation

One minister described his congregation as 'time poor, money rich'. The temptation to use money rather than time, to employ professionals rather than to enable human contact, can be a powerful one. 'Structures of participation' sound more impressive than rotas: the reality is the same. A rota may sound boring, but the reality can be liberating. Over-busy people actually can still get directly and personally involved in transforming the world around them. As those busy people offer what limited time they have, so the mission benefit will be far greater than if money had been offered instead. A two-way opportunity for transformation has been opened up. Those in need are helped. The church, in turn, has the opportunity to be freed from the drabness of its 'suburban captivity', church members developing 'story-rich' lives as they work, not with theoretical issues, but with real people.

2. Being out and proud

Pushing one's views on other people may cause offence. Rather than concealing the very beliefs that motivate our participation, a more positive way forward can be to encourage Christians to be 'out and proud'. A simple honesty that 'I am here because . . .', especially in the context of actions to accompany words, need not be threatening. It simply tells it as it is. It may actually be more honest than a self-conscious reticence. After all, people *expect* churches and Christians to have something to do with God! In a world of widely varying views and lifestyles, Christian believers have as much right as anyone else to say, 'This is who I am, and I have a right to be openly and unashamedly myself.'

3. Taking opportunities for apt liturgy

In *Journeying Out*, Ann Morisy develops the significant potential of 'apt liturgy'. Apt liturgy is not worship, which demands too much of those of uncertain or inchoate belief. Rather it is a shared recognition of the *possibility* of God, an articulation of the sense that God is alongside in the universal struggles which Christians and others share together.

Apt liturgy is about naming moments, articulating emotions, working to recognize the struggles and questions borne by those encountered through community ministry. While the idea can seem challenging, it is in fact one thing in which churches have enormous experience and expertise on which to draw. As Ann Morisy comments: 'Apt liturgy is about the churches doing what only they can do. It is an art that churches are becoming increasingly adept at expressing.'[4]

One church living community ministry

St Mary Ashley Road is a parish church in north London. Faced with multiple problems of poverty and homelessness on the surrounding streets, the church took the bold step of reordering its buildings. A transparent screen now divides the church in two. At one end, the worship area is retained as a quiet place, specifically for worship, yet still visible to all users of the building. At the other end, nearer the main entrance, pool tables and sitting space provide room for recreation and a place to relax in the warmth. Food, hot showers and a laundry service are available. Advice is offered on a range of issues, and access is facilitated to specialist services including health care, mental health, housing and addiction.

The buildings at St Mary's do a great deal to speak of holistic mission. People using the facilities are welcomed into the church building itself, not just into some adjoining hall. This is clearly church, welcoming and designed to be useful, but still maintaining its identity as a holy place. But the strength of the work there is not only a matter of buildings. Centre users, volunteers and paid team members pray and share in leading worship together. The vicar and centre manager share a vision for community ministry that empowers people to become independent yet also longs for them to develop a true dependence on God. Small groups, some therapeutic, some skills based (gardening and carpentry groups run alongside a depression self-help and a men's anger-management group), encourage people to develop self-esteem.

A Christian beginners' group starts not with a fixed programme, but with listening and with centre users' questions. This is process evangelism, but for people who have for so long had no voice, the need is first to be listened to, to come to terms with the long story of how they got to be where they are. God's story matters too, but the way to encountering it comes more often through seeing God at work somewhere in their own story: the story of Jesus may less often be the easiest point at which to start.

Community ministry: things to think about

A long-haul strategy

Community ministry is not the best route forward for a church looking for speedy growth. The stories of changed lives in both the helpers and the helped (and often it is not clear who comes into which category) are deeply moving and speak powerfully of the authenticity of the gospel. But they are not neat. The inspiring testimony is very likely to be followed by disaster as soon as it has been aired in public. If the journey to faith for most people is confusing and multifaceted, the faith journeys of those at the bottom of society's pile are almost inevitably even more characterized by U-turns, contradictions and outbursts of frustration.

It may take considerably longer before those who come to faith through the support provided by community ministry can exercise leadership in many 'standard' churches. Even those with less chaotic lives, but whose faith journey has been encouraged by helping as volunteers alongside Christians, may have different priorities from some other converts. Church groups and committees appear less important than the work in the community that first helped a community volunteer hear the call of Jesus. It is interesting to note that Ichthus, the New Church grouping that has expended more energy than most on work among the poor, has shown lower rates of numerical growth than other similar church groupings which are located in more comfortable areas. People with chaotic lives who come to Christian faith will be less likely to grow quickly into mature believers, ready to exercise leadership and play a full part in the continued mission of the church.

Keeping a balance

There may be difficult balancing decisions to be made, hard choices in the area of accepting the priority of outreach but noting at the same time the need to build up a core of committed believers. Time and energy devoted to developing discipleship may sometimes be essential if the mission of the church is to continue in a self-sustaining way, but this can look to some committed volunteers more like a retreat into inward-looking churchiness.

The story of the Mayflower Centre in East London is traced by Peter Watherston in *A Different Kind of Church*.[5] It is both an inspiring and a saddening story, as courage, innovation and commitment are interspersed with disappointments and with recurring heart-searching about exactly what the centre was there for. In what represents one of the best known and most long-established ventures into community ministry in recent Church history, the same tensions have been faced that many other churches and projects have encountered. What should be the balance between outreach work and the building of a Christian community? How far should sharing and partnership with the local authority and with secular agencies go, and when must it be limited if the Christian nature of the enterprise is to be retained? If the Mayflower project, served by some of the most imaginative mission thinkers of different generations, has faced such struggles, it is hardly surprising if many others have grappled with similar questions.

Working in partnership

Working in partnership with individuals who share a concern for the needy may not necessarily lead to a search for faith among other helpers. One London vicar detected a distinct 'social work mentality' on the part of many who helped as volunteers. They were deeply suspicious of 'pushing religion' and in some cases had been harmed themselves by the excessive enthusiasm of previous Christian experiences.

Another church found that the great difficulty was drawing *local* people into volunteering. In what was a largely working-class area, people seemed to be using up much of their energy coping with their own lives. Volunteers came from further afield, mainly from middle-class parts of the city. The experiences and the results of their work were extremely important, but the impact on the immediate local community was not as great as might have been hoped.

Community ministry as expounded in Ann Morisy's *Beyond the Good Samaritan* emerges from the experiences of churches in London, where poverty and afflu-ence exist in relatively close proximity. It may be less easy to implement in other areas, where large tracts of poverty or affluence are found. In more comfortable places the needs may be less easy to identify, and where they do exist they may be concealed by embarrassment and the need to keep up appearances. In large, urban-edge local authority estates significant poverty may go unnoticed by most inhabitants of the city. The absence of potential volunteers from within the estates themselves may produce a further and significant barrier to developing effective community ministry.

The dangers of professionalization

Almost inevitably, projects that start small can face pressures to expand. Needs are identified, hopefully as part of a shared process which involves the local people themselves. But volunteers then need to be drawn in, sources of funding identified, and the potential to expand the work leads very easily (and often rightly) to changes in the nature of the project. Finances need to be managed, policies for child protection, disability access and other areas adopted, safeguards put in place and good practice adhered to. Decisions need to be minuted, roles clearly defined. All of this is likely to be good, indeed virtually essential, as initial 'good ideas' evolve into larger organizations. But at the same time the professionalization of the operation will sap the confidence of those whose working experience is not formally 'professional'. Informal community initiatives that were in tune with the culture and instincts of local people will cease to be recognizable as 'they' start to expect more formal working structures. The energy of the individual visionary can be diluted as a vision becomes an organization.

The drift towards professionalization can be an issue in the whole area of finances, as community-based fund-raising (inefficient but highly partici-pative) is replaced by skilled applications for grant funding. Elsewhere money may not be the problem, but the relative lack of local expertise may mean that the leadership of the project is out of the hands of those closest to it. Sam Wells, writing of his experiences as a vicar in Norwich involved in a major Single Regeneration Budget project, has described with impressive frankness some of the tensions inherent in the project's early development:

> Few moments crystallised the process as much as the appointment of the project manager. If a person were appointed from outside the community, would that be saying local people did not know what was best for their community? If the person were paid a large salary, what would that say to people who were struggling to make ends meet on a fifth of that sum? Should the new organisation be run like a local authority, like a business, or like a project in the developing world? Could anyone bridge the culture of the neighbourhood and that of the 'suits' in the public agencies and private sector?[6]

Going on to comment on the effects upon both locals and outsiders, Sam writes:

> At times everyone felt and behaved like a victim of exclusion. Local people, excluded and patronised and undervalued over many years, were highly sensitive to any suggestion that they were not 'good enough' to handle money, take decisions, govern a process or hold executive roles. Others, who felt they had a stake in the community, but due to living on the wrong side of the road or not shouting loud enough (sometimes literally) to make their voices heard, felt they were being ignored. And so-called 'agencies', professionals who had experience and skills and commitment to offer, sometimes felt treated as leeches because they seemed to grow in number as soon as a large Government-funded project appeared.[7]

Individual gifting

The 'Beckham effect' analogy used above depends on the involvement of one of the world's most talented footballers. At its most effective, community ministry must similarly have a place for individual commitment and gifting, for the maverick and the rough diamond. Some of the most effective projects will depend on the presence of someone with the dynamism to set them up, or with the specific gift of evangelism which allows community action to become overt mission.

This may mean that team strategy (to continue the analogy) may have to be shaped around the players available. At St James the Less in Pimlico, a project called 'The Safe' set up a drop-in centre for homeless people. Growing from the prophetic vision and energy of one young woman, it proved highly effective. As well as being a safe and welcoming place, it provided the means by which a number of people came to faith. Eventually, a change in leadership led to the demise of that specific project, but work among the homeless continues in other ways. The project was not a failure – it was rather an important venture, but one with a limited lifespan. Ending is not necessarily failure: it may be the recognition that a person and an opportunity need to be together for a particular expression of community ministry to be effective.

Signs and authenticity

Jesus performed miracles as signs. His healings, for example, most certainly had enormous value in themselves, but that was not the main story. Jesus did not come to establish a Galilean health service. Miracles of healing were indications of the work of God in bringing full healing to the human race: the signs were there as a way of pointing to a deeper reality.

Actions that are used deliberately as signs can be highly significant. If actions speak louder than words, we do indeed have in those actions a powerful means for proclaiming the gospel. Practical expressions of God's love that get noticed, therefore, have a value over and above their immediate effects. Once this is recognized, the symbolic value of actions should be considered very carefully. Undertaking acts of caring with the overt intention of getting noticed may not necessarily be a bad thing. Even those who instinctively hesitate at the idea need to take note of the example of Jesus.

Taking the 'signs' principle a bit further, some churches have adopted a policy of undertaking 'random acts of kindness', gestures that may in themselves be short term or limited in impact but which are signs of the gospel. As I write, approximately 50 young people from my local church are clearing gardens, washing cars and tidying waste ground as a sign to our local community of God's unexpected grace.

Sometimes referred to by its proponents as 'servant evangelism', this has also been written of by detractors as 'gimmick evangelism'. Does it even belong in the context of a consideration of community ministry, which involves the long haul and serious commitment to relationship building? Maybe the answer lies in authenticity. If short-term acts of kindness are to add up to more than a Christian version of *Ground Force* makeovers, they need to be signs of a tangible reality. One-off acts of kindness will speak of a loving God if they are rooted in the long-term life of a loving community.

The Eden project in Manchester seems to be providing one of the best expressions of symbolic action and serious long-haul commitment working in partnership. In August 2000, about 11,000 Christian young people flooded into Manchester as part of the annual Soul Survivor festival. This time Soul Survivor was different from usual, taking part in a project called The Message 2000. In place of the normal Somerset venue, Soul Survivor was relocated to Manchester's Heaton Park. As well as participating in central meetings for teaching and worship, teams of young people moved out across the city. Some of the most deprived urban areas were transformed as overgrown areas were cleared, piles of rubbish removed, buildings repainted and local children and young people drawn into the whole atmosphere. The project was headline news in the local press. Police chiefs recorded an almost complete disappearance of crime in some estates while the project was going on. Manchester had noticed!

It could have been a flash in the pan. It could have left little to be seen a few years down the line. The strength of The Message 2000 was the groundwork that had been done beforehand and the long-term commitment that followed. Working with young people in Manchester for several years before the project, and building partnerships with local churches, the World Wide Message Tribe (a Christian band with a commitment to youth work) had built up a reputation for getting stuck in and staying involved with some of Manchester's poorest. Following on from The Message 2000's big event, a growing number of local groups have been set up, made up of people committed to moving long term into some of the city's most economically deprived areas. Known as Eden Teams, they are another living sign of the perma- nent reality of God's presence. The one-off gesture (in this case a very big one) was partnered by serious, costly commitment once the bulk of the participants had left. The sign was effective because it pointed to solid reality beyond itself.

Keeping the momentum going

Like all aspects of a church's mission, community ministry needs regular reassessment. What are the aims of a particular project? What measure of success can we apply? How does it fit into our overall view of mission? Working with people at the edge of society can be lonely and draining. Physical exhaustion, the feeling that much effort is producing little result, resentment from those being helped whose anger erupts at those closest to them, all can take their toll. Comparison with other approaches to evangelism may not be very heartening: community ministry is not the fastest way to grow a church.

If speedy numerical growth is unlikely, it may be tempting for the local church to adopt other measures of 'success' instead. There is a real danger that success may be measured only by practical and material results. My local church has established a community lunch, free to all comers each Saturday. A rota of regular helpers keeps the meals coming week by week. On one level the lunch is a major success, with a significant number of people getting a good meal. On another level it is also a struggle. The lunch is there, but the community needs to be created. Volunteers to give practical help are not always matched by helpers there simply to eat, to chat and to help people know they are valued for being themselves and not merely for being hungry.

If the sole aim of a lunch is to feed hungry people, then the only route to 'success' will be one that produces more food. Professionalization and even automation may seem the most effective means of achieving that. On the other hand, a mission-focused view will also need to consider the human relationships between helpers and between the helpers and the helped. What other things apart from or along with the meal are entering the lives of those served? More listening and less food-serving may be the best result of a full consideration of the purpose of the project. A rota, and one that is wide enough to draw more people into relationships, may be more important than a well-run but professional catering service.

Community ministry in the mix

Community ministry and church health

Needs-oriented evangelism is one of Natural Church Development's key quality characteristics (see Chapter 9). If evangelism is not meeting people at the point of need, the danger is that it may lack any real impact. An analysis of church health could be one of the things to first point a congregation towards community ministry.

Community ministry and process evangelism

A commitment to community ministry will create a church that exudes authenticity. The church fringe will almost certainly grow, and those involved will be impressed by what they are seeing. They may begin asking more about what motivates the church and what motivates Christians. Process evangelism courses might be a helpful way forward from here. On the other hand, people contacted through community ministry are likely to come with more and with harder questions. They will have seen enough of life to realize that over-simple answers will not do!

If, as we have seen, people being helped through community ministry find they can relate to courses which start with their own questions, it is likely that those doing the helping may also feel the same. Community ministry is a challenge, but the testimonies that emerge have a rough-edged honesty that can be far more powerful than the neater journey to faith that some process evangelism courses might imply. Perhaps there is a lesson in that for every church, whatever form of ministry it is involved in.

New forms of church

It may be through community ministry that a radical reassessment of church life begins. The bridges built by community ministry may be attractive, the church to which they lead alien. People on the edge of society are less troubled than most by the need to be polite or to suffer quietly. The questions they may pose about the shape, timing, location or leadership of worship may be the very things that others have felt but have not spoken out about. If community ministry leads towards a more open, more listening, more tolerant church, that may be a gain from mission that has something to teach all congregations.

Conclusion

Community ministry is not a quick or easy route to evangelistic success, but this in no way diminishes its importance. The temptation to draw back from a genuine integration of evangelism and social action is there on either side. Evangelism can apparently show greater results with the more receptive parts of society. Social action and practical caring on their own are part of the Church's mission, but they are not in themselves evangelism, nor are they a replacement for it. Such is human nature that most Christians will find themselves instinctively at least a little way one side or the other of the dividing line between evangelism and social action. Many with a deep desire for social justice may not even read a book that focuses explicitly on evangelism. Many who are passionate about evangelism will be concerned that a chapter on social action is somehow missing the target. The gospel is most likely to be seen and encountered in all its fullness when those two groups of people are drawn together by a common vision for mission, working side by side to do and to proclaim God's saving work.

Community ministry is about a determination to hold social action and evangelism together. When that happens, something more of the gospel is seen. When it is followed through with the commitment that is ready to face disappointment without admitting defeat, lessons can be learned which can and should colour the Church's whole approach to evangelism and to its mission.

For further information

Visit

http://www.faithworks.info/index.asp

Read

Steve Chalke, *Faithworks: Intimacy and Involvement*, Kingsway, 2003
Steve Chalke, *Faithworks: Stories of Hope*, Kingsway, 2001
David Evans and Mike Fearon, *From Strangers to Neighbours*, Hodder & Stoughton, 1998
George Lings, *Across the Pond*, Encounters on the Edge No. 6, Church Army, 2000
George Lings, *Hope Among the Hopeless, Connecting with the urban poor*, Encounters on the Edge No. 39, Church Army 2008
Ann Morisy, *Beyond the Good Samaritan*, Continuum, 1997
Ann Morisy, *Journeying Out*, Morehouse, 2004

8

Children's evangelism

Mike Booker

> There are only two lasting bequests we can hope to give to our children.
> One is roots; the other, wings.
>
> Holding Carter

Children and the churches: the major crisis area

If Bishop Gavin Reid's assessment of current church life in this country is correct, about 40 per cent of churches, across all denominations, now have no children's ministry at all.[1] Much of the work that does go on with children is underfunded, undervalued and inward-looking. The churches have been losing children at about twice the rate they have been losing adults. In *Hope for the Church* Bob Jackson quotes the Church of England's statistics of Sunday attendance to reveal that all but one diocese are in overall decline (on Sundays, at least).[2] What is striking is that while adult rates of decline varied from 2 per cent to 28 per cent in the period 1989–99, children's attendance fell by between 3 per cent and 58 per cent. There is some cause for hope in the growth of midweek activity, as we shall see, but this is only a partial and limited counterbalance to what are still, quite frankly, frightening figures.

This chapter is different from the rest of the book, in that it aims not to critique a strategy but to urge a priority. For most churches, the priority in children's evangelism is not finding the right strategy – it is having any kind of strategy at all. This is important, not simply because children are part of society and part of the Church: it is more serious than that. The fall-off in work among children is one of the most serious pieces of news for the Church in contemporary Britain. Adopting new strategies of evangelism while leaving children's work untouched is simply postponing disaster. To have hope for the future there needs to be hope in that generation that will become the future. Most of the rest of this book will only make sense if there is another generation growing up which knows something more about Jesus than that he is a swear word.

The neglect of children's evangelism means that the renewed energy being put into adult evangelism may be too late. Most adult converts to Christian faith come with at least some background of Christian experience during childhood. *Finding Faith Today* reported that the vast majority of people who came to faith as adults were actually coming back to something they had previously experienced in childhood:

> The importance of early encounters with the church can be seen in the figures for those who had no contact with the church. Only 10% never went to Sunday school or church and another 13% went only occasionally. *Thus 76% of those who became Christians as adults had a reasonably prolonged contact with a church during childhood – this is a good deal higher than the population at large.*[3]

Reflecting on a lifetime in Christian ministry characterized by a passion for evangelism, Gavin Reid quotes church growth researcher George Barna's findings in the USA to underline the importance of people having Christian contact as children. Working with a sample of 4,000 people, Barna's research group 'concluded that if people do not make a commitment to Christ by the age of fourteen, the likelihood of ever doing so is slim'.[4] Convictions about individual freedom and the grace of God may make us reluctant to accept such comments meekly, but the statistical evidence is powerful. If much of the rest of this book contains a message that evangelism in Britain today is challenging, that may be because the church is reaping the rewards of serious and increasing neglect of children's work. If there is to be hope for the future, then it is at the level of children's evangelism that part of the answer must be sought.

This chapter is also different from much of the rest of the book in another very important way. The 'How do we get people to come?' question pervades much adult evangelism. When working with children there is no reason why this need be the case. The opportunities are there for the taking. There is ample evidence that good children's work, so long as it is ready to change as our society changes, can and does still draw large numbers of children. My own experience of leading mission teams has repeatedly reinforced this impression: while we puzzle over how to attract adults, children will come and come in large numbers if the event, time and place are right. There is encouragement in the midst of the bad news!

Avoiding the hard sell

Some people have reservations about doing evangelism at all, so it is not surprising that those reservations are especially strong when it comes to children. Our culture accepts a wide range of things between consenting adults, while striving to shield children from most of them. Evangelism is likely to fall into this category. Many people in our society see children as innocent and easily led, and think they should not be subjected to an evangelistic 'hard sell' before they are able to respond with appropriate adult wariness.

Such reservations fail to spot at least two very important factors. The first is that our society is in no sense neutral. The hard sell of consumerism is already fully in operation by the time children are old enough to watch Teletubbies. Materialism hits young children powerfully on a daily basis, followed frighteningly soon by the sexualized images which not only aim to sell products but also introduce the message that worth is found in physical attraction. There is not, quite simply, a safe, 'neutral' world in which children can grow and explore life's options. If the Good News of Jesus Christ is not heard among the competing and persuasive voices around them, children have no chance of making a free choice about their worth and their future.

Secondly, and backed up by significant recent research, it is evident that children are not simply blank, secular slates upon which religious ideas are imposed by adults. David Hay and Rebecca Nye have noted the widespread evidence of spiritual awareness in young children. In listening to children speak of their spiritual experiences, the stories varied considerably, but there was in many a pervading presence of what Hay and Nye call 'relational consciousness'. This involves a sense that there is a wider reality, beyond the purely secular, which the child has a sense of belonging to. The danger, then, is not that religious ideas will be forced upon children, but rather that secularization is denying them the language to express what they feel. The Church's first task in our secularized culture is therefore that of 'helping children to keep an open mind'.[5]

In the light of the already-present spiritual sensitivity of children, evangelism is not about imposing beliefs upon them: it is about helping them to give shape to a sense of the divine that is already there. Rather than evangelism being an imposition, it is the lack of evangelism that is in reality serious neglect. If Christians take seriously the strong words of Jesus about those who cause (or allow?) one of these little ones to fall (see especially Matthew 18.1–7), the Church's failure to evangelize children may be seen as one of the most scandalous examples of child abuse in our contemporary society.

Children, evangelism and conversion

Evangelism with children is more than simply a matter of pressurizing young people to 'accept Jesus'. Process and crisis, journey and decision interplay in children's lives as they do in adults'. Children have a will to exercise, and they are certainly able to make choices. It is quite appropriate for a child to decide to follow Jesus; it is probably not appropriate to expect that decision to be the one defining moment in a whole lifetime. The journey continues, and faith needs to keep growing.

There is a growing recognition that faith develops through childhood and on into adult life. Francis Bridger outlines some of the key thinking in this area.[6] Probably the most accessible is that of John Westerhoff,[7] who identified four stages in the development of faith:

- experienced faith (characteristic of babyhood and infancy);
- affiliative faith (characteristic of childhood);
- searching faith (as the search to think it out for oneself is undertaken);
- owned faith.

The child growing up in a Christian environment will typically move from a simple acceptance of the security offered by the home environment to a conscious acceptance of the faith of those s/he knows and trusts in the Christian community. Growth to maturity may then typically involve an element of struggle before a clearly grasped, independent adult faith is reached.

In the light of this, children's evangelism involves a number of elements. Children need to belong. This is a fundamental human need, but Christians see it as a need that will only fully be met through belonging in the body of Christ. Affiliative faith may simply involve that belonging, joining in a caring, fun, welcoming Christian group. Saying 'yes' to Jesus may in practice mean saying 'yes' to good Christian children's work, but there is nothing wrong in that. Faith like this needs to keep growing, but it is faith nevertheless.

For growth to continue, that faith will need both taught stories and living stories. The content of the Christian message is no longer common currency in today's British culture. Faith will grow if the Christian story is communicated in words and in lives. Good teaching content and good, caring relationships will provide the framework in which faith can flourish. The intention to follow Jesus can become a lifetime commitment if the building blocks of Christian truth are in place, and if those blocks are seen to be part of the living temple of the Christian community.

Facing up to current priorities

In overstretched and financially strapped churches it is not possible to do everything. However, priorities are often exposed by the things that are allowed to drop first. The disappearance of children's work is marked and startling in this category. What lies behind this collapse of work with children?

1. Finance

Good-quality work with children needs money. It may not need a very large amount of money when compared with a roof appeal or an organ fund, but money is important nevertheless. Good-quality resources, well-equipped meeting rooms, exciting trips and activities all communicate to children that they matter. They also communicate to parents that reaching children matters to churches. Given the absence of children from the governing structures of nearly all churches, it is a particular responsibility of adult members to make sure that children's work is made a financial priority.

Today's children are the most technologically aware generation ever. In the course of a primary school activity day I found that one of the girls seemed very excited about her church. I asked her what made it so special. 'It's great!' she replied. 'We've got our own recording studio and we can make television programmes!' I'm not suggesting that something as ambitious as that would be within the reach of most churches – but set alongside the sums involved in roof repairs or organ appeals, it might well be attainable by rather more congregations than one might expect. That may be an ideal which is still some way off; nevertheless, money, used wisely for appropriate resources, can communicate to children and their families that the gospel is not out of date. Children faced only with colouring-in as regular weekly church fare will conclude the opposite!

Money is also needed to fund the training, materials and support that will encourage the next, even scarcer resource: leaders.

2. Lack of high-quality leaders

Children's work needs leaders. The difficulty in finding sufficient leaders appears sometimes to be a national characteristic. Churches of all sizes regularly struggle to have enough people to run an adequate children's programme, and those who do volunteer can be among the least supported in the church. There seem to be multiple reasons behind this.

In some larger churches which run a wide range of activities, children's work can be viewed as a lower priority than 'adult' activities like small-group leadership, being on the church council or preaching. Our society suffers from a strange type of snobbery which accords higher status to those who have least opportunity to influence people. Put at its starkest, a university lecturer (who works with people whose characters are already formed) is accorded higher status than a primary school teacher (working with people who may be far more open to change), who is in turn viewed as more important than a nursery nurse (who may have the potential for the greatest influence of all three). Seeping into churches, such an attitude means that work with children is undervalued, and sometimes left in the hands of less able leaders. Children's work is for beginners, so the accepted wisdom seems to believe, adult leadership for the wise and mature. The priority given to children by Jesus (see for example Luke 9.46-48, and especially verse 48: 'Whoever welcomes this child in my name welcomes me') is sadly not always shared by his contemporary followers.

It may not simply be a matter of low priorities. Children's work may have to compete for leaders with increasingly complex church programmes, while at the same time many Christians have less free time available. Worship groups replacing organists, meetings and committees which seem to have a self-propagating energy all of their own, lay involvement in readings and intercessions when previously a member of the clergy might have conducted the whole service alone, all have their value but all take up time. If work with children is being squeezed out, there may be a case for taking some long, hard looks at the other church activities that are doing the squeezing.

Added to priorities and time pressure are changing church age profiles. There are fewer young adults to lead energetic and up-to-date children's activities. This is not to undervalue the faithful work of older church members. It is often older people who have continued children's work when they might long ago have wished to hand over to someone with more youth and energy. As one experienced children's and youth worker commented, 'the trouble is not that the young people are postmodern, it's that the leaders are postmodern'. Long-term commitment comes less easily to younger leaders than it did to the preceding generation, and commitment, familiarity and secure relationships matter a great deal to children. If commitment is to be maintained then children's leaders need support, spiritual and practical. But in practice those who work with children are often unable to share in the main acts of weekly worship: the least-fed members of the congregation are those who teach children.

3. Undervaluing children as people

'Now the children will leave us for their classes' is an often-heard statement in those churches that still have children's groups. The 'children leaving us' mentality communicates that children are a minority group, separate from 'normal church'. This need not in itself be a bad thing – it is possible that special groups for children reflect a special interest in their spiritual growth. However, the implication that children are not 'us' can be part of a subtle message that they are less than a full part of the church. When families arrive at a service, if parents and other adults are greeted with a smile and a service sheet while the shorter people in the family are ignored, it simply adds to the message received by children that they are less than full members. Small, symbolic messages communicate to all present that children are a lower priority.

What is true within the church is true on the edge of the church as well. In the specific area of children's evangelism, the tragedy is that hugely successful events can go almost unreported. Thirty new children at a summer holiday club, several hundred hearing the Christian message at a special assembly in the local county primary school, may pass virtually without mention. When this happens, not only are children undervalued, but an enormous opportunity for encouragement is overlooked. Few outreach events for adults would attract anything like the same number of outsiders in most churches. When working with adults, the question may often be 'Will anybody come?' Children will come, and come regularly, to special events in large numbers, but our undervaluing of children means that the chance to celebrate a major evangelistic success is missed.

4. Fear

Last week an experienced vicar sat opposite me and listed the local churches that had curtailed their children's programmes. The reason was not only that leaders were in short supply. Some who had been leaders were becoming uneasy about continuing. Even when people were eager to continue, they sometimes faced pressure from their husband or wife to move out of the 'risky' area of work with children. In the midst of a right awareness that child protection is important, some volunteers (and even some whole churches or organizations) are concluding that the safest thing is to avoid contact with young children altogether.

Children, like adults, come to faith primarily through relationships. In Christian homes this will normally involve a relationship with their parents, and for all children friendships with their own age group are of enormous importance. But in addition to that, genuine and caring relationships with trusted adults have a central place. Increasingly, fear on the part of adults is denying children that life-giving friendship.

A significant part of the strategy I was trained in as a young Christian leader on a boys' summer camp was 'personal work'. We were encouraged to pray for opportunities to talk individually with boys about God, about their personal relationship with him and about the need to make a step of Christian commitment. Whether or not the approach itself sounds formulaic, the result was significant, with younger teenagers hearing first hand of the faith that motivated someone a few years older than themselves. The current question for many might well be, 'Is it worth the risk?' However worthy the motives might be, they are open to misinterpretation. Even when good practice is rigorously enforced, the temptation is to conclude that it is safer simply to discourage such close personal contact. Yet how many adult Christians in churches across the country came to faith through personal conversations which would now be either impossible or at best discouraged?

When something goes wrong, those taking part in children's work may find themselves on the end of considerable criticism, and at worst of press coverage or legal action. Those who do nothing will go unnoticed. Yet across the country there are children whose lives are blighted by the lack of positive role models, who face long unsupervised weekends or evenings because the local church no longer feels able to take the risk of working with them. Our fear of involvement leaves children facing greater risks on their own. Closing down children's work leaves children vulnerable, either alone on the streets or in the 'care' of other adults whose motives and concern may well be far less healthy. It is essential that churches work to ensure good practice,[8] but, if that begins to look such a challenge that the temptation is to withdraw from children's work altogether, it is important to remember that the worst practice is to do nothing.

5. Looking inwards

A large church recognized the potential for reaching local children and families, and appointed a children's and families worker. Motivated by a deep concern for evangelism among local people, the woman appointed soon found herself pulled in two directions. Her first desire was to reach local families and build bridges between them and the church. The first priority of the church members who paid her was to see their own children well catered for. In the end, the ones who paid the piper called the tune, and a full and exciting programme for church children took priority over building bridges to people outside the church.

The *Children in the Way* report[9] published by the Church of England in 1988 made a strong case for the inclusion of children in church life and specifically in the main act of worship. As the report was launched in deaneries, an accompanying video portrayed the plight of a child who was excluded from the colour and beauty of worship and pushed out into a children's group in a damp hall. Children need to be welcomed and affirmed within the church, and bad children's work in damp halls is indefensible. But the danger of the report's approach was that it majored on the need for greater involvement of those children already within or on the edges of church life. This is important, but if the needs of the church as it is, and even the needs of children in and around the church as is, are allowed to set the agenda, then our focus can easily cease to be evangelistic. The great majority of children are now outside the churches, come from families which do not attend church and have 'better' things to do on Sundays. Welcoming children and giving priority to finding the best leaders for the children already in the churches will fail in themselves to meet the evangelistic challenge presented by children's work today. Inward-looking churches find it hard to see evangelistic opportunities.

Putting children first

How then can and should the churches begin to address the crisis in children's evangelism? One way forward is to revisit the five aspects of the crisis outlined above.

1. Finance and resources

Great Shelford Free Church is a middle-sized independent congregation just outside Cambridge. Following the tragic death of their associate minister, the church made the bold decision to appoint instead not another minister but a youth worker. The result was remarkable. Not only did the work with young people expand so that a group of up to 70 were meeting regularly: the whole church experienced a change in attitude. Having committed themselves in practice to a new emphasis on youth work, the older church members supported, prayed for and felt a genuine pride in what was being done with young people.

The story above is primarily about work with teenagers. There is no reason why it could not be repeated with younger children. Devoting money and energy to children's work will not only have an impact because the resources themselves allow more to be done. Money concentrates the mind wonderfully, and older church members with a larger financial stake in what is happening with children will find that that area of work moves up their list of priorities for prayer and for practical support.

2. Leaders, volunteer and professional

So does the future lie with professional children's workers? We noted in Chapter 7, on community ministry, that there are limitations in professionalization. For many larger churches the step of employing a children's worker may be necessary, but if that worker is then expected to *do* the children's work the results will be disastrous. Experiences abound of exhausted children's workers whose time is constantly taken up with trying to recruit more volunteer leaders. Those leaders who do volunteer need training and support, and a professional children's worker may be essential in providing this. Good children's work needs planning and attention given to good practice, and a children's worker may be able to enable that, providing direction for the uncertain and confidence for the fearful.

Many smaller churches will be unable even to contemplate appointing a paid leader. For all churches, regardless of size, it is the volunteers who will bear the bulk of the load. Training, recognition, a priority in pastoral support, can all communicate to leaders that they matter. If a major disincentive to volunteering is the example of old, faithful leaders who have been involved for 30 years, limits to the expected time commitment can make the task seem manageable. There is an inevitable trade-off here. A rota which allows some weeks working with children and some weeks off, or a one-year limit to new voluntary responsibility, can make the task of volunteering more attractive. The downside is that these can also preclude long-term involvement and relationship building. Whatever the pattern, children still need to hear loud and clear that work with them is a priority and a privilege.

3. Valuing children in the church

At one church down the road from me you may experience some difficulty finding the vicar just before the service begins. He is often to be found talking with the children, sometimes lying on his stomach to be down at their level. Children matter to him as much as the adult church members, and the way he uses his time in the busy minutes before Sunday worship begins signals that to the whole congregation.

For some churches, valuing children is expressed in allowing them to receive Holy Communion. This is a major, theologically rich and highly contentious area, and one that will not be examined at length here; it has been more thoroughly covered elsewhere.[10] There is a danger in over-concern with Communion, and it is twofold. Firstly, it can obscure the wider question of our attitude to and welcome of children. Holy Communion is deeply symbolic, and children's participation in it must be a symbol of our practical welcome to them in all parts of the Church's life. Secondly, admission of children to communion, before confirmation but after baptism, still fails to address the question of the Church's welcome for children from non-church families. Greater inclusion of those children who are part of families clearly within the church community may not be entirely positive if the downside of it involves exclusion of unbaptized children, who receive the signal that they 'do not belong'.

Welcome can be quite simply that, a clear and cheerful 'hello' to the child who comes into church. It may involve children in the planning of all-age worship, or in carrying out tasks like taking up the collection. If we believe that children can and do exercise Christian faith, then there may also be much more that can be expected of them. Instead of the minister praying for the children before they 'go out', perhaps the children could pray for the rest of the congregation. More radically, the rest of the congregation could 'go out' on at least some weeks if building space allows, leaving the children to take over the main worship area. If the vicar or senior minister leaves the sermon to somebody else on a regular basis in order to be with the children, a clear signal of priority is given.

Truly valuing children involves valuing the work God is doing in them. They have a part to play, and gifts to share with people of all ages in the church to which they belong. Mark Ireland relates the following story:

'A few years ago I was preaching at a large cell-church in Malaysia, St Patrick's Tawau, as part of a mission team from Lichfield Diocese. After the service a young boy, who could only have been five or six years old, came up to me with his mother. His mother said, "While you were preaching, my son had a prophetic word for you. May he pray for you?" I was gobsmacked, but sat down on the dais while the boy laid his hand on my shoulder and prayed for me. The boy had never seen me before – I had literally flown in the night before – yet his simple little prayer was so relevant to the work I was going back to in Britain. I was profoundly moved by the experience, and humbled by the experience of being ministered to by a young child. But what really challenged me was the thought that if that boy belonged to my own church back in England, what opportunities would he have there to exercise such a gift? Yet Joel 2.28 clearly says, "I will pour out my spirit on all flesh, your sons and your daughters shall prophesy . . . ."'

The purpose of the above account is not to make a theological point about the nature of spiritual gifts. Whatever you think spiritual gifts are, if they are given to children they are given for a purpose, and should make a difference wherever children spend their time. This may be at school, in the playgroup or wherever children are involved outside church. Adults learn by doing, and so do children. Much of the most effective children's evangelism is done by children. If we wait until they are older before we trust them to minister, then they may no longer be there.

4. Working for the possible

Jesus will be real to children if he is encountered in and through real people. Good practice in child safety must be a priority, and churches must make use of all the resources and training available. But an over-concern for safety must never drive God's people away from a determination to share themselves with children as well as adults in genuine, life-giving relationships. The attitude adopted to working with children must be one of determination to allow relationships to flourish within those boundaries essential to ensure safety. The need for good practice with children is an incentive to work even harder to allow relationships to flourish, but to flourish appropriately, just as the need for audibility in the pulpit should be an incentive to provide an effective amplification system. Abandoning children's work in the one case is no more a solution than abandoning preaching would be in the other!

5. Looking outwards

Much of what has been considered so far relates to the need for the best possible work with children who are already in or around church life. If this has sounded challenging, the task of children's evangelism beyond the church fringe will stretch commitment and imagination even further. This point was brought home to me most forcefully during a weekly shopping trip to our local Aldi store, the cheerful discount supermarket that keeps the family food bill down to a manageable size each week. In front of me was a single mother, with three boys hanging on to the edge of her trolley. Shaven heads, ear studs, strong language and broken ketchup bottles made it clear to me that the gulf between my church and many of the people around it was very wide indeed. I had been wondering how well behaved my well-churched and generally polite child would be at the all-age service the next day. But how could I even begin to expect the family in front of me to cope in my church? Our all-age worship is shaped by the tolerance limits of polite children.

An outward-looking church will shape its activities around the children it hopes to reach, not merely around those it already has. On one level this will mean simply being ready to welcome children if some appear! The number of children needed to begin children's work is not one but none. If there is at least a provisional plan of action in place should a child come to church, then there will be some hope that a child who does come will want to return.

Money, leadership, respect for children and a determination to work effectively with them, all can be aimed at those children already 'within the fold'. This is vital work, and a flourishing group of Christian children will provide one of the main incentives for other children to be drawn to faith, but it cannot be sufficient in itself. Truly evangelistic children's work will seek to look outwards and target outreach at children on the fringes of the church and those way beyond them.

Some national encouragement

Voluntary organizations have for many years provided excellent resources in children's evangelism. CPAS and Scripture Union stand out, with a long track record of training, providing resources and running evangelistic summer holidays. The Church Army have for many years included children's evangelism as one of their key areas of work, with Church Army children's evangelists working in a number of parts of the country.

Within the Church of England a further encouragement has been a move to raise the status of children's evangelism, with the appointment in 2001 of an Archbishop's Officer for Evangelism among Children. The national awareness of the priority of children's evangelism is slowly growing. The challenge now is to establish a concerted momentum from concern to action, to use the resources available and to think how best a response can be made to our changing national culture.

New directions in children's work

Shifting the balance away from Sundays

For previous generations the chance to go to Sunday school may have been one of the highlights of a drab weekend. The competition today makes that decidedly unlikely! The excitement of ice skating or mini rugby, or the more poignant but vital chance to visit a separated parent, can make Sunday children's groups inaccessible. Even where there is no strong competition, the culture that encouraged non-attending parents to send their children to Sunday school has faded. But at the same time, midweek opportunities are flourishing.

A village church in mid-Devon had found the children's group shrinking to the limits of viability. When the vicar's boys were not there the group effectively ceased to exist. Helped by a visiting mission team, the church began an after-school club, which attracted half the pupils at the village primary school during its first week. The initial burst of energy subsided, but from it emerged a weekly group of about 15 children, most of whom would never have come to a Sunday activity. The problem had been the day and the time, not the willingness of children to come to a Christian group.

After-school clubs may well provide the most fruitful meeting time for children's work, but they happen at a time when few volunteer helpers will be free. Part of the attraction of the timing to parents is the opportunity for childcare at the very time of day most adults are busy working! If the after-school slot is not free, midweek evenings may still provide openings which Sundays simply no longer deliver.

New life in old places

Effective work with children need not always involve the new and the ground-breaking. There may be the potential for more life than is normally realized in some of the traditional links that churches have with children. This dawned on me over a period of years as I saw the impact of a children's choir in a very ordinary parish church.

> Wendy's choir was more than just an opportunity for children to sing. Yes, the choir led adults in singing on Sunday mornings, and that was in itself an important affirmation of the children's own ministry, but there was more to it than that. Choir practices taught children the theology of worship. The God whom they worshipped was also encountered in prayer, as children were prayed for by adult choir members, and as they prayed for one another. Wendy took time to explain to the children why they were singing the words in front of them. She also took time to listen to them, to hear the stories of the day they had been through before coming to choir practice, of how they had been struggling to live out the faith they sang about. The choir was not merely a choir, it was also a junior discipleship group.

Other channels for involvement will be present in the life of many churches. If the way children are enabled to take part allows them not only to learn how, but also to learn *why*, then there is the chance for genuine disciple-ship to develop. It may not provide a new way in for many, but for some children the chance may be life-changing. If they are there because they are *doing something*, playing a part that matters, that may be a route into Christian fellowship that appeals more than even the most exciting social programme.

Children's work in the mix

It is sad but true that we did not find much awareness of children in most of the approaches considered in the other chapters of this book. Often the main concern seems to be that babysitters can be found so that adults can get to events. There is a need to put a child-focused element into each of the ready-made programmes on the market, but in most cases the energy and initiative to do that will have to be home-grown.

Where an approach to evangelism is more flexible and less based on prepared materials, involving children will be far easier. Certainly, a parish mission event that ignores children is almost bound to be missing out on a huge amount of fun, not to mention a major evangelistic opportunity.

Community ministry and contacts with the international church may be especially fruitful places to think how children might be involved. Not every community ministry project will be appropriate, but some, like visiting a lonely older person along with another adult, for example, or helping prepare sandwiches for rough sleepers, could give a child a life-changing insight into the reality of faith.

Meeting believers from other cultures through overseas links can cut through the high-tech, commercialized consumerism that confronts most children today. For my own children, meeting Joseph from the war zone of the southern Sudan suddenly put the attractions of the Nintendo fairly and squarely into perspective!

Conclusion

During the last generation or so there has been a tragic and seemingly unnoticed collapse in the involvement of British churches with children. Yet the door is still open. The exact way it is open may have changed, with the levels of Sunday school attendance of the earlier twentieth century being irretrievable, but there are still clear and welcoming ways in. Evangelism with children gives them the opportunity to be the people they were created to be, the people that (at some deep level, at least) many already sense they are. To neglect it is not only to neglect a key evangelistic opportunity, it is to deny children the chance to realize they are made in the image of God. Getting stuck back into children's evangelism may be the most important gift the Church can give to the next generation.

For further information

Visit

http://www.churcharmy.org.uk
www.cris.org.uk
www.biblewonderland.co.uk/

http://www.godlyplay.org.uk/
http://www.heartforchildren.com/
http://www.request.org.uk/ (an excellent resource for RE work in schools)

Contact

Church of England, National Children's adviser, Church House, Great Smith Street, London SW1P 3AZ: mary.hawes@c-of-e.org.uk

Read

Francis Bridger, *Children Finding Faith*, Scripture Union/CPAS, 1988/2000
Claire Dalpra, *Small Beginnings: Church for under 5s*, Encounters on the Edge No.31, Church Army 2006
Penny Frank, *Every Child a Chance to Choose*, CPAS, 2002
Claire Gibb, *Building New Bridges*, National Society/Church House Publishing, 1996
David Hay and Rebecca Nye, *The Spirit of the Child*, Fount, 1998
Margaret Withers, *Not Just Sunday: Setting Up and Running Mid-week Clubs for Children*, Church House Publishing, 2003
Margaret Withers and Paul Doherty, *Where are the children? Evangelism beyond Sunday morning*, Barnabas, 2005
Margaret Withers, *Mission-Shaped Children: moving towards a child-centred Church*, CHP 2006

9

Focusing on church health

Mike Booker

> To carry out their mission in the Church, Christians must open their ears and hear what the Spirit says to the churches. It is not enough for them to listen to the Church unless the Church, through its leaders, is listening to the Spirit.
>
> Avery Dulles

Natural Church Development: sounds a good idea, but what is it?

Students of church growth have noted for many years the tendency of growing churches to share certain characteristics. Perhaps more obviously, the patterns of *unhealthy* church life, leading to stagnation and decline, can be identified in numerous congregations. Most readers will be familiar with scenarios such as:

- the all-out-for-evangelism church which has no time for the care and nurture of new converts and sees a haemorrhaging of members out of the back door as new ones enter through the front;
- the cosy fellowship which enjoys familiar worship and cares for its members, but lacks the courage to address the concerns of those outside, and which eventually declines as the congregation grows old together;
- the busy church which falls apart as things just don't seem to work, where the complaint that 'there's no communication in this church' reveals a lack of adequate organization.

Healthy, growing churches, so claim the proponents of church health, can be identified by the signs of life they bear, just as living organisms are fundamentally different from rocks and minerals and healthy plants are distinguishable from the stunted and dying.

But what exactly are those key characteristics? Many writers have developed lists based upon a combination of observation and conviction. The best overview can be found at http://www.easum.com/FAQS/Healthly_Churches.html, which gives full details of the similar but clearly not identical lists of the components of church health produced by a number of writers. While the number of contributors gives a degree of confidence that there must be something in this general approach, the task of identifying the most helpful list among the different options available may not at first sight be easy.

This chapter will concentrate primarily on one particular set of church health characteristics, and on the wider approach to church life within which this list originates. Natural Church Development (NCD), an understanding of church health developed by a German church growth specialist called Christian Schwarz, provides the fullest readily accessible church health package in the UK. It also has the advantage of having the broadest statistical basis. It draws on initial research in 1,000 churches worldwide, but undergoes continual modification as further data is fed into the system.

NCD is now a major phenomenon on an international scale. Within Britain it is far less well known, but that is no reason to overlook it. NCD can provide a framework for understanding and transforming the local church, and this is a useful tool for mission in itself. More importantly in the context of this book, it can dovetail with many of the other resources and approaches to local church life and mission under consideration.

The basic approach of Natural Church Development is outlined in Christian Schwarz's book of the same name.[1] There is a growing range of accompanying literature, making it increasingly possible to use the whole NCD 'package' as more is translated from the original German.

NCD operates as a network on a worldwide scale, local partners working in each country in cooperation with a very small central team in Germany. The British partner, Healthy Church UK (contact details are available at the end of the chapter), oversees the survey process at the heart of the NCD approach, provides consultancy and is still often the only source of literature. This may have been something of a handicap for NCD in Britain. A larger UK partner may well be needed for NCD to achieve a higher profile. Sadly, Christian bookshops are still often without any NCD material on their shelves.

The basics of the NCD approach

Armed with a set of assumptions which he found in earlier church growth writing, Schwarz set out to investigate the actual statistical correlations between numerical church growth and other aspects of church life. Those aspects he found to be most important he refers to as 'quality characteristics'. It must be stressed that the quality characteristics were identified in relation to numerical

growth alone. Only those things that were found most often in *growing* churches were recorded. Other things that are also fundamental to the gospel (such
as concern for social justice) will not be reflected in the quality characteristics
because they do not correlate with numerical growth.

The eight quality characteristics identified (in no particular order of priority)
were as follows:

- Empowering Leadership
- Gift-orientated Lay Ministry
- Passionate Spirituality
- Functional Structures
- Inspiring Worship Services
- Holistic Small Groups
- Need-orientated Evangelism
- Loving Relationships.

In Schwarz's initial research, these qualities correlated strongly both with each
other and with numerical growth. In all the cases Schwarz encountered in his
worldwide investigations, churches that had all these qualities to a significantly higher degree than the national average were found to be growing over
a five-year period. A far smaller number among those that lacked high overall
quality were found to be growing. Most churches with weak expressions of
the key qualities were in decline.

However, this list of quality characteristics is only one part of the NCD approach.
Natural Church Development aims to be just that, an expression of church
life which is as natural as plant or animal growth. Along with the number-
crunching and the jargon, which can jump off the pages at times, NCD also
exudes a conviction that what is going on should be natural and organic.
Drawing on a conviction that the promise of Jesus 'I *will* build my church'
(Matthew 16.18, italics mine!) is expressed in growth as natural as that in
any other part of creation, the language of seeds, soil and fertilizer pervades
Schwarz's writing.

Steven Croft's recent description of NCD and allied approaches as 'Quality
control' perhaps misses the mark slightly in the light of this.[2] Schwarz sees
the church not as a factory, not even as agri-business, but as a plant, which
will inevitably grow and flourish providing it is given the right conditions to
allow it to do so. This is what is referred to in NCD literature as the 'all by
itself' principle, drawing on Jesus' image of the seed which sprouts and grows
unseen (Mark 4.26-29).

Principles rather than models

How can the hard-pressed and sometimes dispirited congregation hope to see growth? In response to this question, the answer has often been to look at large, growing churches (or at least, at large churches which have grown in the past) and to attempt to emulate them. Small church choirs, for example, struggle to cope with an anthem somebody heard at the cathedral. Eager evangelical congregations launch into Willow Creek-style seeker services. The temptation is to think that something that works in one place will provide a formula that can be transplanted elsewhere with similar effects.

Sadly, experience shows that this is often not the case. At best, the approach of the large church becomes less appropriate as the scale or cultural setting of church life gets further from the original. At worst, what results is the 'we tried that once but it doesn't work here' mentality which can stifle new ventures of any kind in the future.

Schwarz's research also shows (as does Bob Jackson's with reference to British church life[3]) that growth is more often a characteristic of small churches. The high-profile success stories may not be able to keep up with their reputations: Paul Yongghi Cho's Full Gospel Church in Korea, for example, has been described by Schwarz as 'the fastest declining church in the world'![4] Copying large churches is not the best way to grow small churches.

NCD makes the bold claim that it can identify the universally applicable principles that correlate strongly with healthy church life across the whole range of churches surveyed internationally. Although those principles themselves may be transferable, their implementation will vary from place to place. One healthy church may therefore look very different from another. Genuine church health depends upon fittedness to the specific context, be that the denomination and theology of the church concerned or the local cultural setting. This means that the quality characteristics identified in the list above are sufficiently non-specific to apply in a great range of local church settings. NCD should, in theory at least, be equally valuable regardless of the culture or traditions of the church concerned.

The significance of the minimum factor

There is one fundamental insight which, to many, stands out amongst all the rest of the NCD package: the minimum factor. Grasping this is probably the best way to latch on to the way NCD works.

If there are eight quality factors to be kept up to scratch all the time, how can any church hope to keep working on them all? The key thing, Schwarz suggests, is to focus on the minimum factor. A church will be only as healthy as its weakest characteristic, since this is the primary thing that will be holding back the growth God desires. This may come as a surprise to churches that have prided themselves on their distinctive strengths or grown to see themselves as specialists ('Yes, our small group life is pretty weak, but our focus is on preaching ministry . . .'). Yet the key insight of NCD is that even a church which scores well above average in several ways will be held back in terms of its overall health (and therefore in its potential for numerical growth) by just one weak area.

Schwarz uses a number of analogies from life and from natural processes to press home this point. For example, if a diet is generally good but deficient in one vitamin, ill health will result because of that one weakness regardless of how good the rest of the diet is. Similarly, crop yields in a field will be limited by whichever essential fertilizer is present in the smallest quantities.

The most helpful way to grasp how the 'minimum factor hypothesis' works is through the milk barrel image: indeed, for a number of church leaders this illustration has probably been the single most important learning experience in encountering NCD. In Switzerland, milk has traditionally been kept in barrels made from vertical slats of wood. If these slats are of different lengths then the amount of milk that can be held will depend upon the height of the shortest slat. Barrel capacity can only be increased by making the *shortest* slat longer – any changes to other parts of the barrel are a waste of energy.

So, to apply this image to church life, the cosy congregation which cares for its members well, the outward-looking evangelical fellowship and the church

Figure 9.1 NCD – 'the minimum barrel'

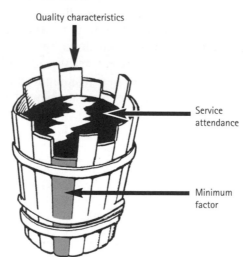

Quality characteristics

Service attendance

Minimum factor

Source: Schwarz, *Natural Church Development*, p. 53.

which is known for the excellence of its worship (be it choral or charismatic) all very clearly have significant strengths. Love, evangelism or worship might be seen in each case as the single most important characteristic of church life, and each church might even see itself as specializing in one of those. NCD insists that truly balanced and healthy church life, and by implication sustained growth, can only be achieved if the minimum factor is addressed. The loving church will be stronger if it makes the effort to look outward. The evangelistic church may need to recognize the role of caring, for both congregation and converts. A worshipping church might need to release the untapped gifts of the passive recipients in the pews. All will be healthier and more open to natural (rather than forced) church growth as a result.

In response to the relative weakness of the minimum factor, Schwarz then encourages the church to move on to the next step, using its strengths to address the weaknesses. This could lead to the transformation of the situations mentioned above. Love can flow out into concern for those beyond the congregation. Evangelistic energy sees people's *need for* God, but it can also be redirected to focus on the need to *keep close to* God. Worship can be transformed to employ a wide range of gifts rather than remaining a slick performance by the few. In each case the strengths of the church are exercised, but they are used to address the weakest part of church life.

Once the minimum factor has been strengthened, further growth in church health can follow, and will continue until a different minimum factor makes its presence felt. This will then need to be addressed in turn if further growth is to be possible.

Putting it into practice

The quality characteristics we have considered are clearly important. But if the NCD approach is to work out in action, there needs to be a way of measuring what are frankly rather nebulous criteria. In some cases this may be quite easy, as both the leadership and the congregation of a church may have a pretty good idea of what their weak area is. If that's the case then the next step is relatively straightforward: to work to strengthen the weakest characteristic.

In practice it may not be that simple. Personal relationships and internal church politics can hold people back from speaking out what most of them know only too well ('Yes, I know Jane's not really the right person for that job, but it's not easy to say that now she's been doing it for so long . . .'). A shared awareness of the cost of change can lead, possibly at a subconscious level, to collusion that denies the problem. We are all human, and we all have blind spots that prevent us seeing some of the biggest weaknesses, especially if we are part of them!

NCD aims to help churches by providing an objective assessment of their quality areas. It does this by asking the church leader and 30 key members at the heart of church life to fill in a fairly extensive questionnaire. The questions aim at objective responses rather than opinions, most using 'I', 'we', 'our' wording to encourage a sense of ownership. There is no indication on the questionnaire of how the scores relate to the final quality characteristic profile, and that makes it hard for respondents to try to guess the 'right' answers. The church then sends the completed questionnaires to the British NCD partner organization for processing. An alternative is to buy from the national NCD partner a computer program which will allow this analysis to be done on a PC by a local church member with a moderate level of IT skill.

The resulting church profile provides an overview of the strengths and weaknesses of congregational life. Each characteristic will receive a score out of 100, which is calculated against national average figures for churches that have undertaken the survey. However, the numbers are not the important thing – what matters is the relative sizes of the scores for each quality characteristic. There will be higher scores against certain quality areas, and that provides scope for affirmation as the first response. Experience indicates that human nature needs this to be given time and attention: we are all more likely to face up to the challenges revealed by minimum factors once the good things God is doing have been recognized and celebrated. The major challenge is then to get to work on the one or two weakest areas revealed. An *Implementation Manual*[5] provides guidance at this stage, and a network of local coaches who can give on-the-spot advice is slowly developing.

Fundamental to this stage is the application of what the NCD books describe as 'biotic' principles. These are approaches and strategies which retain a fluidity and a relation to natural growth processes. Maybe 'organic' might be a better translation. Definite goals do need to be set, but they are not in the area of church attendance. The intention rather is to aim at specific improvements in the *quality* of church life, leaving the growth in terms of numbers to God. Most specifically, the healthiest current areas in the church's life provide the key to future strategy. They are the strengths that can be used to address weaknesses.

What should then follow is in many ways the most important and (from Christian Schwarz's observations of worldwide trends) often the most neglected part of the process: undertaking a second survey. To judge whether there has been positive development in the life of the church a second survey (using the same questions) is designed to take stock, to indicate progress and to point out the next area of church life in need of attention.

The recommended time between surveys has initially been six months. This seems to allow ample time for church life to be transformed in many other cultures, but the great majority of British churches seem to wait considerably longer than this. Eighteen months or even two years may be a more realistic response to the slower-moving reality of British church life.

The reality: some British local church experience of NCD

The number of churches that have gone through the full process of survey and profile production is still relatively small. By early 2005 just over 500 congregations across Britain had been or were still involved: a significant number, but a long way off the scale of involvement in better-known programmes such as Alpha and Emmaus. While the number of congregations that have received inspiration from NCD or made informal use of the principles is undoubtedly much higher, the amount of measurable data is still relatively limited. Of those participating as paid-up members, the number that have gone on to complete a second survey is smaller still. By early 2005, 25 per cent of churches involved in the full NCD survey process had continued this far. Although NCD in Britain is still in its early days, 16 per cent of churches had completed a third survey by then, and one has now moved on to go through the survey process six times.

Among the small number of churches that have gone beyond the first survey, there is strong evidence that NCD works. Two-thirds of the repeat surveys showed an increase in the recorded quality of church life. Only one-third were unchanged or recorded a fall in average quality score, many of these citing external reasons for this anomaly.

It is an interesting comment on British church life that the most common recorded weak areas were Empowering Leadership and Inspiring Worship Services. If there is one thing clergy are likely to see themselves doing it is exercising leadership, and if there is one thing churches are expected to do, it's having services. In both cases, many of these are not doing it very well! Leadership and worship are going on, but it would seem that they are often neither empowering nor inspiring.

On the positive side, the most frequently recorded maximum quality characteristic to emerge from church analyses in Britain to date is Gift-orientated Ministry. In many congregations, people know and are using the gifts and expertise they bring. This bodes well for the future if many churches are able to draw on these gifts among lay members to develop the weaker aspects of their corporate life.

However, the full national picture has yet to emerge. In the absence of large-scale statistical data, the story of one parish church in southern England may provide a snapshot of NCD in practice.

One church puts NCD into practice

St Michael's is a medium-sized parish church in an area of mixed housing on the fringes of Southend, with an average Sunday attendance in the region of 160 adults ranging over three services. Peter Nicholson, vicar of St Michael's, discovered *Natural Church Development* when browsing in a bookshop. The immediate attractions were the international nature of the research and the 'principles not models' concept underlying the thinking. This seemed a useful tool for producing an effective church audit.

The first survey
A first set of surveys was distributed among those in positions of lay leadership in the summer of 1997 – 40 copies to ensure that at least 30 were returned. All the PCC were given surveys, plus other lay leaders. The resulting profile emerged (scores out of 100):

Empowering Leadership	54	Inspiring Worship Services	28
Gift-orientated Lay Ministry	38	Holistic Small Groups	56
Passionate Spirituality	51	Need-orientated Evangelism	60
Functional Structures	45	Loving Relationships	47

St Michael's was committed to ongoing evangelism, with Peter a local Alpha resources adviser, so the highest score for evangelism was not an enormous surprise. The low score under Inspiring Worship Services, although in tune with the national pattern noted above, was less expected.

Worship: the first minimum factor
St Michael's has a mixed congregation with traditional, charismatic and evangelical strands. Within this mix it may not have been easy to perceive a general dissatisfaction with the quality of worship in the church. On reflection it was agreed that worship had indeed been rather overlooked, and a small NCD team was set up to ensure implementation of NCD principles and that the church neither neglected the results nor went overboard on goal-setting. The survey results were announced at the annual parochial church meeting and statistics were presented so as to make the whole congregation aware of the focus for the coming year.

To address worship (the 'minimum factor' in the first survey) a number of strategies were adopted, partly in response to the guidance in the NCD *Implementation Manual* – prayer before services, a Saturday workshop on worship, assigning welcomers to each service, a rota for intercessions, job specifications for those involved in worship leading, lay leaders going away on worship conferences, with the Worship team setting two or three achievable goals at any given time. A new amplification system was put into the church building and a new overhead projector purchased.

Encouragement from survey 2
A second survey 18 months later revealed not only an improvement in the score relating to worship but also a significant increase in the overall average:

Empowering Leadership	59 (+5)
Gift-orientated Lay Ministry	50 (+12)
Passionate Spirituality	63 (+12)
Functional Structures	58 (+13)
Inspiring Worship Services	53 (+25)
Holistic Small Groups	56 (unchanged)
Need-orientated Evangelism	69 (+9)
Loving Relationships	69 (+22)

It would appear from the results of this second survey that the steps adopted to improve the worship at St Michael's were beginning to have a marked effect. But there was also something else going on. The fresh sense of purpose and of working together seems to have had the most marked spin-off in encouraging loving relationships. Perhaps this was developed as church members set about projects together. Similarly, gifts were put to use in making changes, and people were more committed in their personal spiritual life since shared action stretches faith and encourages prayer. Thus passionate spirituality became more marked. Structures had to become more functional if things were going to get done by a wide range of church members. The process of change had an impact across most of the quality areas, not only in the weakest one.

The second survey led to a teaching and action programme on spiritual gifts, while at the same time work continued on developing a vision for worship within the church.

On to survey 3
A third survey some time later revealed a very marginally lower overall average score, but more significantly a change in the minimum factors, with functional structures and holistic small

groups (rather left on the back burner, as Peter puts it) now scoring lowest. It is unclear at this stage whether the slightly lower scores represent a neglect of these areas in the light of efforts put into worship and spiritual gifts, or whether growing involvement had produced rather higher expectations on the part of those completing the questionnaires.

Certainly the overall rise between the first and second surveys was not repeated, but nor had the progress been lost. The effect on overall church health of a sense that something positive was going on, while not producing ever-rising scores, does seem to have resulted in a lasting and all-round perception that this was a better church to be part of, quite apart from the specific strategies adopted to address the minimum factors.

Taking stock

After a pattern of gentle decline in the years before NCD was introduced, St Michael's now shows small signs of numerical growth. While not of a scale to be statistically significant, it combines with the growing sense of commitment and expectancy revealed by the surveys.

St Michael's was working through a £300,000 building project during the period of the NCD process. While it saps energy and makes demands on leadership time, such an undertaking also has the effect of galvanizing God's people, encouraging spiritual commitment (there's nothing like a big projected budget deficit to get us praying!) and releasing gifts which might otherwise lie dormant.

A cell-based future?

In response to the third survey, with holistic small groups as the new minimum factor, Peter made a decision to experiment with cell groups. Two small groups have started using cell-church principles and there is the possibility of a post-Alpha group becoming a cell group. It is proving quite difficult persuading existing group leaders that this is the way to move forward. As will be discussed in Chapter 10, transition to cell church can be a challenging process. At St Michael's this has meant that the NCD survey-taking process has been put on hold until there is more time for the church to stop and catch its breath and find new NCD implementation team members to replace three of the five who have left.

Assessing NCD

An undervalued resource

NCD has a far lower profile in Britain than it deserves. It provides a highly valuable tool for taking stock of church life, giving an overview of strengths and weaknesses and pointing to strategies that will help a church move forward from where it is. There is also a liberating feel about much of its message: the task of the church's leadership is not to struggle and strain to force a church to grow but rather to shape the life of the church in such a way that God's gift of growth is able to flourish.

Once one has absorbed the language of growth and of natural life processes, the full implementation of NCD procedures can come as something of a surprise. A relatively extensive questionnaire, computer analysis and technical language (biotic principles, bi-polarity and growth automisms are not the usual subject matter of after-church coffee conversations) can give the impression of a complex technical process which probes with scientific precision into the unseen forces that lie deep beneath congregational life. However, it is important to grasp the role of NCD within the whole life of a church. Unlike things like the Alpha course, or the widely publicized build-up to a parish mission, NCD as an investigative process is something that will largely affect only the minister(s) and a fairly small circle of key church members. Apart from possible decisions relating to the cost of the operation, the main impact on the wider congregation and the community beyond will be through the plans and programmes that may be initiated in response to the questionnaire analysis. The public face of NCD may ultimately be another programme altogether, even though it has been put into effect in response to NCD analysis.

NCD fatigue?

Our parish case study above shares with a number of other churches something of an experience of NCD fatigue. There is a slowing-down in the rate at which successive surveys are undertaken, with longer periods of time needed to implement changes. On one level this may be a realistic reflection of church life in Britain and in western Europe more generally. NCD has grown out of worldwide research, and the reality of church growth in much of the two-thirds world far outstrips anything that is normally seen in contemporary Britain. The challenge to church leaders may be to 'hang on in there' in continuing the process, with the benefits of NCD being seen as the work continues after the initial burst of enthusiasm has died down.

Behind NCD fatigue may lie another issue that is more specifically related to its approach. It is questionable just how regularly a plant can be uprooted and examined before its growth starts to be affected! That may be an unfair analogy, since clearly a plant can be watched without uprooting, but the detail of the NCD questionnaire and the anxiety of waiting to see what emerges as the minimum each time round may sap energies that could be put to better use elsewhere.

How and when to use NCD

It may well be most effective to introduce NCD at a time when a church is already in the process of taking stock and reconsidering its direction. In a number of cases the arrival of a new minister, with the adjusting of relation-ships and the re-evaluating of priorities that that will necessarily involve, may be the moment to begin working in this way. A survey undertaken as a new minister arrives cannot be interpreted as a judgement on his or her leadership in the past, and is therefore more likely to lead to action. The converse is probably also true: it may be a bad idea to undertake a survey if the minister has been in post a long time and lacks the energy to make changes, or if he or she is frankly not very competent and easily threatened!

Certainly it seems that a good case can be made for longer periods between surveys, allowing a congregation to get stuck into a given area of focus. Change takes time and energy in the current cultural climate of British church life. Schwarz reports the significant value of using outside consultants in helping churches to implement change, and British experience backs this up. Moving from survey results (important though they may be) to action takes wisdom and energy, and an outsider's perspective on the realities revealed and on possible ways forward may be vital. Some Anglican dioceses are beginning to respond to this, and other denominations such as the United Reformed Church are beginning to offer consultancy at regional level.

A few reservations

Quite apart from the process, there are questions to be asked about the content of NCD. Since it derives from a study of numerically growing churches, the quality characteristics are inevitably related to numerical growth. The 'health' that they indicate will reflect a balance of church life which certainly seems to encourage increased numbers of worshippers. On the other hand, we may be theologically convinced that other things, although not directly correlated with numerical growth, are essential for a church to be truly healthy. Most obviously, the quality characteristics make no specific reference to the need for churches to be active in issues related to justice, peace and the integrity of creation. This may be indirectly addressed under Loving Relationships or Need-orientated Evangelism, but many would see commitment to the needs of the oppressed to be central to wholehearted discipleship even when it cannot be fitted into this particular mould.

NCD in the local church?

The strengths of NCD may well lie mainly in its diagnostic value. Cumbersome though it may be, the extensive NCD questionnaire analysis is able to identify areas of weakness in a particular church and encourage a focused response. At the same time it will hopefully indicate at least some areas of strength that can provide affirmation and encouragement.

A further strength of NCD can be found in its flexibility in contextualization. There are relatively few prescriptive instructions as to *how* a particular quality characteristic might be raised. In complete contrast, when referring to worship, American church growth analyst George Barna states that church growth seems to need at least 20 minutes of uninterrupted worship songs in any given service(!).[6] Schwarz's NCD is open to considerably more variety in worship than this, commenting in the *Implementation Manual*: 'This is the area where you find most diversity of style (and liturgical "rules"), so it is impossible to give a single model which is useful for every church.'[7]

Commendable though such flexibility may be, it carries with it the inherent danger that the local church leader might feel more personal responsibility for implementing change. It is not possible simply to say: 'We have to take this next step now since the book tells us to.' Ideally, working with NCD will move a congregation into patterns of natural growth that *feel* spontaneous rather than forced. Inevitably, the reality will still involve hard work. The experience of the farmer in Mark 4.26-29, who 'goes to bed at night and gets up by day, and the seed sprouts up and grows', might not be paralleled by every church leader who is struggling to respond to the results of a survey analysis!

As an international programme with the majority of its material currently available only in German, immediate usage of all the NCD training literature and resources is not at present an option for any but the most able linguist. On the other hand, this obliges church leaders to look outside the NCD framework and to see how many of the other options available might link in with an overall strategy.

More NCD materials are planned for translation, and these may well be very useful. However, this might also be a disadvantage for the British reader, who is already surrounded by an extensive array of other approaches from other sources. A more relevant response to the local context may come from integrating these resources with the results of NCD analysis. An understanding of church health can play a central role within the mix of other evangelism strategies. One alternative route to assessing church health has appeared slightly more recently, and this is also worth serious consideration.

Another way of looking at church health

In response to concerns about both the unwieldy nature of the NCD questionnaire process and the restrictions of the eight quality characteristics, Robert Warren, previously of Springboard, has produced a modified set of quality characteristics as part of the *Healthy Churches* programme. The list is similar to that used by NCD, but not identical:

Healthy Churches . . .

- are energized by faith
- have an outward-looking focus
- seek to find out what God wants
- face the cost of growth and change
- operate as a community
- make room for all
- do a few things and do them well

The advantages of *Healthy Churches*' approach would appear to be ease of use (the questionnaire is significantly shorter) and greater breadth of content. Coming from a specifically English background, based on pilot work in Durham diocese, it may well be that *Healthy Churches* is more immediately useable in the British local church setting.

The *Healthy Churches' Handbook* provides a clear and easily-implemented outline of how to use the programme. It is also a major addition to the literature addressing church health in general, providing some helpful pointers as to how the Healthy Churches programme overlaps with NCD and containing as an appendix one of the most extensive lists of resources related to local church mission currently in print.

Healthy Churches is a significant resource, but it also has its weaknesses. There is less direct relation to the extensive statistical basis that underlies the international NCD package. The *Healthy Churches* questions are rather more transparent, and it may therefore be easier for prejudices and personal opinions to skew the results that emerge.

In Natural Church Development and *Healthy Churches*, British congregations now have two ways in to assessing church health. Both are valuable, and a most fruitful way forward may be to attempt to draw on both sets of resources. That will be a challenge, but it may well repay the effort.

Church health in the mix

Church health and process evangelism

Alpha, Emmaus and other process evangelism courses have considerable potential to work symbiotically with NCD. They offer openings for developing gift-orientated ministry, and if they work well they should lead into and further develop holistic small groups. They can provide scope for empowering leadership as group leaders grow in confidence and independence. Ideally there should be a 'biotic' feel to the way those who come to faith through one course then share in the next one and invite their friends to it. If a church is strong on functional structures and holistic small groups but weak on need-orientated evangelism, Alpha may be the natural way forward. If passionate spirituality or inspiring worship is the weakest area then Alpha may not necessarily be the right next step.

It is in this chapter on church health that it may be most relevant to mention the Beta course. Despite its name, the team producing Beta have no links with Alpha and the material does not form a particularly natural follow-on from it. Process evangelism it is not, but church health may benefit significantly from its content.

Beta is designed primarily as a course to encourage better understanding of how people function, drawing both on Christian teaching and insights from psychology. Looking at issues like relationship, forgiveness, loss and change, Beta has the potential to be a useful tool in developing informed pastoral care and healthy relationships. This in itself can play a part in helping churches as well as individuals become healthier places. There may also be the potential within Beta to open up understanding of the dynamics of church life, and to give deeper shared understanding of why it is that the changes diagnosed by NCD or Healthy Churches are so painful to implement.

Church health and community ministry

If loving relationships are to develop outside of the sometimes forced atmosphere of church social events, partnership in shared tasks could be a fundamental step forward. Many men (and certainly many women too) find it more natural to build a friendship in the context of working alongside others. If loving relationships are to spill out beyond the core congregation, and if needs-orientated evangelism is to listen for the felt needs of others as well as the perceived needs from a church perspective, community ministry may be a significant partner to NCD in developing the mission of the local church.

Church health and cells

On a world scale, much of the data that feeds into the NCD project has been drawn from cell-based churches. Cells provide holistic small groups *par excellence.* They have scope to encourage passionate spirituality, to grow gifts and to energize leadership. The current questionnaires used for NCD analysis may require a little explanation in order to work in a cell setting, but the potential for NCD and cell-based church life to work in partnership is considerable.

Conclusion

Assessing the current state of a church's health can be crucial in helping that church to find the way forward. NCD is a valuable tool for this: it is objective and based on considerable research, and it deserves far wider usage. On the other hand it is expensive and relatively cumbersome to use. Springboard's 'Healthy Churches' material is slimmer, cheaper and easier to use (it could be undertaken in the course of a church leaders' day away, for example). It lacks the range of follow-up materials, however, and is perhaps more easily swayed by subjective opinions. The best approach may be to draw on the strengths of both, and to seek outside support and guidance in interpreting the results so that an effective strategy can be developed.

For further information

Visit

http://www.ncd-international.org/
www.healthychurch.co.uk/ncd.html
http://www.beta-course.org

Contact

Healthy Church UK, PO Box 100, Sandy SG19 1ZR. Tel: 01767 692938

Read

Christian Schwarz, *Natural Church Development Handbook,* BCGA, 1998
Robert Warren, *The Healthy Churches' Handbook,* Church House Publishing, 2004

10

Cell church

Mike Booker

> If people come together to care for each other, it is because they feel
> more or less clearly that they have a mission. They have been called
> together by God, and have a message of love to transmit to others.
> Jean Vanier

Small is beautiful

While big churches may catch a greater share of public attention, the secret
is beginning to get out: smaller churches have much to offer which large ones
do not. Not only is the quality of relationships and the ability to spot and
welcome newcomers higher, smaller churches are on average far more likely
to grow than large ones. This is not to say, of course, that any one small church
will be able to add more new members than one large church – all things
being equal, this is extremely unlikely. What it does mean is that added together,
a large number of small congregations are likely to end up with more new
members than would be the case for one single larger church. Bob Jackson
identifies this trend from his examination of attendance data from the 1998
English Church Attendance Survey when compared with records from 1989
(see Figure 10.1).[1]

Similar patterns were found in the Church of England, particularly in the
Diocese of St Albans (see Figure 10.2).

Although avoiding decline may not of itself be the most inspiring of goals,
the trend is still clear: smaller churches are far less likely to be in decline and
much more likely to show overall growth in attendance. Small churches involve
their members, draw out stronger senses of loyalty and commitment, and allow
for face-to-face contact and a welcome to newcomers as they are seen and
identified rather than being lost in the crowd. This is important news for the
Church nationally, and deserves serious consideration in large-scale planning:
closing small churches may not necessarily be the best way forward in many
cases. It is also a major piece of encouragement for small churches across the

Figure 10.1 Church growth and decline in all denominations, 1989–98 (grouped by size of church in 1989)

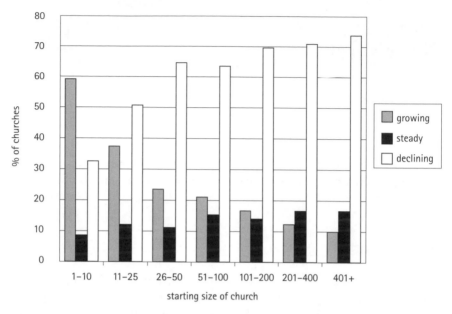

Figure 10.2 Change in usual Sunday attendance in St Alban's Diocese, 1991–9 (grouped by size of church in 1991)

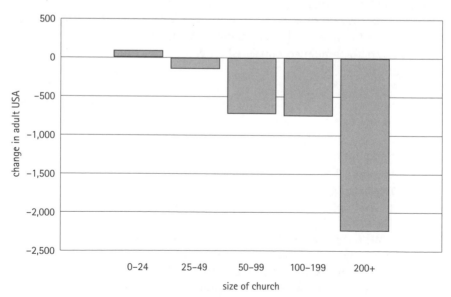

country: they may feel insignificant, but churches like them are one of the main sources of hope for the future.

Where the 'small church = greater growth' equation is less helpful is in the immediate application to larger churches, by which we mean any local congregation above the very smallest. We are not advocating waiting until attendances have dropped below ten people in the hope that growth will then follow! This is where cell church has much to offer: large churches can replicate the benefits that small churches experience. The rest of this chapter will focus on cell church as one expression of small-church benefits within larger church life. This will involve assessing what makes cell church distinctive, its history and the culture in which it has emerged, together with some thoughts on how cell church may work in the British context. Most specifically, consideration will major on how cell church relates to the central theme of this book: evangelism.

Encountering cell church

So what is cell church? At its most basic it means recognizing the small group as being the central unit of church life. Small groups are not news in the life of the Church, although they have sometimes been overlooked for centuries at a time. Cell church provides one challenging and accessible way through the 'Can only small churches grow?' question. In essence it allows larger congregations to foster some of the characteristics of small churches, and so makes it easier to exhibit those qualities of church life from which growth flows. Cell church also comes as part of a package. It is not a branded package that can be bought from one source, but there is nevertheless a clearly defined identity to 'genuine' cell church. That identity involves a commitment to certain values as well as to a foundational size of church unit. With those values comes a distinctive language, which is part and parcel of most writing from the cell church stable. If the pages that follow appear peppered with unusual new terminology, this is deliberate: the easiest way to get under the skin of cell church thinking is to learn the language. The task of translation into words and concepts common to a wider section of church life may then be necessary, but that can happen only when cell church has first been understood on its own terms.

Something old

Small groups are by no means a new phenomenon in church life. Since the call of Jesus to the twelve, small groups based around face-to-face contact have been part of the Christian community. The development of the early

Church as recorded in the New Testament shows evidence of small-group life. Doubtless many of the churches of the New Testament were only small groups themselves, but in larger centres there appear to have been smaller groups within the whole church of the city, with Aquila and Priscilla standing out as especially dedicated home church hosts, recorded as having churches meeting in their homes in both Ephesus and Rome (1 Corinthians 16.19; Romans 16.5). Paul records teaching in Ephesus 'both publicly and from house to house' (Acts 20.20). Perhaps more significantly, the repeated language and imagery of belonging, relationship and mutual accountability (for example, Romans 12.3-8; Galatians 6.1-2) reflect a pattern of church life where involvement in small groups was the norm.

While much small-group life may have been lost from the mainstream Church for centuries, it found expression again at the evangelical revival of the eighteenth century. John Wesley's organization of the early Methodists at this time stands out in particular. John Pollock records a sympathetic curate's report to a hostile bishop:

> A class is between twelve and twenty persons of any age or sex that live near each other, who meet together to sing and pray with their leader once or twice a week. The leader of the class examines each person with respect to the state of their soul, gives some short admonition and makes a report to the preacher of the society [who could expel them if unrepentant].

The society in the curate's neighbourhood numbered 250 members, though three times as many might attend the twice-weekly evening meetings; on Fridays they fasted and met for intercession. The pattern was not simply one scale of small-group life, as the curate went on to explain:

> When they have made some considerable advancement, and have, as they express it, received justifying Faith, they are united into Bands. A Band is 5 or 6 such persons of the same age and sex, which when they meet together are more unreserved, and declare, as they say, the inmost secrets of their hearts.[2]

Home groups

Not exactly 'old', but by now a remarkably well-established part of church life, house groups have been around for a generation in much of British church life. It may be easy with hindsight to underestimate the importance of small group development. In my parents' evangelical Anglican church in the years after the Second World War, the midweek 'Bible study' was a lecture delivered to the assembled faithful by the vicar. The freedom to sit together in a home, study the Scriptures and discuss together their meaning was a major change which should not be discounted. In other churches small groups have grown up primarily as prayer meetings, in many others as temporary gatherings during Lent, Advent or other special occasions.

Home groups can at their best provide support, allow for spiritual growth, engage with their local communities and be vehicles for evangelism. In effect they can be mini-churches, replicating all that is good in the small church while sharing the back-up and belonging provided by their being part of a larger congregation. David Prior outlined an impressive vision for groups such as this in 1983, in his book *The Church in the Home*, but even then he was identifying what he called a 'steady disillusionment' with small groups.[3] Small groups in churches, Prior argued, failed to become real local churches because they were stuck at the stage of responding to felt needs. They had become stuck, inward-looking, and were not responding to what Prior viewed as the 'divine imperatives' of holistic small-church life.

Base communities

A further source of inspiration for small-group life has been the example of base ecclesial communities (often known simply as base communities), primarily in Latin America. Inspired by liberation theology, and rooted in the needs and concerns of the poor in the local community, base communities have aimed to work with a 'bottom up' approach, listening to the perspective of local people as they see the issues around them, and working together to see how this relates to the Scriptures and in turn to action.

Something new

So how is cell church different from home groups or from base communities? Is it simply more of the same, or is there in cell church thinking a new strategy that can bring fresh direction to church life?

Cell church is certainly a small-group strategy. It represents a prioritizing of small groups in church life of an order far beyond the secondary role assigned to home groups in most churches. Rather than working with the model of a church *with* small groups, cell sees a church *of* small groups. Membership of a small group is primary, and as much as possible of the life of the church occurs in or is delivered through the small groups. In theory, church life should be 'two-winged', involving both the larger congregation and the smaller cell group of between six and twelve members. In practice, the Church's neglect of the latter for centuries leads cell church enthusiasts to emphasize the small group as the fundamental level of church life.

This emphasis on small groups as the primary expression of church life clearly marks out cell church from the older home group philosophy of most congregations. Cells are to have a whole-life concern, relating to worship but also to working life, personal relationships, personal discipleship and evangelism. They are not to be Bible study or prayer groups only. But cells are also very different from base communities. The difference lies in their theology and their origins, and in the direction from which power is exerted.

Cell church has very largely emerged from within Pentecostal and evangelical church life in the two-thirds world. Much of the thinking has come from Asia, with Korea and Singapore playing a major role. Less has been written about cell group life in the growing churches of China and Latin America, and these may well be more varied in expression and less formally structured. Cell church, as generally encountered in the literature available, comes from a cultural background that is ordered, hard-working and deferential towards authority. This has implications for the next distinctive characteristic: the direction from which power and control originate.

If base communities are 'bottom up' in the development of their theology, cell church can more accurately be described as 'top down'. Within our Western culture this may not be very openly or enthusiastically expressed. Writing from a Korean perspective, Paul Yonggi Cho has no such reservations. The pyramidal pattern of organization (see Figure 10.3), with the senior pastor standing at the pivotal point between the whole church and the Holy Trinity, expresses the top-down philosophy behind some cell church thinking with startling clarity.

Evangelical and Pentecostal Christianity is committed to a certain number of non-negotiable truths, and the following of those truths by church members is a high priority to leaders. Yet cell church gives a very considerable degree of autonomy to the small local group. That autonomy has the potential for doctrinal divergence, for thinking outside the approved limits. It is therefore perhaps inevitable that cell church usually has a clear hierarchical pattern, since practical group autonomy is not intended to allow theological independence.

In one seminal work on cell church, Ralph Neighbour outlines what he sees as a biblical pattern of church leadership, with senior pastors overseeing zone servants who in turn oversee shepherd-group leaders.[4] The terminology here is not the important thing, and it would be a grave mistake to write off cell church because the language employed in some books does not easily cross cultural divides. The important thing to note is that, although leaders are to be involved and relationship is of fundamental importance, cell church expects a considerable degree of oversight to be exercised. There is an important reason for this: cell church may appear to be based around new structures, but those

Figure 10.3 The pyramidal structure of leadership in one Korean cell church

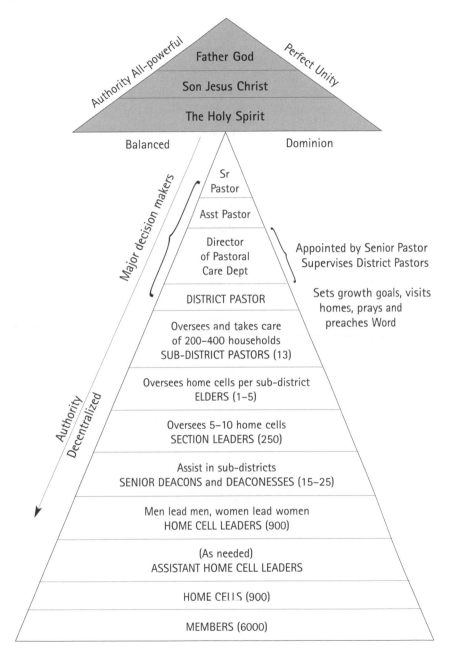

Source: P.L. Kannaday (ed.), *Church Growth and the Home Cell System*, Church Growth International, Seoul, 1995, p. 137.

involved in working with cell will tell you that it is actually the values behind the structures that are by far the most important thing.

Principles: values and structures

Cell church books and resources provide a number of different lists of values, but there is broad agreement on their nature. Anglican Cell Church Network's web site, using cell church terminology in a British context, provides an accessible summary as follows:

- **All involved:** Every member ministry – the aim is for everyone to become involved, from breaking the sound barrier and sharing in the group, to everybody in the church discovering and then pursuing their gifts.
- **Becoming disciples:** Not just knowing our faith but applying it in an accountable way.
- **Creating community:** Cell is a way of life and never just a meeting.
- **Doing evangelism:** The emphasis here is on doing it instead of just talking about it. And cell church is totally committed to helping every Christian to become a witness, and to do it seriously, continuously and strategically in very simple step-by-step ways.
- **Encountering God:** 'Jesus be the centre' is the cell church motto, and it pursues that value in very practical ways.[5]

Therefore, the normal cell meeting follows a distinctive pattern, designed to embody the above values, and conveniently alliterated to help each member remember why they are there:

- **Welcome:** An 'icebreaker' question is asked of every cell member, who all give their response in turn. Each member participates from the outset, hears their own voice in the meeting and feels included from the start rather than being a mere spectator.
- **Worship:** This could be sung worship if there are musicians in the group. If not it could be anything that exalts the Lord in the meeting, e.g. the reading of a psalm and pause for reflection and prayer.
- **Word:** This section is based around personal application of a teaching, perhaps from the Sunday service or other source. Often at this point there will be opportunity for corporate prayer for those who request it – an opportunity for the cell to minister one to another.
- **Witness:** Based around the corporate aim of making friends with non-believers and seeing them come to Christ, this section is often used for planning strategy and prayer.[6]

In particular, the witness of a cell focuses upon what is called the '*oikos*' group of each member. Using the Greek New Testament word for 'household' (*oikos*), this concept assumes that each cell member will know a circle of friends, family, colleagues and neighbours, wider than the contemporary nuclear family. Just as people like Lydia (Acts 16.15) were baptized with their household, so the expectation is that evangelism will occur most naturally within the *oikos* group of each cell member.

But is it British? Contemporary cell stories

How well can cell church work out in contemporary British life? If the patterns it uses have largely grown up in the ordered and hard-working culture of south and east Asia, can it really sit easily within a national personality more characterized by making do and muddling through? More specifically, can cell church easily be expressed within the traditions and patterns of life that are found within our mainstream denominations?

Making the change

Certainly, there are encouraging stories of the growth and effectiveness of new cell churches where church planting has led to their establishment. Harvest Time Anglican Fellowship in Margate has emerged from a more traditional parent congregation. Starting from scratch with a committed and gifted leader, the church has grown steadily if unspectacularly in the kind of socially downmarket area that seldom produces rapid church growth.

One of the struggles as church planting has developed has been to ensure the right 'DNA' for new congregations – that is to say, to find ways of ensuring that new churches are committed to ongoing growth, and will not simply replicate the relatively static patterns of life that are found in many local churches around them. The values of cell church and the clear way in which they are communicated through individual meetings and overall structures seem to provide considerable potential for creating new churches which will continue to grow. They have the 'DNA' within them that will allow continued growth and life, and are not merely clones of ageing, traditional churches.

Elsewhere the picture is more complex. 'Transitioning' to cell (a term that is widely used) is a costly process. To make the change in one fell swoop will inevitably mean considerable disruption in existing patterns of small-group life and activity. Home groups will need to be closed, or at least very significantly overhauled, rotas and teams disbanded or completely reorganized. Making space for most church members to be able to belong to a weekly cell requires a radical pruning of all the other meetings and activities that take up people's time. To make a change on this scale will take time in preparation, time in helping the whole congregation see the significance and understand the values that underlie cell church. Failure to do this will leave people feeling that there is simply yet more unnecessary tinkering with structures going on at a time when financial and staffing constraints may already be forcing change upon them.

The alternative is to go for a pilot scheme, establishing one or more cell groups within an existing structure and working to bring more of the church life progressively within cell patterns. At the same time, within the Church of England especially, the expected duties of the church to hold Sunday worship accessible to all (cell members or not) and to undertake occasional offices will continue. Deanery, diocese, area and elders' meetings will all continue within whatever denominational pattern applies. The wider congregation may struggle as they see a new 'cell' group which doesn't seem to be playing the same part in the existing life of the church as others do. The model of cell thus provided may prove attractive and ensure that in time others are eager to move in that direction, but, as Howard Astin points out in his account of the development of cell church at St John Bowling, in Bradford, bad news travels faster than good.[7]

Making the change may be challenging however it is undertaken. The temptation may be to moderate the demands of cell church, drawing on some of its ideas without implementing them fully. Some churches seem to make a point of avoiding cell terminology, adopting their own names for groups and values. This may well make cell feel more indigenous and easier for many congregations to accept. The downside may be uncertainty about just what it is that is different from the home groups the church has always had. It also makes the pastor's job more difficult. By avoiding terminology and modifying some aspects of cell church thinking, there is less opportunity to use cell church 'off the shelf' and more work to be done in producing home-grown materials.

In spite of the challenges involved in making the change, the response of church leaders who have been introducing cell ideas is overwhelmingly positive. Small groups in church life have achieved a new sense of purpose where in many cases there had been a sense that they were running out of steam. Leadership gifts have grown, and the values and structure of cell have enabled leaders to understand what they are about, to exercise independent initiative but still to know they are part of a network and to work closely with others who can guide and support. Welcome as an element of each meeting strengthens group identity; worship (which need not necessarily involve singing – cell resources are strong in introducing new ideas in this area) and the application of the word of God are accessible and relevant. Linkage of the cell meeting with teaching at the congregational level allows more time for the application of the word to shared lives, less for sitting in a puzzled circle trying to work out the 'right' answer to the vicar's questions on an obscure Bible passage!

A number of clergy report growth in numbers as the small-group life of their church has been strengthened. The most common pattern is for Alpha to provide the main evangelistic vehicle, with new believers joining cells or forming new cells from their Alpha group. There are many ways in which cell church certainly does work for contemporary British congregations.

Cells and evangelism

'Well, it's worked very well for three of the four W's, but we struggle with the Witness.' As my conversations with and visits to churches that are introducing cell church progressed, I found a clearly detectable trend. Indeed, it was often mentioned before I even began to ask about the idea. Cells in Britain struggle with evangelism. One church in Derby which has cell-based youth work explained it this way:

> The most notable gain has been the growth and development in the young people. They spend time in prayer and preparation, and model that to others. Young leaders have been stretched, frustrated, excited and envisioned, as they have been given tasks beyond their strength and have had to rely on God to see them through. There has been an increasing hunger and passion to see God act – the young people started and run early morning prayer meetings in several schools around the city, with a central cross-church one midweek. They show greater confidence to take part in their own meetings, but also in mixed-age meetings, in every aspect, including ministering in the power of the Spirit. The openness and honesty within groups and the sense of greater accountability has resulted in increased commitment to daily discipleship. And there has been a releasing and recognition of gifting amongst those involved – preachers, pastors, teachers, evangelists . . . On the other hand, evangelism has not developed as rapidly as we would have liked. There is still a 'two world' culture ingrained into some of our young people, though an increasing number of them are sharing our frustration . . . Good friendships are forming, and some people on the fringe are making a definite commitment.[8]

On one level this is unsurprising. Britain shares the western European cultural phenomenon of slow church growth. Even in places where churches are growing, once transfer from other fellowships is accounted for the rate of growth through conversion is far less than is the case in most other continents. But it is disappointing in the light of cell church's vision of cells multiplying like yeast, constantly expecting them to grow and divide into two new cells. Cells certainly can grow and divide, as one church's story will reveal below, but this is currently the exception rather than the norm. As one church leader put it, 'strangers are an enormous problem for a cell group'. British reserve is a major barrier to small groups becoming the main entry point into church life. This appears to be two-way, with enquirers feeling happier with the open atmosphere of an Alpha group or the anonymity of a main service, and cell members being more comfortable grappling with their faith in the safety of an all-Christian group. As the cultural gulf grows between church and the society in which we live this problem is unlikely to diminish. Indeed, the high level of commitment expected within cells can itself lead to a deepening of a separate church culture and a wider gulf which must then be bridged.

The alternative difficulty (although one much less commonly found) is that cells are so open to outsiders that the opportunities for Christian growth and nurture are diminished. Another church involved in cell-based youth work found that committed Christian members of its cells were frustrated by what they perceived as the low spiritual temperature of the cells, containing as they did a considerable proportion of young people who were unsure of their Christian commitment and uncommitted to Christian lifestyle. As a result the more committed young people formed an additional group of their own for prayer and mutual support. More evenings were taken up with another church event, and cells as the foundational units of church life were called into question.

One church's strategy

Cell church may not be an easy route forward for the traditional Anglican parish church, but one church's story provides an encouraging illustration of how things might work out.

St Mark's, Haydock, has worked for longer and with more commitment than most other British churches to see cell church principles working out. Even so, Phil Potter, the vicar, is realistic about evangelism, recognizing that evangelism is always a hard slog! Cell church is reflecting the national pattern, with Witness usually the last W to get tackled. However, he puts a positive spin on this lack of evangelistic energy, pointing out that the rest of cell church life is so good it's easy for people to settle for all that. Cells are expected to multiply every two–three years, considerably longer than the expectation in many other parts of the world.

Phil estimates that it took two years for the church's culture to shift from 'normal' church to cell church, to learn what it means to have fellowship with Christians in a 'normal' manner, doing ordinary and not only churchy things. If cells engender a stronger Christian culture, that culture itself clearly needs to be changed. Christians have explicit permission to be themselves and have fun, and to share that with non-Christians. Bridge-building is built into the cell agenda, with each cell expected to be aware of and praying for the immediate circle of family, friends and colleagues known to each cell member.

To free up time to make this possible, pruning has to be accepted as a way of life. This includes pruning back the demands of Sunday worship, with cell members expected to attend only one of the different Sunday congregations. However, it has also involved some pruning of the weekly commitment to cell life, so that there is more space for social involvement with others around. Every fourth week all cells have a social or prayer night, some cells majoring on prayer, some on social activities. The aim is to build up a monthly 'fringe' to each cell, people who begin to feel they belong even if they only join in occasional events. Social events bringing in outsiders are based upon the interests of those people for whom the group has been praying. As the individuals around the cell are regularly prayed for so events run by the cell or by the whole church can be shaped to fit the needs and interests of the cells' contacts. Some cells are specifically focused on community issues, drawing around them a fringe of people who are served by the cell or share in its community concern.

Central to the realism of this approach has been learning to celebrate real testimonies; stories of small steps in bridge-building are shared and affirmed, not only dramatic conversions. The structures themselves are like an enormous, ever-moving jigsaw. If the monthly social gathering is not really 'them' then people move to another cell group. The communication and support offered by local pastors helps in this, enabling the structures to respond to the people, rather than people being fitted into an over-rigid framework.

Where contact at the edge of a cell leads on to overt interest in the Christian faith, enquirers may join an Alpha course. In this case a friend may leave cell to join Alpha with the enquirer, or the whole cell follows Alpha. The pattern of cell life is secondary to the priority of evangelism.

A high-cost strategy

Moving to the full adoption of a cell model is a high-cost strategy. A church can run a process evangelism course and then choose to discontinue, can undertake an NCD or 'Healthy Churches' analysis without being bound to the findings. Cell is different. Making the change to cell church is demanding, and will inevitably affect the whole congregation. Without significant reductions in the older patterns of church life it (or the congregation) will collapse under the weight of the demands generated.

On the other hand, the stories of some of the early adopters are overwhelmingly positive. The message from those who have worked hardest to take on cell values and structures is that it is worth the struggle. By giving both priority and a degree of autonomy to small groups, some of the advantages of small-church life are made accessible to members of larger congregations in a way that older home groups have seldom achieved. In this we need to note that cell church is at a very different stage from Alpha. The Alpha course is now very widely used, and provides a package which most local church leaders can pick up and put into action. Cell church is still the preserve of the more adventurous. As such it is currently being used by some of the most imaginative and adventurous clergy in the Church. An evaluation of its usefulness for most average churches will take more time.

One thing that is clear is that cell is not in itself a panacea. Evangelism will not 'just happen' because cell structures are adopted, and even when cell values are communicated it seems that the focus on evangelism is the priority that takes longest to work out in action. Cell structures may enable exponential church growth in other cultures where the dynamism for growth is already there. In this they are providing a pattern through which growth can flow unhindered, but it may be that much of the energy for growth is not coming directly from the cell structures themselves.

The desire to know, pray for and structure outreach around the needs and interests of those known to church members would seem to be a way in which cells and evangelism can begin to work in effective partnership in the current British church scene. This model is one that could be taken up by most churches. Where cell has specific value is in encouraging and enabling this approach through the life of the small group, and in guiding and encouraging church members and leaders through the patterns of oversight that accompany small group life.

Some possible modifications

One helpful and broader insight has recently come from Steven Croft, who has been involved for a long time in small-group evangelism and is one of the authors of the Emmaus course. In his recent book *Transforming Communities*, he examines many of the issues that cell church also addresses, seeing in small groups the place where lives and their surrounding communities can be transformed.

Read alongside some of the literature that is more clearly tied in with cell church thinking, *Transforming Communities* gives another perspective on cell thinking without employing the same terminology. It also has a number of other important emphases to add, not the least of which is a recognition that contemporary culture in all its diversity needs opportunities for people to come to faith in more than one way. For some that will be through the closeness of relationship within a small group. For others it will be through the space and anonymity provided by a church building and larger public events. The role of small groups may be in part to maintain the life of the church so that those larger opportunities continue to be provided.

Transforming Communities also goes further than much cell church writing in stressing the need for an integration between church involvement and working life. Interestingly, there is also more of a focus on listening to the local context and letting it shape vision and theology. In this there may be at least a pointer towards cell church and base ecclesial community thinking coming together. After some initial discussion in the early 1990s it would appear that those involved in these two movements have had little contact with each other. Divided as they are by theology and style, the shared focus on a renewed place for small groups in the life of the church nevertheless leaves much that could be learned were a new process of two-way listening to begin.

It may be that the small group is not in itself the only or the best way to respond to the need for belonging within British culture. Two of the largest and most imaginative churches in Britain are Holy Trinity Brompton in London and St Thomas, Crookes, in Sheffield. Both have made a major focus the group size above that of the cell, with 'pastorate' and 'cluster' groups respectively providing a middle-scale between small groups and the whole congregation. Where possible, active church members belong both to a small group which is in turn part of a medium-sized gathering.

Medium-sized groups can welcome those who need more personal space than cells alone can provide. They can also reduce some of the pressure towards uniformity, giving scope for small groups of different sizes and different intentions, since small groups do not have to deliver all parts of church life. This can have a particular value if a process evangelism group wants to continue once the course has finished; while it may not have the balance of membership to become a 'proper' cell, it could quite easily continue as a small group while also belonging to a larger grouping that would form the link to the wider church community.

Of course, models drawn from very large churches will not always transfer to the smaller church. Many churches are already not much bigger than a cell group, but for churches with an active membership of one hundred or more, a medium-sized, pastorate level of group belonging may well be worth considering. Like process evangelism courses, this is an approach to church life which is emerging from within the British cultural setting, and like process evangelism, it may well be more in tune with our national culture than 'pure' cell church with its origins outside western Europe.

Cells in the mix

Taking on the full message of cell church can seem a major task in itself. In practice, the number of links and overlaps with some of the other sections of this book are considerable.

The link with Alpha has already been mentioned. A cells-plus-Alpha pattern seems to be well established in a number of churches, with the Alpha course providing a way in to church life which compensates for some of the difficulties that cells experience when they try to welcome enquirers by themselves. The predominance of Alpha reflects both its national profile and the overlap in theology between the cell church and the Alpha approach. There is no reason why a similar synergy should not develop between cells and other process evangelism courses. Similarly, Alpha or other process evangelism groups could form the basis of new cells.

A move to cell church thinking could be an effective follow-on from a Natural Church Development survey if holistic small groups were revealed as a minimum factor. Overseas links might prove effective in opening up the eyes of a congregation to the priority of group commitment and of evangelism, although some stories of exponential cell-based growth from other cultures might prove challenging. Cells with a shared focus on community action might form the starting point for the development of those relationships with partners in action from which a cell fringe will grow.

Conclusion

Those church leaders who have taken on the challenge of cell church wholeheartedly were amongst some of the most enthusiastic people we spoke to in researching for this book. On the other hand, half-baked moves to become a little more cell-like can leave church members feeling that all that has happened is a change in terminology. Introducing cell church can have far-reaching positive results, but it is also hard work. This is not a low-commitment option, but it may be a pattern of church life which is increasingly seen to be effective and one that becomes more and more accepted in the future.

For further information

Visit

http://www.celluk.org.uk/
www.cell-ideas.co.uk

Read

Steven Croft, *Transforming Communities*, Darton, Longman & Todd, 2002
Michael Green, *Church Without Walls*, Paternoster, 2002
Phil Potter, *The Challenge of Cell Church*, BRF, 2001

11

Fresh expressions of church

Mark Ireland

> The Anglican church's credentials are its incompleteness, with tension
> and travail in its soul. It is clumsy and untidy, it baffles neatness and
> logic.
>
> Archbishop Michael Ramsey

A new phrase has entered the language. 'Fresh expressions' is not, as you might
be forgiven for thinking, the name of a new brand of aftershave, but rather
a phrase coined by the *Mission-shaped Church* report to describe emerging
forms of church created to reach sections of the population not being attracted
by inherited models of church. The remarkable impact of *Mission-shaped
Church*, which was published by the Church of England in 2004 and sold
15,000 copies in its first year, has brought church planting back to the top of
the evangelism agenda after a decade dominated by the success of Alpha.

The thrust of *Mission-shaped Church* is that a fast-changing mobile society
presents significant new opportunities to engage people through networks
rather than neighbourhoods, and that in a more fragmented culture we are
going to have to develop much more diversity in styles of worship and church
if we are to 'proclaim afresh' the gospel of Christ to a new generation. This
does not mean abandoning the parish system – which still draws a million
people every week to public worship – but rather developing new patterns
alongside it to meet new challenges the old structures were never designed
for. As Rowan Williams has put it,

> We have to ask whether we are capable of moving towards a 'mixed economy'
> – recognising church where it appears and having the willingness and the
> skill to work with it.[1]

The report contains many examples of fresh expressions of church, from café
church and school-based congregations to new services within existing
buildings, but the crucial thing about becoming a mission-shaped church is
not copying other people's *models*, but absorbing the underlying theology
and *values*, and then seeking to express those values in developing a new

model appropriate to one's own context. Churches that simply try to adopt new models without first working through the underlying theological values will quickly fail. According to the report there are five core values for missionary churches:

- A missionary church is focused on God the Trinity.
- A missionary church is incarnational.
- A missionary church is transformational.
- A missionary church makes disciples.
- A missionary church is relational.[2]

Mission-shaped Church was overwhelmingly endorsed by the Church of England's General Synod and has received powerful top-level support – which will be vital in turning assent into action. Archbishop Rowan Williams has appointed Steven Croft to head up a new Anglican/Methodist agency called Fresh Expressions to promote the development of fresh expressions of church. At the same time General Synod has also been working on a new Pastoral Measure, designed to give legal recognition and provide an enabling framework for new non-parochial expressions of church. The Church Commissioners have reviewed how their funds are used and have begun to make grants to dioceses specifically for new initiatives in mission, which will be a vital source of seedcorn for planting new churches. In parallel with this a new 'mission' criterion (H) has also been added to the selection criteria for ordained ministry, which requires candidates (for the first time) to show potential as 'leaders of mission'.

What is church planting?

To speak of 'church planting' is to use a biological metaphor that may be unfamiliar to some. To explain the principle, it is helpful to think about what an apple tree is for. The ultimate aim of an apple tree is not simply to produce apples but to grow new apple trees. The core of an apple that falls to the ground contains the seeds of a new apple tree. In the same way, so the thinking goes, a healthy church should be aiming not simply to produce new Christians but to replicate its own life by the formation of new churches. And just as a young apple tree grows more vigorously than an old one, so young churches also have the potential for more vigorous growth than those that have been around a while.

Church plants aim to bring the church to where the people are, rather than expecting the people to travel or to change their culture in order to join the church. This is of course not a new idea, and many of today's traditional churches began life as 'missions' or 'daughter churches' in new housing areas.

The typical church plant in the 1980s or 1990s involved a core group of perhaps 20–30 people being sent out from one church to start a regular Sunday morning service in a hired building, often a school, with a short, informal, 'family service' style of worship. The core group is usually a key part of church planting strategy, providing a nucleus of lay people to give leadership to the new church, rather than one minister having to start from scratch by him- or herself.

Church planting in the 1990s

The story of church planting in Britain over the last ten years is one of both success and failure. A major interdenominational congress held in Birmingham in 1992 adopted the bold vision to evangelize Britain by planting 20,000 new churches by the year 2000. However, despite much hard work, mostly by free and 'new' churches, the actual number of new churches planted in the 1990s was about 2,000, well short of the original target. The Baptist Union planted 135 churches. The Methodists challenged every circuit to plant a church, and 100 were planted. The Salvation Army closed 88 churches and planted 70 new ones, a reminder that pruning and planting are needed for healthy growth – as Robin Gill has commented: 'Simply pruning induces decline, but simply planting leaves intact the long-standing excess of churches and chapels . . . both pruning and planting are needed for effective numerical growth.'[3]

Within the Church of England, church planting peaked in the early 1990s, with almost 40 Anglican church plants per year. The majority of these plants were within existing parishes, but the ones that made the headlines tended to be where a church was planted into another parish, sometimes without the permission of its incumbent. Vicars tend to guard jealously the 'cure of souls' of the particular geographical area entrusted to them, in a way that does not always foster effective evangelism – the great charge levelled by clergy against John Wesley was that he preached in other people's parishes without permission. Sensitivity and courtesy are required towards clergy who may have had a long-standing work in a particular area, but parish boundaries were designed to facilitate mission, not prevent it. As Graham Cray, Bishop of Maidstone, reminds his clergy, the role of a priest is 'to serve your parish, not defend it'.

Another approach to church planting, pioneered by Holy Trinity Brompton and now undertaken with the active support of the Diocese of London, has involved injecting new life into existing structures by transplanting a member of staff and a core group into a struggling church faced with closure when the parish becomes vacant. HTB has now been involved in 15 such church plants since 1977, and by 2002 the total membership of the 15 churches involved was 6,617. The original membership of these churches before planting totalled 878, which shows that planting has been a significant cause of growth among Anglican churches in London.[4]

Church planting does, however, offer no guarantees of growth. Not every church plant flourishes – it is estimated that 20 per cent of church plants fail and close.[5] As every gardener knows, not every seedling survives transplant, and Jesus taught in the parable of the sower that tender new plants are vulnerable to drought and thistles. A particularly vulnerable time for new church plants is when the original leader moves on to new work, especially if that person is not replaced.

Why the slowdown?

The gradual decline in the number of new church plants in the late 1990s can be attributed to a number of factors. First of all, the most 'obvious' church plants have mostly already been done, for example into areas of new housing, or into neglected areas of existing housing. One significant factor seldom noted by those involved in church planting is that the overall decline in the health and strength of large churches (documented in Bob Jackson's *Hope for the Church*) means that fewer churches are in a position to give away a significant proportion of their most committed members without seriously weakening their own life. There have been a number of examples where the formation of a lively church plant has been at the expense of the mother church, which has failed to recover from the loss of some of its most committed core. The lesson here seems to be that planting out of a large but declining church may simply hasten that church's decline, whereas planting from a church that is experiencing growth is more likely to multiply that growth.

New church plants are becoming increasingly specialized and need more creative energy to lead, as they minister to the needs of a particular community or cultural group rather than offering a standard 'family service'. With all denominations strapped for cash, the lack of resources to employ paid leadership is also a factor in the slow-down in church planting. There is now greater recognition of the limits of unpaid lay leaders, who often have many other pressures on their time. A number of young church plants have also been stunted by a lack of continuity in ordained leadership – led by a succession of assistant curates, none of whom stays very long, with long gaps in between. The recent development of ordained local ministry within the Church of England could provide valuable pastoral continuity for small church plant congregations. Ordained local ministry is an attempt to identify, train and authorize indigenous local leadership. Ordained local ministers are unpaid and are authorized to exercise their priesthood only in their local context.

Church planting today

As we have already noted, church planting is going through a period of rapid and very significant change, building on the experience in the 1990s of both success and failure and responding to the changes in culture, particularly among those under 40 who seem increasingly distanced from traditional models of church. Church planting is becoming much more diverse in style, with less emphasis on geographical location and more emphasis on working through networks of relationships. Alongside fewer of the traditional 'daughter church' plants, there are now an increasing number of much more innovative plants, aimed at evangelizing networks of people who share a common culture, age group, work or leisure interest.

The Church of England's parochial system, which covers every inch of the country, is no longer as effective a tool for mission as it used to be. A system that worked brilliantly when people lived, worked, socialized and were buried within the same geographical location is under increasing pressure in a highly mobile society where younger people's sense of belonging is much less related to 'place'. People live, work and socialize in many different places, with no knowledge or interest as to which ecclesiastical parish they might be in. Research quoted by Michael Moynagh shows that people feel little sense of identity with their neighbours or those who come from the same town, but feel they have much more in common with those who have the same hobbies, with members of their own family and with their work colleagues (see Figure 11.1). On the evidence of Moynagh's table, future church planting is likely to be network-based.

Figure 11.1 People have little in common with their neighbours

'In general, how much would you say you have in common with the following?' (where 4 = a lot, 3 = a fair amount, 2 = only a little, 1 = virtually nothing)

People who have the same hobbies as you	2.82
Your parents	2.74
Your siblings	2.69
People who work at the same place as you	2.49
People who do the same type of job as you	2.44
People who enjoy the same type of television programmes as you	2.38
People who go to the same pubs as you	2.36
People who like the same music as you	2.31
People who are the same age as you	2.29
People with the same educational qualifications as you	2.17
People who read the same newspaper as you	2.07
People who support the same political party as you	1.97
People who wear the same kind of clothes as you	1.89
People who come from the same town or areas as you	1.82
Your neighbours	1.81

Source: *Planning for Social Change*, The Henley Centre, 1995/6, quoted in Michael Moynagh, *Changing World, Changing Church*, Monarch, 2001, p. 151

A creative recent example of a network church is B1, which meets in Birmingham city centre. This initiative arose out of the realization that the recreational centre of Birmingham is packed at weekends with young adults whose culture is light years away from that of most parish churches. The bishop appointed Geoff Lanham as 'deanery missioner' for the city centre, with a brief to establish a 'complementary' church evangelizing the networks of young adults who come to the city centre for work, leisure and sport. The church began with a core group of 29 adults, mostly drawn from the church where Geoff was previously curate. They began with a monthly 'cabaret-style' evening in the upstairs room of the Walkabout Inn, an Australasian-themed pub in the centre of town.

These evenings are designed to be a place of dialogue with non-Christians, very different from the 'seeker service' model where people just watch and receive. People are not told what to think, but given a safe place to ask questions. Everyone who comes has a say in how the church develops, including the children and the not-yet Christians. They are trying to model an inclusive church, getting 'belonging, believing, behaving' in that order. Those who are attracted by the 'cabaret-style' evenings are fed into the regular worship, which takes place in another pub on Sunday mornings. Once a month they have no meeting on a Sunday and meet instead on a Wednesday evening for 'alternative' style worship.

Discipleship takes place through cell groups and enquirers' groups. In the first ten months they added 18 adult members plus children, a growth of 68 per cent in numbers. None of these new members came from other churches in Birmingham, which had been one of the fears of local clergy. Growth since then has been more modest – one of the features of young adults in Birmingham is mobility, and there is a high turnover as work commitments change and people move into and out of the area.

Network churches like B1 are having success in evangelizing adults in their 20s and 30s in various parts of the country, and are particularly attractive to young professionals who have their own transport. Of course, this raises questions about the Church's mission to the poor, who might get left behind precisely because they do not have mobility. The long-term challenge is to see whether network churches can also work in areas of social deprivation, where fewer people have their own transport and where there is still a strong sense of local identity and rootedness.

Stoke-on-Trent is just such an area, having come 376th in a recent quality of life survey of 376 local authority areas. Of the 126,000 young adults aged 15–39 who live in the Stoke-on-Trent/ Newcastle-under-Lyme area, scarcely 1,000 belong to the Church of England. This has led the diocese to recruit a 'missionary to young adults', a creative young church planter/mission priest whose brief over a seven-year contract is to create a new worshipping community by evangelizing the networks of young unchurched adults who live, work, socialize or pub and club in the conurbation. None of the churches in the area was large enough to provide the core group for a church plant, but gradually over the first eighteen months a nucleus of about 25 adults and children has emerged. Having outgrown the priest's living room, the 'Church Without Walls' now meets in a local club at 4pm on Sunday afternoons.

Reworking our theology of mission

The need to develop such creative new types of church plant to evangelize a fast-changing culture requires us to rework our theology of mission. As George Lings has pointed out, over the last 30 years or so Britain has moved from being an evangelism field to being a mission field (see Figure 11.2). In an 'evangelism field' the role of the evangelist is to go out from the Church, recall people to faith and bring them back into the existing churches. In a 'mission field' the role of the missionary is to take the gospel into a new culture and seek to build a worshipping Christian community that belongs authentically to that culture. Now that the majority of the population have never experienced what it is to belong to a worshipping Christian community even as a child, Britain has become a mission field.

A mission field requires a different approach. Instead of evangelistic campaigns designed to get the lapsed back into church, the challenge is much more long-term and incarnational – to take the gospel to the people around us in their diverse cultures and help them to become disciples of Jesus Christ within those cultures. Instead of trying to get new believers from a very different culture to fit into the inherited culture of our existing churches, the challenge is to build church around those new believers within their own culture. This requires new forms of church for a new missionary situation.

In this task it is vital we learn from the history of Christian missions in the nineteenth and twentieth centuries so that we avoid the mistakes of those courageous Victorian missionaries to Africa and Asia who took so much of their culture with them and replicated styles of worship and church architecture that

Figure 11.2 From evangelism field to mission field

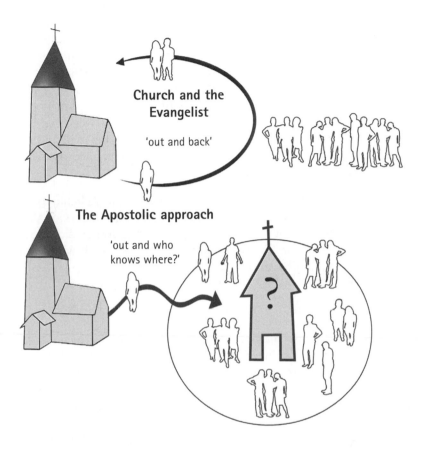

Source: Based on a Powerpoint slide by George Lings

were completely alien to local culture. I vividly remember the shock of arriving at an Anglican church in Lahore, Pakistan, as a young teacher and encountering a fully robed choir perspiring heavily in the heat as they struggled to sing Mattins in 1662 English to the tune of Merbecke! As Jesus reminds us, new wine requires new wineskins, and we cannot afford an evangelism strategy that requires unchurched young adults to renounce their own culture in order to be accepted within the Christian Church. Learning how to appreciate Radio 3 music and understand Tudor English may be valid educational targets for some, but they can hardly be justified as preconditions for becoming a disciple of Jesus.

There is an important parallel here with the beginnings of the Gentile mission in the Acts of the Apostles. The first Christians were Jews and had an enormously valuable religious tradition that had nurtured them and for which they had much to give thanks. However, once they began to evangelize Gentiles they had to make a decision about how much of their own tradition it was right to impose upon new believers from a pagan background. The apostle James's conclusion in Acts 15.19 is equally crucial for the Church today: 'It is my judgment, therefore, that *we should not make it difficult* for the Gentiles who are turning to God' (NIV, italics added). The apostolic decree of Acts 15 shows that one can be proud of one's heritage without seeking to impose it on others. If the Judaizers, whom Paul opposed so strongly in his letters, had won the day then all Gentile converts would have had to be circumcised and become subject to the Jewish law. Christianity would have remained a Jewish sect instead of becoming a world faith.

As we seek to make disciples for Jesus Christ in the rapidly changing cultures of our own day, we have to decide what are our equivalents of the non-negotiable elements of the faith, and what are our equivalents of the Jewish dietary laws. For example, in an emerging workplace church with just a few members, does singing have to be a necessary part of worship?

Incarnating the gospel

The inspiring testimony of Vincent Donovan in *Christianity Rediscovered* shows how a culture can be most effectively evangelized from the inside. Donovan was sent as a young Roman Catholic priest to work among the Masai in northern Tanzania. Realizing that building mission stations with Western-style churches, schools and clinics had had almost no evangelistic impact, Donovan pleaded with his bishop to be allowed to go and live outside a Masai camp, taking nothing from them and simply waiting until the chief trusted him enough to be willing to let him explain the Christian gospel to the elders. Donovan did so in terms that resonated with their own tribal culture. After an extended period of dialogue and teaching, which caused Donovan to rethink every aspect of the gospel as he translated it into their culture, the whole camp decided to embrace Christ and be baptized. Donovan repeated his painstaking work in other villages and so a truly indigenous Masai Church was born. When he returned to America he wrote these prophetic words:

> I realised, when I came back to America,
> that on the home front
> I had left behind me one of the most exotic tribes of all
> – the young people of America.
> They have their own form of dress . . .
> food, music, ritual, language, values –
> these are the things that make up a tribe,
> or a subculture as they have been called.

> It is to that tribe, as they are,
> that the gospel must be brought . . .
>
> You must have the courage to go with them to a place
> that neither you nor they have been before.[6]

Donovan's pioneering work incarnating the gospel in Masai culture reminds me of Jeremy Sylvester, a priest I met in South Africa in 1995, just after the election of Nelson Mandela. Jeremy was chaplain to a 'squatter camp' (or 'informal settlement') called Vlakfontein on the edge of Johannesburg. Like most such informal settlements, Vlakfontein was at that time a lawless and very deprived community, with no roads, sewerage or electricity, where landless people made shelters out of whatever they could find. Jeremy had agreed to serve the people of Vlakfontein on one condition, that he could live among them. He invited me to stay in the corrugated iron shack he had built for himself in the middle of the village. When I asked Jeremy why he had chosen to live there, rather than in the comfortable vicarage he had been offered, he replied, 'You can't share the Good News with someone until you first find out what their bad news is. And you won't find out what their bad news is until you are alongside them and they trust you.'

This total commitment to getting alongside people in their own culture and situation is at the heart of Paul's missionary strategy in the New Testament. Even though he was proud of his Jewish heritage (cf. Philippians 3.4-6), yet he was able to describe his method in these terms:

> To those outside the law I became as one outside the law (though I am not free from God's law but am under Christ's law) so that I might win those outside the law. To the weak I became weak, so that I might win the weak. I have become all things to all people, that I might by all means save some. (1 Corinthians 9.21-22)

Reworking our ecclesiology

> Church is what happens when people encounter the Risen Jesus and commit themselves to sustaining and deepening that encounter in their encounter with each other. Rowan Williams[7]

In commending *Mission-shaped Church* Rowan Williams has been keen to encourage Anglicans to do some fresh thinking about the nature of the church. He grounds his mission theology in the event of the new creation, as people are transformed through encountering the Risen Christ. Church is 'the beginning of God's reclaiming of the territory of human life and of creation as his own and God's pouring into creation of his saving and transfiguring power so that the world will once again show radiantly who and what he is as God.'[8] Williams chides those whose first reaction to any fresh expression of church is to ask nervously, 'Is it Anglican?' rather than approaching it first with gratitude, and then seeking to apply 'passionate patience' in seeking to discern how the Spirit is at work in these new communities.

Our understanding of what makes 'church' is inevitably shaped by our own experience of it, which in Britain is likely to include special buildings, paid ministers and raising money. Robert Warren defines church in 'inherited mode' as

church = building + minister + stipend

This is hardly a New Testament model – the early Church grew rapidly with no buildings and few paid leaders. The defining marks of the Church in the New Testament are worship, community and mission, and so a more biblical equation would be

church = worship + community + mission

These are the hallmarks of church in 'emerging mode', which Warren defines as 'engaging faith community'.[9] If our primary understanding of church becomes a 'worshipping missionary community' then this throws up many new possibilities. Church exists wherever there is a community engaged in worship and mission, wherever they choose to meet, and on whatever day. A group of Christians meeting at their place of work to worship, care for one another and reach out to their colleagues is surely church. Likewise, a group of young mothers who can't get to church on Sundays but who meet on Wednesdays for prayer and Bible study and who lead a toddler group that reaches out to other young mums is also church. Conversely, one could ask how far a group of people who may attend a service in a church building but have no evident sense of community or mission really is church.

If church exists wherever there is a worshipping missionary community, then this throws a whole new light on the evangelistic potential of the social and outreach activities of local churches. Many churches expend a lot of energy organizing a whole range of social and community activities to reach out into the community, and then spend a whole lot more energy trying to persuade those who come to midweek activities to join the Sunday congregation. A much more creative approach is to look at all the midweek activities of a church and try to identify what elements of worship and mission are already present and build on these in order to create a worshipping missionary community where the people are already gathered.

Such an approach is not without its pitfalls, however and those engaged in planting new forms of church need skills in practical ecclesiology as they explore and press the boundaries of church. George Lings helpfully defines the four dimensions of church as In, Up, Out and Of (see Figure 11.3). One potential problem with giving the name 'church' to every worshipping mission-ary community is the danger of fragmentation. However local and small-scale the church may be, it needs a clear link and identity with the wider church – otherwise there is the danger that the eye might indeed say to the hand, 'I have no need of you' (1 Corinthians 12.21) and so bring division.

Churches that have successfully planted new congregations need to develop new patterns of leadership and oversight. A number of larger churches with several existing weekly services and several new church plants have adopted a 'multiple congregations' model of church life. This was the approach adopted in Sheffield some years ago by Robert Warren, and more recently by Chris Neal, Team Rector of Thame in Oxfordshire.[10] In this model, each service has a distinctive style and a particular target group it is seeking to attract. Each service also has a designated leader or team within the overall church leadership responsible for organizing worship, pastoral care and outreach. The vicar or senior pastor then becomes the focus of unity within the church, moving between the congregations and training and caring for their leaders.

Figure 11.3 Enduring dynamics of church

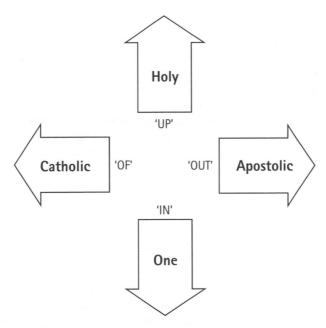

Source: George Lings, Powerpoint slide. Reproduced with permission

Church planting midweek: examples

A number of churches that have seen a drop in Sunday attendance have also seen an increase in midweek attendance – either at traditional midweek services, or at Alpha courses, informal worship events or post-Alpha groups. As Sundays become ever busier for people, opportunities to worship midweek will be increasingly important in helping people to grow and live as Christians.

One creative example takes place each Monday afternoon after school in Stoke-on-Trent. The traditional congregation had been unable to offer a Sunday School for some years because there was no one available to lead it and the worship style had been difficult for children to engage with. Finally, in desperation, Tim, the Church Army captain, decided to try out something after school, when he and his wife would be available to lead. They sent a leaflet home with the children of the adjacent school, inviting children and carers to come to 'React', an informal worship experience at 3.15pm on Mondays, straight after school. They thought they might possibly get half a dozen children, and were bowled over when 25 turned up the first week. As the children arrive from school they are given a drink and a biscuit and a video is playing. Then, when they are ready to start, Tim leads everyone in singing the Peruvian Gloria and children lead a procession into church carrying a cross, a Bible and candles. Once in church they have an interactive child-focused service, with lots of visuals and powerpoint. This is not an all-age event, it is a place for *children* to worship. For the children who come, this is not a bridge to church, this *is* church.

Another example is the J Gang, which meets three times a week on a deprived estate in Walsall. This group began when three or four bored children wandered into church one Tuesday evening whilst the vicar was saying Evening Prayer and asked, 'What's going on? Can we stay?' The few ladies who were there made them welcome and tried to explain what was going on. The next evening the children came back with ten other friends, who were very curious but completely confused by the liturgy. At that moment the vicar and one of the ladies realized that this was an opportunity they had to seize, so they invited all the children back the following Wednesday to the church hall for the first meeting of the J Gang.

Five years later the J Gang meets three times a week and has almost 100 children, aged 8–16, on the books. On Wednesday evenings the group meets at 5 p.m. for the J Gang Certificate, which is basically an hour of Christian teaching following a home-made confirmation course. Then at 6 p.m. they break for games and a variety of activities. On Friday evenings they meet with no programme, but simply take the opportunity to talk among themselves about their particular needs and issues. On Sundays they take part in the morning Eucharist, and they also now have an informal evening service every six weeks led by a music group from a larger church nearby. Over 50 of the J Gang have now been confirmed, and the original members, who are now 16 years old, are beginning to take responsibility for the day-to-day running of the group. Mandy Keay, who has led the group from the beginning, comments, 'A key factor in their journey to faith has been that they feel valued because we respond to their ideas. We answer their questions honestly and never judge, yet we have seen such changes in their lives.'

St Mary's in Leamington Spa has had a thriving coffee morning for senior citizens for many years. Centred upon friendship and welcome, the group had limited overt spiritual content until one or two members met with Revd Marjorie Warnes and decided to start up a brief devotional meeting before the coffee morning. Over the course of a few weeks, the group grew to around 15 meeting for worship before the main coffee and chat, and eventually this became a simple service of Holy Communion. Several members of the group were already worshipping at other services, but many others were not. Initial clergy conversations about 'how to get these people to come to church' missed the point. In a small and very unspectacular way a congregation had been planted. For a number of members this *was* the church, far more accessible than the noisier Sunday morning all-age worship, among people who expressed their faith in a way which others at the coffee morning could relate to, and at a time when it was natural to be there. Very unspectacular, but nevertheless important: a new way of being church, discovered by accident.

Workplace Church

A natural extension of planting into networks is the concept of workplace cells or congregations. Peter Brierley records that one branch of Asda opens half an hour later one morning a week so that staff can attend communion.[11] Many cell churches have cells which either meet in the workplace or which are mostly drawn from that workplace. A number of the cell groups at St Thomas's, Sheffield, have a mission focus towards a particular type of job or profession. Workplace cells or congregations are another way of bridging the gap between Sunday and Monday, between faith and work. Industrial missioners have a long history of chaplaincy within the workplace, helping Christians to relate faith and life. The development of workplace cells or congregations could be a natural extension of that ministry and a powerful way of helping people to do their paid work in a distinctively Christian way. In a world where work is becoming both more demanding and more fulfilling for many people, local churches are often slow to make the connections that equip people to apply their faith to their work situation.

Workplace church will be a new idea to some, but it is only an extension of a kind of ministry of which others who work in residential communities like schools, the armed forces and prisons have had long experience. It is worth noting that the first Christians met for worship on Sunday, which was a normal working day, and so some who had a sympathetic employer may naturally have worshipped at work – as Christians sometimes do in Malaysia and other Muslim countries today. There is an intriguing glimpse of a possible workplace cell in the New Testament itself – in Philippians 4.22, where Paul writes, 'All the saints greet you, especially those of Caesar's household.'

Conclusion

Planting fresh expressions of church is likely to be a key part of any evangelism strategy for the coming years if the Church is to be faithful in responding to the work of the Holy Spirit. The focus of church planting will continue to evolve, from unchurched places to unchurched networks of people. New church plants will increasingly target particular age groups or cultural groups rather than geographical areas. As our culture becomes more diverse we can no longer work on the 'one size fits all' approach to worship provision. Too often the emphasis has been on persuading new wine to fit into old wineskins, rather than building new patterns of church around those who are coming to faith.

Keeping doing the same old thing when everything is changing around you is not actually doing the same thing. A survey of large churches in Lichfield Diocese showed that those churches that had made no change in their service pattern during the previous five years were all declining numerically. As in horticulture, not every new plant flourishes, but the overall figures show that church plants are much more likely to grow than existing congregations. Future shapes of church are more likely to be smaller scale, more local, more fragile and more contextualized to local situations. The key will be to identify the networks and groups that exist in any locality and find ways into those networks through 'men and women of peace' who are sympathetic and will help in the creation of worshipping missionary communities. These emerging congregations will then need to forge strong links with the rest of the Body of Christ, so that they are able to contribute to and be nourished by the wider Church.

For further information

Visit

Fresh Expressions (a new Anglican/Methodist agency for promoting fresh expressions of church) at www.freshexpressions.org.uk
www.emergingchurch.info ('a touching place for the emerging church', supported by Church Army and CMS)
Anglican Church Planting Initiatives (Bob and Mary Hopkins) at www.acpi.org.uk
The Sheffield Centre (George Lings) at www.encountersontheedge.org.uk
Reaching the Unchurched Network at www.run.org.uk

Read

Archbishops' Council, *Mission-shaped Church*, Church House Publishing, 2004
Paul Bayes, *Mission-shaped Church*, Grove Books, Ev67, 2004 (a short readable introduction that focuses on the values that lie behind the report)
Steven Croft, *Transforming Communities*, Darton, Longman & Todd, 2002
Vincent Donovan, *Christianity Rediscovered: An Epistle from the Masai*, SCM Press, 1982
Michael Frost and Alan Hirsch, 'The Shaping of Things to Come: Innovation and Mission for the Twenty-first Century Church', Hendrickson, 2003 (a more radical vision of what church for the non-churched might look like)
George Lings, *Thame or Wild?*, Encounters on the Edge No. 8, The Sheffield Centre
Michael Moynagh, *emergingchurch.intro*, Monarch, 2004 (an excellent guide to understanding emerging forms of church, with lots of examples)
Robert Warren, *Being Human, Being Church*, Marshall Pickering, 1995

12

Engaging with the search for spirituality

Mark Ireland

A Mother may feed a child with her own milk, but our precious Mother, Jesus, feeds us with Himself, courteously and tenderly, with the blessed Sacrament, the blessed food of life.

Julian of Norwich

Back in 1995 Robert Warren identified 'from doctrine to spirituality' as one of the 'enriching trends' during the Decade of Evangelism.[1] Postmodernism is not so much interested in the 'Is it true?' questions of apologetics as the 'Will it work for me?' questions of spiritual experience. Yet most process evangelism courses still start by assuming that people are asking questions about what Christians believe and whether it is true. It is vital for effective evangelism that we understand the extent of change in our culture and society and the massive implications this has for mission.

Whereas the Church used to be regarded as boring and irrelevant, it is seen by many seekers today as unspiritual, and therefore as having nothing to offer them in their spiritual quest. Just as Philip came alongside an Ethiopian official who was searching for God and began by listening to him and asking him a question, so we need to come alongside today's searchers after spiritual reality and engage with the profound questions they are asking.

The aim of this chapter is to explore some of the ways in which this search for spirituality challenges the spiritual life of the Church, and to consider ways in which churches can reach out to or reconnect with those who are searching for spirituality but have never thought that Christianity might have anything to offer them.

Spirituality as a route to faith

Despite the apparent decline of interest in institutional religion in western Europe, one thing is clear – spirituality sells. To witness the massive shift in interest from organized religion towards do-it-yourself spirituality you only need to go to your nearest bookshop. In my local bookshop in Walsall the 'Religion' section (covering Christianity and all the main world faiths) comprises just one stack tucked away in the back corner of the first floor, whilst in prominent position at the top of the main staircase are three large stacks entitled 'Body, Mind and Spirit', covering everything from aromatherapy, reflexology and alternative medicines on the one hand to crystals, astrology and occult spiritualities on the other. This section has recently overflowed onto a fourth portable bookcase with a full range of tarot cards for sale.

Likewise my local newsagent, who doesn't stock any religious newspapers or magazines, is heavily promoting a new magazine dedicated to 'Enhancing your mind, body, spirit'. The first issue covers a wide variety of topics, from herbal cures for the common cold to how to cast simple spells and engage in tantric sex, and comes complete with free lavender oil and a 'starter' quartz crystal. The spiritual search that this all points to seems to be stronger in women than in men – also in my newsagent is a recently started women's magazine, *Spirit & Destiny*, which offers a mix of complementary medicines, cosmetics, horoscopes and witchcraft 'for women who want the best possible future'.

Generation X

The fact that New Age spirituality is such big business points to a deep underlying hunger for spiritual experience among Generation X (those born between 1961 and 1977). They may have accepted the popular wisdom that science has disproved Christianity, but they do not believe that science has all the answers. Research by David Hay and Kate Hunt at the University of Nottingham into the religious or spiritual experiences of adults (male and female) in Britain shows a remarkable rise in the period 1987–2000 in the number claiming to have had some supernatural experience in their lives – up from 48 per cent to 76 per cent of the sample in just 13 years. The greatest increase was in the recognition of a transcendent providence – 'a patterning of events in a person's life that convinces them that in some strange way those events were meant to happen'. Hay concludes that in reality there has been no great change in the frequency with which people have spiritual experiences, but that the rise of postmodernity has greatly increased the 'social permission' people have to talk about such experiences.[2] Hay's findings are summarized in Figure 12.1.

Recent research

A significant study in Coventry of the spirituality of people who don't go to church has shown a remarkable level of interest in the big questions of life.

Figure 12.1 Frequency of report of religious or spiritual experience in Britain, 1987 and 2000 (David Hay and Kate Hunt, reproduced by permission)

	1987	2000*
A patterning of events	29%	55%
Awareness of the presence of God	27%	38%
Awareness of prayer being answered	25%	37%
Awareness of a sacred presence in nature	16%	29%
Awareness of the presence of the dead	18%	25%
Awareness of an evil presence	12%	25%
Cumulative total	(48%)**	76%

*The data for 2000 is taken from the nationwide Soul of Britain survey conducted by the BBC in May 2000.
**This includes totals for respondents to two additional questions asked in 1987 about 'a presence not called God' (22%) and 'awareness that all things are One' (5%), i.e. the total of 76% for the year 2000 is quite likely to be relatively speaking an underestimate.

People were asked, 'If there is one big question you could have the answer to, what would it be?' Among the variety of answers given, by far the six biggest categories were:

- Destiny – what happens after we die?
- Purpose – why are we here?
- The universe – accident or design?
- Is there a God?
- What about the supernatural?
- Why is there so much suffering?

The striking thing about these questions is that they are all ones about which the Christian faith has a great deal to offer – and yet the respondents had little concept that church might be a place for them to find the answers. This poses a major challenge to the churches. The findings of the Coventry research and their implications for evangelism are the subject of the next book in the Explorations series, *Evangelism in a Spiritual Age* (Church House Publishing, 2005).

A major research project into the spirituality of those who live in the English market town of Kendal has also just been published.[3] The findings show a significant movement away from involvement in church congregations towards involvement in various forms of holistic or 'new age' spirituality. They also reveal that those congregations which allow most expression of the experiential in worship (the charismatic ones) are holding up in numbers compared to those with more traditional styles of worship. One caution though is that the research doesn't really prove there is any great upsurge of interest in spirituality among the unchurched population – it may simply show a change of allegiance among the 10-20% of the population who are in some way religiously inclined. This raises the question as to what the other 80% of the population are doing – probably shopping!

Generation Y

How far this spiritual quest is shared by the under 20s (sometimes known as Generation Y) is uncertain. Preliminary findings of a two-year research project by the Centre for Youth Ministry in Cambridge and Theology Through the Arts into the hopes and aspirations of those born after 1980 show that spirituality barely gets a mention, and that many of them 'do not even have an echo of the Christian memory'. Analysis of 26 focus groups studying the role of clubbing, soap opera and advertising in young people's lives indicated their main concerns were to do with getting on with their friends and making a go of life. Traditional religious ideas had little or no relevance, and neither were they interested in alternative or eastern forms of spirituality. This lack of spirituality in their lives did not appear to have led to disenchantment or alienation, but rather to the pursuit of happiness now. They had a story line or world view which was more modest and local than the grand metanarratives of religion or Marxism. Their focus was on the happiness and welfare of themselves and those closest to them, their families and friends.

> Given post-modern readings of culture we expected to find amongst the young people a 'pick and mix' smorgasbord of beliefs. Instead we found a coherent narrative that undergirds the worldview (via the popular arts). We call it the **Happy midi-narrative**. This world, and all life in it, is meaningful as it is. There is no need to posit ultimate significance somewhere else . . . Happiness *is* the goal in life . . . 'Happiness is the ideal you aim for.' (Case 14/male)[4]

These findings suggest that evangelism among Generation Y should not be based on the false assumption that young people have a latent spirituality simply waiting to be activated. This may explain why attempts to evangelize club culture have proved so difficult, if clubbing is not a kind of pseudo-spirituality but simply a desire for a good time. For many other young people computer games are the dominant thing, and the addictive nature of the games allied to the sinister and violent content of some of them may exert a spiritual influence that makes it harder for some youngsters to be aware of the Christian story. Writing to a young church in a city full of different spiritualities, Paul commented that 'the god of this world has blinded the minds of the unbelievers . . .' (2 Corinthians 4.4). The challenge for the youth evangelist is to show that Jesus is relevant to young people's search for happiness – 'I came that they may have life, and have it abundantly' (John 10.10) – without at the same time losing the essential counter-cultural challenge of the gospel – 'If any want to become my followers, let them deny themselves and take up their cross and follow me' (Mark 8.34).

Failure to connect

The disturbing fact for the churches is that those non-Christians who are searching for spirituality today naturally turn to bookshops, evening classes and magazines rather than to church. They do not appear to make any connection between 'spirituality' and the familiar church building on the corner of the street. And, to be honest, who can blame them sometimes? Most church noticeboards make no attempt to connect with the spiritual searching of those who walk past, or to explain how what happens 'at 10 a.m. on the second and fourth Sundays' will help them find God. It is ironic that those who are looking for literature about how to meditate are more likely to find it in W H Smith's or Waterstone's than in church. On a recent walking holiday my wife and I were pleased to discover a number of churches that were left open during the week. We decided to look around, imagining that we knew nothing about Christianity and trying to find out what we would learn solely from the literature and notices on display. Sadly, we learnt almost nothing about Jesus on our visits, and our conclusion was that any complete outsider would think that 'church' must be an organization focused on architecture and raising money.

Cathedrals are rediscovering their role as showcases for spirituality, and some clearly have a well-thought-out strategy to help tourists become pilgrims. One good example is St Albans Cathedral, which has attractive large-print notices by items such as the altar, lectern, font and choir explaining their religious significance, with photographs showing them actually in use. In both St Albans and Birmingham cathedrals I picked up eye-catching leaflets explaining who Jesus is and what it means to follow him. In the chapter house of York Minster I saw a superb professional display using pictures of stained glass, sculptures and works of art in the minster to explain what Christians believe and why. In a number of small village churches I have found simple photocopied leaflets of prayers freely available for people to use and take away. These appear to meet a real need for people who rarely get to church on Sundays but do have the chance to call in during the week. Clergy I have spoken to are usually amazed at how many leaflets are taken each week.

The desperate burden on some local churches of constant fundraising to maintain historic buildings may blind congregations to the fact that large Gothic buildings with stained-glass windows are a significant evangelistic resource where they can be kept open. Many people visit church buildings during the week who do not attend worship on Sundays – sometimes for the architecture and history, sometimes to visit a grave, sometimes for the sense of sacred space where prayer has been valid for generations, sometimes just looking for a quiet oasis and space to think. Such people often spend more time reading the notice-boards and displays than the regular church members do, and their needs should be borne in mind.

Security is a big worry for many churches. Many church buildings are now kept locked because of fear of theft, which hinders their potential for mission. However, research by Ecclesiastical Insurance shows that churches that are open and staffed by volunteers are less vulnerable to crime than those that are kept locked. The Open Churches Trust, founded by Andrew Lloyd-Webber, is dedicated to helping open up locked churches during the week, and can provide help and expertise in keeping churches open and reducing the threat of crime.

Athens revisited

The great smorgasbord of religious ideas around today has parallels with the situation Paul encountered in Athens in Acts 17 where a multiplicity of differ-ent gods were worshipped and the citizens of the city 'spent their time in nothing but hearing or telling something new' (17.21). It is worth noting that Paul took the message of Jesus and the Resurrection not only into the syna-gogue but also into the marketplace (17.17). When called before the Areopagus Paul does not begin by condemning their syncretism, as some contemporary Christians might, but by commending their attempts to be religious. Rather than quoting verses of the Old Testament, he quotes their own authors to affirm the dignity of human beings as children of God (17.28), before chal-lenging the elders to repent of their ignorance and turn to Christ who will one day be their judge.

Paul's approach challenges Christians today to engage constructively with the spiritualities we see around us and to start where people are, rather than ignoring New Age ideas or condemning them out of hand. I can't help feeling that if Paul were alive today he would be keen to attend the psychic fairs and 'body, mind and spirit' festivals and to engage their leaders in dialogue. John Drane quotes an interesting contemporary example of this approach by Ross Clifford, a theological college principal in Sydney. Clifford visited a psychic fair and was particularly taken with the biblical imagery in the tarot cards, so he opened a stall at a later fair under the banner 'The Real Meaning of the Tarot' and attracted a crowd to discuss with him the pictures on the cards. In this way he used the cards to point searchers to the God of the Bible.[5]

Many churches are running process evangelism courses but really struggle to get enquirers to sign up because the courses fail to connect with this popular search for spirituality. In a world where people are much more interested in spirituality than in doctrine, the way ahead may increasingly be to start by giving people hands-on experience of prayer and meditation and then move on to explaining the underlying doctrine afterwards. One of the reasons that Alpha has done so well is that it does blend teaching with spiritual experience, although the main spiritual experience (the weekend away) only comes after week 6.

rejesus web site

Another sign of the ways in which people today are searching for spirituality is the popularity of the recently established 'rejesus' web site, sponsored by the major Churches (www.rejesus.co.uk), which already has a million hits a year. The most visited part of this site, *which is designed for non-Christians*, is the daily prayer space, where people can light a virtual candle, read a verse and say a prayer online. Another popular part of the site, which has a fascinating postmodern approach to inviting a response, is 'Steps of Faith' – a locker room with 20 pairs of shoes. Visitors can choose any pair of shoes as a way of making a step of faith. Some of the steps suggested are deliberately small, whilst other, larger steps are available for those closer to a definite commitment.

Essence

A fresh and creative way into spirituality is the Essence course, which many churches may find valuable to run prior to Emmaus or Alpha. Essence is a short, six-session course designed 'to stimulate a deeper spiritual life, drawing from the teachings of Jesus and the Christian mystics' (see Figure 12.2). It is written by Rob Frost and arises out of theological explorations with John Drane and others engaged in mission in a New Age context. The course is designed to be held in community centres, libraries or health clubs rather than in church, and could be run as an evening class course at a local college. The cover design of the course book (in blues and purples) and the style of the suggested publicity flyers is intended to stand alongside the New Age courses that tend to be advertised in libraries and health food shops and to attract those who would never enter a church.

Figure 12.2 The Essence syllabus

1. The Journey So Far (our own journey)
2. The Journey Within (who am I?)
3. The Journey to a Better World (the environment)
4. The Journey to Wholeness (pain and healing)
5. The Journey to Spirituality (prayer)
6. The Journey to the Future (hopes and dreams, life after death)

A children's version of Essence, designed for those aged 8–11, was published in 2004 under the title kids@essence. As with the adult version an accompanying CD-ROM includes meditations and imaginative exercises, with lively readings from the 'Street Bible'.

Essence aims to start where a growing number of non-Christians are, with the issues that concern them, and to value their own spiritual experiences. The learning style is very experiential, and involves things like relaxation exercises on the floor, making bracelets, smashing pots and modelling in dough. The Bible is used as a resource in all six sessions, each of which ends with a prayer in the name of Jesus. Because the course aims to be open-ended, a lot is expected of the leaders – Penny Horseman, who led one of the pilot groups, commented, 'It was terrifying to lead, but afterwards the leaders were so excited. Part of the secret is that the leaders are not in the position of power or control, and have to depend on the Holy Spirit.' The willingness of leaders to be vulnerable and to adapt as they go along in response to the group is crucial not just in Essence but in all attempts to build contact with enquirers.

So far Essence is only one course, marketed on a fairly small scale, but it perhaps sets a new direction that others will follow. As we look ahead to what may replace Alpha as the market leader in a few years time, future courses may well build on the insights of Essence to offer a more experiential approach that takes seriously people's previous searches for spirituality and yet leads them on towards a clearly and distinctively Christian understanding of God.

Essence and kids@essence are available from Share Jesus International at www.sharejesusinternational.com Tel. 020 8944 5678.

Sunday services

Courses like Essence are a creative way of engaging with people who don't come to church, but there are hundreds of thousands of people in Britain who are searching for spirituality and who already come to church on an occasional or sporadic basis. One of the best ways of engaging with the contemporary spiritual quest is to give careful thought to how we can do well what we already do week by week. As Natural Church Development reminds us, growth comes not by doing more things, but by improving the quality of what we do already. Too often those who lead services seem to assume that those in the congregation are already (or jolly well ought to be) fully committed and paid-up members of the church who don't need any help understanding what is going on beyond being given an occasional page number.

The idea that the experience of worship and prayer can be a route to faith is, of course, nothing new. As we saw in Chapter 1, John Finney's research shows that the majority of people begin to attend and experience worship in a local church before coming to a point of faith and commitment. Research among the 17 churches of Almondsbury Deanery in Wakefield showed that half of all the people who attended church in that deanery during an eight-week period did so only once, and that the total number who attended a Sunday service during the eight weeks was five-and-a-half times larger than the published 'average Sunday attendance' figure.[6] There is clearly a huge pool of people who drift into church occasionally but who are not yet attracted to coming regularly.

Those charged with leading, praying or preaching at regular Sunday services need to be reminded that some of those present at *every* service – not just special services – will be seekers or occasional attenders. The Church of England has a particular obligation to provide 'public worship' which any member of the public has a right to attend. Yet so often it can seem as if worship is provided for the faithful few who know how to take part, while any members of the public who attend are expected to sit quietly and watch. Although every service includes times of prayer, it is remarkable how rarely these are combined with any teaching or guidance on *how* to pray, even on occasions like baptisms and 'family' services where there may be many newcomers or unchurched people present.

A surprising number of those who have stopped coming to church say that a church's lack of spirituality was a significant factor in their decision to drop out of church life. In Richter and Francis's research, published in *Gone But Not Forgotten*, a quarter of all respondents said that a significant part of the reason they left church was that there was 'too little sense of the presence of God in worship'.[7] People can experience the presence of God in church in a variety of ways – through singing, the liturgy, hearing Scripture, the sermon, the sacrament – and one key way that is all too often missing is silence. Although *Common Worship* suggests silence at a number of points, my own observation in visiting a great many churches is that either this is ignored, or the silence is so brief (less than ten seconds) as to be useless.

John Wesley famously described Holy Communion as a 'converting ordinance', and yet for many occasional worshippers or unchurched people, attending parish communion can be a distinctly excluding experience as it is made clear, however gently, that they may not receive the bread and wine unless they are already communicants. As Gavin Reid has commented, 'It is a remarkable fact that in the years since 1950 a graph would show that at the same time as the number of confirmations has fallen steadily, the numbers of churches offering only eucharistic worship on a Sunday morning have risen equally steadily.'[8] If it is true, as we have argued, that belonging comes before believing, then this raises profound questions about our strategy for evangelism. Either churches need more opportunities for non-eucharistic worship – 'services of the Word' or 'family' services – or they need to rethink their eucharistic hospitality and discipline to provide a genuinely open table to all who are searching after God.

There are clear warnings in 1 Corinthians 11.27-32 about the dangers of receiving the sacrament unworthily, but these were directed at Christians who were behaving badly. Is it right that while few churches seriously apply these verses to Christians (the discipline of excommunication being long defunct), yet they are invoked to separate and exclude children and those who are searching for faith? In the Gospels Jesus shared table fellowship with tax collectors and sinners, yet churches today are rather more particular about who may share his bread.

Pick'n'mix spirituality

One of the distinctive and disturbing features of the current explosion of interest in body, mind and spirit is a 'pick'n'mix' approach to spirituality. People may pray and go to church while at the same time taking an interest in crystals, astrology and reflexology. The upsurge of interest in alternative therapies and Chinese medicine as well as in Christian healing means that many people try a variety of different approaches to a problem without realizing that the treatments offered may derive from very different (and possibly even opposing) religious outlooks. A related issue is that in a world where spirituality is being sold as a commodity, a lot of the spirituality tools on offer are really bolt-on extras to a basically secular consumer world view.

On the one hand, dabbling in the New Age offers spiritual experience without the moral demands and total change of life required by wholehearted commitment to Christianity. On the other hand, those who commit themselves to alternative lifestyles can demonstrate a high degree of costly moral commitment in some areas, such as conserving the environment, fair trade and vegetarianism. This stance has challenged the churches to rediscover neglected themes of creation and stewardship of the earth's resources within Scripture. Whilst some Christians are inclined to identify New Age spiritualities and the rise of paganism with 'the spiritual forces of evil in the heavenly places' which

Paul writes about in Ephesians 6.12, there is a clear danger of overreacting. For most Christians the main spiritual battle they need to engage in is, as ever, against the concealed enemies of complacency, consumerism, and self-interest in church and in the world rather than against openly occult groups.

Insights from other faiths

A pick'n'mix approach does not just apply to those attracted by the New Age. There has also been an upsurge of interest in Britain in Buddhism and in Islamic Sufi spirituality, often among people who want spiritual experience without the baggage of orthodox belief. One Muslim theologian we met was scathing about this – he felt that interest in Sufism without accepting Islam was illogical and lacked integrity. However, a comparison of some forms of meditation in Hinduism and Christianity, or of the writings of the Christian and Muslim mystical traditions, shows that different religions are often a lot closer in spirituality than they are in doctrine. And although some Christians may be unhappy about using texts from other faith traditions in worship or teaching, there are important examples of borrowing from non-Jewish sources within the Bible itself, particularly in the Wisdom literature. For example, almost all the sayings in Proverbs 22.17–23.11 can be found in the much earlier Egyptian *Instruction of Amen-em-ope*. If Christians believe, as the evening collect in the *Book of Common Prayer* puts it, that 'all holy desires, all good counsels and all just works do proceed' from the one true God, then they must be open to discerning elements of truth about God in the spiritualities of other faiths.

Another interesting example is Psalm 29, which may have its origin in a beautiful ancient Phoenician hymn praising Baal-Hadad, the weather god, which has been carefully reworked to give honour instead to the name of Yahweh. Weiser comments that this 'proves the vigorous power of absorption, peculiar to the biblical belief in God, which is able to incorporate alien matter without forfeiting its own fundamental character'.[9] Nevertheless, the Old Testament writers continually warn that the most serious sins the Israelites could fall into were syncretism (the mindless mixing of elements of different faiths) and idolatry (offering worship to that which is not God).

The challenge for evangelists, therefore, in today's multi-faith pick'n'mix culture is to exercise the gift of discernment, affirming those things in other spiritualities that are not contrary to the gospel, whilst at the same time witnessing to the Christian revelation that prayer to the one true God is made possible only through Jesus Christ and in the power of the Holy Spirit. Listening and dialogue are not without risks, but, as the Four Principles of Interfaith Dialogue put it, 'dialogue is the medium of authentic witness'.[10]

Authentic spirituality

It is not only the spirituality of the enquirer that is important in evangelism but also the spirituality of the believers who wish to share their faith. If our witness is to carry integrity and authenticity then it must flow out of a deep personal encounter with God. As Stephen Cottrell has put it, 'You can't share what you haven't got.' Robert Warren has identified 'from authority to authenticity' as one of his enriching trends in evangelism.[11]

People are no longer convinced of the gospel because something with authority tells them, but because they see it lived out and demonstrated in the life of a Christian community. If a church not only talks about justice but also serves fairly traded coffee after the service, or if it not only talks about the environment but also uses recycled paper for its service sheets, these are signs of authenticity that will be noticed. As Lesslie Newbigin put it, 'The only hermeneutic of the gospel is a congregation of men and women who believe it and live by it.'[12] Or, as Graham Tomlin has recently written, 'Churches are meant to be places where people can begin to understand and feel and experience what a community might look like that really lived in Jesus' kingdom.'[13]

Knowing God in Jesus Christ is the deepest and fullest experience of spirituality there is, and it is from that encounter with God that the followers of Jesus are called out to share him with others. Therefore, whatever strategy for evangelism a church may have needs to be partnered by a deepening experience of prayer, of growing closer to God. As churches grow closer to God they are more likely to feel God's concern for their local community, and to be able to see where God is already at work in that community. When I was a young curate I used to pray earnestly each morning that God would bless what *I* was planning to do that day. Twenty-one years later, I try rather in my prayer time to ask God to show me *his* plans and what is on his heart, so that I can work with him. As I talk to those involved in evangelism, they affirm that their most fruitful encounters have often taken place in the most unlikely places, where they least expected to find God already at work, or at times when things 'happened' seemingly by chance, so that they were there at just the right moment to respond to a need or opportunity.

Working with God

Being open and ready to respond to God's unexpected opportunity has also in my own experience given rise to very fruitful evangelism. When I arrived as a curate in Blackburn I became friends with a group of unchurched teenagers who were always to be found in the park kicking a football. They turned out to be very open to the gospel, and out of our friendship emerged a church football team (which I managed, despite an obvious lack of skill!) and several confirmation candidates.

For the American wife of a vicar in London's Docklands her love of cheerleading was the unexpected opportunity that has seen a significant number of local girls drawn towards the life of the church and given a new sense of their own worth and ability to achieve. She used her cheerleading expertise to set up a cheer-leaders' group that even performed for Anglican bishops at the last Lambeth Conference.

For Sheila, a country vicar wondering how to evangelize a new owner-occupied housing estate, the unexpected opportunity came when someone with particular gifts in organizing children's dramatic productions offered to start a children's drama group. This group flourished and brought large numbers of new children and their families into the orbit of the parish church.

The likelihood of any of the above examples having the same impact elsewhere is very small. The challenge for church leaders is to discern what might be God's unexpected opportunity in their own situation.

Without constant, undergirding prayer, most evangelism strategies will ultimately fail. Believing prayer (sometimes with fasting) can have a massive impact in moving forward church programmes that have become stuck, in lubricating links between different stages on the journey of faith, and in transforming atmospheres and relationships.

Spirituality in the mix

The increased contemporary interest in spirituality rather than in doctrine means that courses on prayer may well be the right thing to offer as a next step for those who make a response during a mission or a guest service, rather than expecting people to sign up to an Alpha or Emmaus course straight away. Stephen Cottrell, one of the authors of Emmaus, encourages churches to run courses in 'Exploring Prayer' as the first stage of follow-up after missions he leads. Likewise, running an Essence course in a pub or village hall may well be an effective first step towards recruiting people for an Emmaus or Alpha course at church. Alpha's emphasis on meeting with God as a key part of the course (particularly in the weekend away) may well make it an appropriate next step for some groups that complete Essence.

Passionate spirituality is one of the eight 'quality characteristics' identified by Christian Schwarz as being essential for healthy churches, and churches that score strongly on passionate spirituality in a Natural Church Development survey may be well placed to attract unchurched people searching for authentic spirituality. Paul talked about knowing the true God in language that the people of Athens would understand, and the challenge for Christians today is to find ways of communicating the reality of their encounter with God without lapsing into religious jargon that is only intelligible to church members. Churches seeking to develop a more passionate spirituality may well benefit from inviting a church leader or team from Africa or Asia to spend time with them. The testimony of those who have trusted God amidst suffering, poverty or persecution may well inspire and stir up churches that are a bit set in their ways. Other churches wanting to develop a more passionate spirituality may find cell church a helpful approach, with its teaching on the fifth core value of 'encountering God' and the cell group pattern of 'worship–word–witness'.

Churches that are involved in community ministry or have facilities used by community groups need to think out their letting policy very carefully from an evangelistic viewpoint. Churches may refuse to let their halls for yoga classes, but what does that say about Christian concern for the body and physical exercise? Is it enough to say that exercise is all right as long as it is secular, or should one try to offer a positive alternative, integrating exercise and relaxation with Christian forms of meditation and prayer?

Conclusion

All true spirituality is about encountering the living God, and evangelism flows out of an encounter with the living God: as Isaiah cried in the temple, 'Here I am. Send me.' Our culture is hungry for spiritual experience, yet for too long within the churches spirituality has been seen as the special preserve of the keen few who go on retreats, instead of something that should be at the forefront of evangelism. The task facing each local church is to make connections with the spiritual quest of so many outside the churches who are left instead to find their own resources in bookshops, evening classes or New Age gatherings. Sunday services and church buildings open midweek attract hundreds of thousand of visitors who are not yet committed Christians, and there are simple but effective ways in which churches can help such visitors to learn how to pray. Popular interest in 'body, mind and spirit' provides local churches with significant opportunities for evangelism if they can rediscover their vocation to teach all people to pray and to grow in relationship with God, hopefully offering the kind of integrated approach that combines teaching on prayer with a commitment to healthy lifestyle and care for the environment. The

Essence course marks a new direction in evangelism that others may build on. As Brother Roger of Taizé has said, 'When the church becomes a house of prayer, the people will come running.'

For further information

Visit

www.ctbi.org.uk/ccom/ – carries David Hay's report on 'The Spirituality of People who Don't Go to Church'
www.rejesus.co.uk – the 'rejesus' evangelistic web site
www.openchurchestrust.org.uk – Open Churches Trust – Tel. 020 7240 0880

Read

Yvonne Richmond et al., *Evangelism in a Spiritual Age*, Church House Publishing, 2005 (develops further the thinking of this chapter)
Richard Askew, *From Strangers to Pilgrims – Evangelism and the Church Tourist*, Grove Evangelism Series, No. 38, 1997
Ruth Burgess and Chris Polhill, *Eggs and Ashes*, Wild Goose Publications, 2004 (from the Iona community, helps Christians to observe Lent in a way that combines worship and practical action for the environment)
Rob Frost, *The Essence Course*, Kingsway, 2002
Bob Mayo et al., *Ambiguous Evangelism*, SPCK, 2004 (reflects on his research on the spirituality of young adults in 'Generation Y')
Lesslie Newbigin, *The Gospel in a Pluralist Society*, SPCK, 1989
P. Richter and L. Francis, *Gone But Not Forgotten*, Darton, Longman & Todd, 1998
Graham Tomlin, *The Provocative Church*, SPCK, 2002

13

Conclusion

Mike Booker

> May you live in interesting times.
>
> Chinese proverb

Life in interesting times

This is a challenging time to be part of the Christian Church in the Western world. The last vestiges of Christendom are disappearing, and the Christian world view is less and less prevalent. Within this broad picture, the local church also appears to be in crisis. Certainly overall Sunday morning attendance figures continue to drop, but the pattern is by no means simple.

While the number of people in church on a typical Sunday morning may indeed be falling, the number attending at other times in the week has shown significant growth. Those attending church but attending less frequently than might have been the case in the past are also beginning to attract attention.[1] While many parish churches record fewer people on Sundays, others, from cell groups to cathedrals, have experienced growth. The number of full-time paid clergy is certainly going down, but at the same time there are more professional youth workers in churches than ever before.

It is not only life within the Church that is interesting. The last generation has seen a more complex pattern of social change than just a slippage in the Christian basis of society. Few people 30 years ago would have confidently predicted the collapse of communism and the global growth of a newly self-confident Islam. British 1960s secularism has been challenged, if not fully replaced, by postmodern pluralism. Christians may no longer be able to claim the possession of unchallenged truth, but when making it clear they are speaking from a faith basis they can find as much freedom to communicate their views as would a member of any other faith community.

The world is changing, but that change is ongoing and patchy. The new is emerging but the old is still here. The challenge facing Christians today is that of living in two worlds.

Living in two worlds

Some of what we have considered in this book will be immediately useful in many churches. Alpha, Emmaus and other process evangelism courses have been proving their worth for some time. Most churches could host a parish mission or invite an overseas team to visit. Natural Church Development, though less well known, provides a valuable tool that can point many congregations towards the next manageable step forward. If the holistic nature of the gospel has been grasped, community ministry will already be on the agenda for most churches, although we would suggest that in many cases it would benefit from a radical review.

Some of the other issues we have addressed have the potential to steer the local church in more radical directions. Cell church, and the range of other new ways of being church that we have considered, sit less easily within traditional structures. Some church leaders will rightly decide that they are called to take up the challenge to transform the local church in its entirety. In many other cases this will simply be too much to ask. There is still a great deal of life in the recognizable patterns of 'standard' church life across the country, and whether it be new music, women's ordination or *Common Worship*, most congregations (not usually among the most radically forward-looking people in society) have already absorbed a considerable amount of change.

The way forward in many cases will be one that involves living in two worlds. Church leaders, lay and ordained, need to be able to work well within and encourage growth within a currently recognizable expression of church. They need at the same time to be asking what else might be growing up alongside it. Each of the areas we have considered has the potential to do far more than merely add on to current patterns of church life. Most of the resources could lead on further if the question asked was not only, 'How can this resource or approach fit into our church?' but also, 'Where might things grow in new and unexpected ways if we follow what the Spirit seems to be doing through this?'

We live at a time when the Church of tomorrow is and should be coming to birth alongside the Church of today. We have encountered much that can help in that process.

A richness of resources

The last few years have been an almost unprecedented period of Christian creativity. We are conscious that we have not explored all the possible sources of guidance and inspiration that are out there, but even within the resources and approaches considered here there is a huge amount that is of value.

Without any central coordination of approach, a whole array of material has been produced. The scale of this has been almost unnoticed, but the impact is immeasurable. It seems almost impossible now to imagine the church without Alpha, yet we now have not only the Alpha course itself being widely used, but also a range of Alpha-inspired alternatives from across the theological spectrum.

Working in the English language provides access to a far greater variety of materials from around the world than is the case for Christians in most other countries. Even so, the remarkable fact is that the great bulk of what we have considered actually originates from within Great Britain itself. If we have a feeling of disappointment it is not that the tools needed to do the job are unavailable. Our concern is that they clearly are, but that there are few guides as to how the best toolkit with a good range of those tools in it might be assembled. We have made our own attempt to bring together a number of things which have the potential to be even more useful together than apart. It is our hope that the authors and publishers of these, and of other materials in the future, will take up this challenge themselves, and devote time and energy to thinking how their contribution might best fit in with the other things that God is doing in and through his Church.

What else is out there?

Our considerations have been limited by our own time and expertise. We are aware that there are other important things going on in the area of evangelism. Some, no doubt, we have simply overlooked. Others we have not included because, although they are of great value, they belong more in the area of tactics than of strategy. In particular we have focused on the strategies that might be employed at local church level. There is a great deal more to the whole Church of God than that.

Witness outside the Church, especially in the world of work, is of fundamental importance, and our desire is most certainly not to suggest that the only focus of Christian witness should be in and around the local congregation. God's people are called to live out whole lives of Christian witness and discipleship, and although it is not the main focus of this book, we would encourage church leaders to remember that this must be part of the balance of Christian living for the members of their congregations.

We have also largely overlooked the place of para-church organizations. Groups and networks working with young people or with women, for example, have a major part to play in complementing what a local congregation can do. Similarly, large Christian gatherings as diverse as Spring Harvest and the

Walsingham pilgrimage can be essential in broadening the horizons of the local congregation, giving people courage to look beyond what is to what might be. Neither is in itself a local church strategy for evangelism, so neither has been considered within this book, but a full overview of what God is doing needs to include these perspectives too.

Trusting the God of surprises

Carefully planned strategies will only get us so far in understanding God's way forward. This is not to diminish their importance in any way. Christian leaders have a God-given responsibility to use their powers of reason and of intellect. But the experience of God's people again and again has been that it is God's surprises rather than their own plans that open up the future in remarkable ways.

Some strategies will be unexpectedly effective, others will turn out to be disasters when they worked perfectly in the church down the road. Key people will move out of town at the very worst moment, but then perhaps a church member will 'just happen' to bump into someone with new and unexpected gifts. God is a God of life and growth, and growth is irregular and unpredictable, but also irrepressible and thrillingly beautiful. If our book points in one direction, but God seems to be leading somewhere else, our advice is to go for God every time!

Hope for the future

In writing this book, we have deliberately worked to communicate realism. Effective evangelism is not helped in the long term by over-optimistic promises of dramatic success. But a realistic view for the Christian must also be a view characterized by hope. This is still ultimately God's world, and always will be. God is working out his plans for the future, and the promise of Jesus Christ that he will build his Church still holds. A great deal has emerged over the last few years that can give shape to that hope, and it is this that has been the focus of our writing. We hope, and we pray, that God will continue to lead his Church forward. The same God who has inspired the richness of thinking that we have described will continue to inspire his people and to lead them on in new and different ways as the next years unfold. We believe and trust in him.

Notes

Chapter 1 Mission, evangelism and the Church of God

1. John Finney, *Finding Faith Today*, Bible Society, 1992.
2. J. Andrew Kirk, *What is Mission? Theological Explorations*, Darton, Longman & Todd, 1999, p. 68.
3. Finney, *Finding Faith Today*, chapter 11.
4. Sara Savage, 'A psychology of conversion – from all angles', in M. Percy (ed.), *Previous Convictions*, SPCK, 2000, pp. 3–4, quoting C. Liu, 'Becoming a Christian consciously vs. non-consciously', *Journal of Psychology and Theology*, 19, 1991, pp. 364–75.
5. I am grateful to my predecessor at Ridley Hall, Amiel Osmaston, for the thinking behind these diagrams.

Chapter 2 Alpha

1. Quoted in *Alpha News*, November 2002, p. 2.
2. In 2004 members of HTB gave, individually and through the church budget, a total of £911,000 towards the cost of running Alpha, equivalent to 19 per cent of the church budget.
3. *Alpha* Copyright Statement, quoted in Nicky Gumbel, *Telling Others*, Kingsway, new edn, 2001, p. 224.
4. 'Seven common mistakes' are listed in *Maximising the Potential of Your Alpha Course*, available from the Alpha office.
5. J. Drane, *Cultural Change and Biblical Faith*, Paternoster, 2002, p. 111.
6. Finney, *Finding Faith Today*, p. 25.
7. The findings of the English Church Attendance Survey are summarized in P. Brierley, *The Tide is Running Out: What the English Church Attendance Survey Reveals*, Christian Research, London, 2000.
8. P. Brierley, *Church Growth in the 1990s*, Christian Research, London, 2000, p. 41.
9. Gumbel, *Telling Others*, pp. 201–3.
10. S. Hunt, *The Alpha Enterprise*, Ashgate, 2004, p. 7.
11. Hunt, *The Alpha Enterprise*, p. 195.
12. P. Brierley, *Leadership, Vision and Growing Churches*, Christian Research, 2003, p. 18.
13. Finney, *Finding Faith Today*, p. 11.

14. S. F. Brian, *The Alpha Course: an analysis of its claim to offer an educational course on 'the meaning of life'*, PhD thesis, University of Surrey, 2003.
15. Based on an idea by John Finney.
16. 'We are finding that on Alpha belonging comes before believing for many people.' Gumbel, *Telling Others*, p. 31.
17. J. Clarke, *Evangelism That Really Works*, SPCK, 1995, p. 14.
18. Gumbel, *Telling Others*, p. 224.
19. P. Ward, 'Alpha – the McDonaldization of Religion?', *Anvil*, 15/4, 1998, pp. 279–86.
20. G. Ritzer, *The McDonaldization of Society: An Investigation into the Changing Character of Contemporary Social Life*, Pine Forge Press, Thousand Oaks, California, 1996, p. xvii.
21. See V. J. Donovan, *Christianity Rediscovered: An Epistle from the Masai*, SCM Press, 1982.
22. Ward, 'Alpha', p. 286.
23. See for example Donovan, *Christianity Rediscovered*, pp. 84–91.
24. Gumbel, *Telling Others*, pp. 38–43.
25. See John Wimber, *Power Evangelism*, Hodder & Stoughton, 1985.
26. M. Percy, '"Join-the-dots" Christianity', review in *Religion and Theology*, 3, 1997, pp. 14–18 (p. 15).
27. Percy, '"Join-the-dots" Christianity', p. 16.
28. Gumbel, *Telling Others*, p. 60.
29. Brierley, *Church Growth*, p. 41.
30. Bob Jackson, *Hope for the Church*, Church House Publishing, 2002.
31. The United States office alone has approaching 20 staff. Figures provided by Mark Elsdon-Dew, Director of Communications at HTB.
32. Nicky Gumbel, *A Life Worth Living*, Kingsway, 1994; *Searching Issues*, Kingsway, 1994; *Challenging Lifestyle*, Kingsway, 1996; *The Heart of Revival*, Kingsway, 1997.
33. Both were using Gumbel, *A Life Worth Living*.

Chapter 3 Emmaus – a 'journey' approach

1. (The high percentage (30 per cent) of people coming to faith on the Credo course needs to be treated with some caution. The statistical sample is much smaller – only 12 parishes were using Credo, compared with 91 for Emmaus and 148 for Alpha – and half of those recorded as coming to faith on Credo came from a single parish, where the particular incumbent's enthusiasm for this particular course may have influenced his interpretation of the question asked.)
2. P. Brierley, *Leadership, Vision and Growing Churches*, Christian Research, 2003. (Available from Christian Research, Vision Building, 4 Footscray Road, Eltham, London, SE9 2TZ, price £1.)
3. P. Ball, *Adult Believing*, Mowbray, 1988, and *Adult Way to Faith*, Mowbray, 1992.
4. See Church of England, House of Bishops, *On the Way: Towards an Integrated Approach to Christian Education,* chapter 3.
5. C. Smith, *Emmaus, The Way of Faith,* on http://home.onet.co.uk/trushare/ JA97BOOK.TXT
6. P. Richter and L. Francis, *Gone But Not Forgotten*, Darton, Longman & Todd, 1998, p. xii.

7. Charles Freebury, *Alpha or Emmaus? Assessing Today's Top Evangelistic Courses*, private publication (see p. 32), 2002, p. 21.

Chapter 4 Other courses – or write your own?

1. R. Tice and B. Cooper, *Christianity Explored*, Paternoster, 2002, p. 12.
2. Personal conversation with Canon Robert Warren at my home, 29 August 2000.
3. Charles Freebury, *Alpha or Emmaus?*, p. 22.
4. P. Meadows and J. Steinberg, *Beyond Belief*, Word Publishing, 1999.

Chapter 5 Missions and evangelists – a crisis within the process?

1. Frank Colquhoun, *Harringay Story*, Hodder & Stoughton, 1955, p. 232.
2. Colquhoun, *Harringay Story*, p. 233.
3. Derek Williams, *One in a Million*, Word, 1984.
4. From personal conversation, January 2003.
5. Church of England, Archbishops' Council, *Good News People*, Church House Publishing, 1999, p. 47.
6. Colquhoun, *Harringay Story*, p. 47.
7. From personal correspondence.
8. C. Peter Wagner, *Your Spiritual Gifts Can Help Your Church Grow*, MARC, 1979, p. 177.
9. Robert Warren, *The Healthy Churches' Handbook*, Church House Publishing, 2004, p. vii.

Chapter 6 Learning from the world Church

1. M. Sheard, 'The history, purpose, principles and future of companion diocese links in the Church of England' (paper presented at conference at High Leigh, February 2002).
2. Bob Jackson, *Hope for the Church*, Church House Publishing, 2002, pp. 87–8.

Chapter 7 Going beyond the Good Samaritan: community ministry and evangelism

1. Ann Morisy, *Beyond the Good Samaritan*, Mowbray, 1997, p. ix.
2. Morisy, *Beyond the Good Samaritan*, p. 5.
3. Faithworks Charter, Service to the Community, section 3.
4. Ann Morisy, *Journeying Out*, Morehouse, 2004, p. 156.
5. Peter Watherston, *A Different Kind of Church*, Marshall Pickering, 1994.
6. Samuel Wells, *Community-led Regeneration and the Local Church*, Grove Books Pastoral Series 94, 2003, p. 8.
7. Wells, *Community-led Regeneration and the Local Church*, p. 9.

Chapter 8 Children's evangelism

1. Gavin Reid, *To Canterbury with Love*, Kingsway, 2002, p. 36.
2. Jackson, *Hope for the Church*, pp. 37–8.

3. John Finney, quoted in Reid, *To Canterbury with Love*, p. 29, italics in the original. The percentages are each rounded down – there is no missing 1 per cent!
4. Reid, *To Canterbury with Love*, p. 40.
5. David Hay and Rebecca Nye, *The Spirit of the Child*, Harper Collins, 1998, p. 163.
6. Francis Bridger, *Children Finding Faith*, Scripture Union/CPAS, 1988/2000.
7. John Westerhoff III, *Will Our Children Have Faith?*, Seabury Press, 1976.
8. In addition to Anglican dioceses and many regional bodies within other denominations, the Churches' Child Protection Advisory Service is an important resource. (CCPAS, PO Box 133, Swanley, Kent BR8 7UQ. info@ccpas.co.uk)
9. Church of England, Board of Education, *Children in the Way*, National Society/ Church House Publishing, 1988. This report provided an important warning of the developing crisis in children's work. We question some of its emphases, but not its concern.
10. Within the Church of England, the *On the Way* report helpfully set the discussion of this issue in the wider context of Christian nurture.

Chapter 9 Focusing on church health

1. Christian Schwarz, *Natural Church Development Handbook*, BCGA, 1998.
2. This is in the context of his far wider study of church life in *Transforming Communities*, Darton, Longman & Todd, 2002, which is an excellent resource for church leaders.
3. Bob Jackson, *Hope for the Church*, Church House Publishing, 2002, p. 109.
4. From personal conversation.
5. Christian Schwarz and Christoph Schalk, *NCD Implementation Manual*, BCGA, 1998.
6. George Barna, *The Habits of Highly Effective Churches*, Regal Books, 1999, p. 98.
7. Schwarz and Schalk, *NCD Implementation Manual*, p. 90.

Chapter 10 Cell church

1. Jackson, *Hope for the Church*, p. 109.
2. John Pollock, *John Wesley*, Hodder, 1989, p. 160.
3. David Prior, *The Church in the Home*, Marshall Pickering, 1983.
4. Ralph Neighbour, *Where Do We Go From Here? A Guidebook for the Cell Church Group*, Touch Publications, 1990.
5. Source: http://www.accn.org.uk/whatiscell/whatiscell.htm#values
6. Source: Cell Church UK web site, http://www.cellchurch.co.uk/
7. Howard Astin, *Body and Cell*, CPAS, 1998.
8. Karen Hamblin from St Alkmund's, Derby, in *Cell Church Stories as Signs of Mission*, ed. Bob Hopkins, Grove Evangelism Series 51, 2000.

Chapter 11 Fresh expressions of church

1. *Report of Proceedings of General Synod*, July 2003, p. 238.
2. *Mission-shaped Church*, Church House Publishing, 2004, pp. 81f.
3. R. Gill, *A Vision for Growth*, SPCK, 1994, pp. 60–1.
4. Figures from G. Lings, *Encounters on the Edge* No. 15, Sheffield Centre, 2002, p. 5.

5. Presentation by Bob Hopkins and Claire Dalpra, record of Together in Mission/ Group for Evangelisation Church Planting Consultation, London Colney, 4–5 December 2001, p. 4.
6. V. J. Donovan, *Christianity Rediscovered: An Epistle from the Masai*, SCM Press, 1982, preface.
7. Foreword to *Mission-shaped Church*, p. vii.
8. Address to the Mission-shaped Church conference, London, 23 June 2004.
9. Robert Warren, *Being Human, Being Church*, Marshall Pickering, 1995, pp. 88–92.
10. See G. Lings, *Thame or Wild?*, Encounters on the Edge, No. 8.
11. P. Brierley, *The Tide is Running Out*, Christian Research, London, 2000, p. 161.

Chapter 12 Engaging with the search for spirituality

1. R. Warren, *Signs of Life: How Goes the Decade of Evangelism?*, Church House Publishing, 1996, p. 69.
2. David Hay and Kate Hunt, 'Understanding the Spirituality of People Who Don't Go to Church', University of Nottingham, 2000, p.14.
3. Paul Heelas and Linda Woodhead, *The Spiritual Revolution*, Blackwell, 2005.
4. Bob Mayo, 'Researching "Generation Y"', Ridley Hall newsletter, July 2003. See also Bob Mayo et al., *Ambiguous Evangelism*, SPCK, 2004.
5. Quoted in Church of England, Board of Mission, *Setting the Agenda: The Report of the 1999 Church of England Conference on Evangelism*, Church House Publishing, 1999, p. 14.
6. See S. Cottrell and T. Sledge, *Vital Statistics*, Springboard/Archbishops' Council, 2002.
7. P. Richter and L. Francis, *Gone But Not Forgotten*, Darton, Longman & Todd, 1998, p. 116.
8. G. Reid, *To Canterbury with Love*, Kingsway, 2002, p. 211.
9. Arthur Weiser, *The Psalms*, SCM Press, 1962, p. 261.
10. *In Good Faith: The Four Principles of Interfaith Dialogue*, The Council of Churches for Britain and Ireland, 1991.
11. Stephen Cottrell and Robert Warren, speaking during the Springboard Travelling School of Evangelism, Lichfield Diocese, March 2001.
12. Lesslie Newbigin, *The Gospel in a Pluralist Society*, SPCK, 1989, p. 227.
13. Graham Tomlin, *The Provocative Church*, SPCK, 2002, p. 60.

Chapter 13 Conclusion

1. Making statistical sense of attendance patterns is an area of live current debate. One brief and helpful way in is through Paddy Benson and John Roberts's booklet *Counting Sheep*, Grove Books Pastoral Series 92, 2002.

Bibliography

W. Archer and M. Finch, *Diocese of St. Albans: Adult Nurture Survey*, 2001

Howard Astin, *Body and Cell*, CPAS, 1998

Peter Ball, *Adult Believing,* Mowbray, 1988

Peter Ball, *Adult Way to Faith*, Mowbray, 1992

George Barna, *The Habits of Highly Effective Churches*, Regal Books, 1999

Paul Bayes, *Mission-shaped Church*, Grove Books, Ev67, 2004

Francis Bridger, *Children Finding Faith*, Scripture Union/CPAS, 1988/2000

Peter Brierley, *Church Growth in the 1990s: What the English Church Attendance Survey Reveals*, Christian Research, London, 2000

Peter Brierley, *The Tide is Running Out*, Christian Research, London, 2000

George Carey et al., *Planting New Churches*, Eagle, 1991

Steve Chalke, *Faithworks: Intimacy and Involvement*, Kingsway, 2003

Steve Chalke, *Faithworks: Stories of Hope*, Kingsway, 2001

Church of England, Archbishops' Council, *Good News People*, Church House Publishing, 1999

Church of England, Archbishops' Council, *Mission-shaped Church*, Church House Publishing, 2004

Church of England, Board of Education, *Children in the Way*, National Society/Church House Publishing, 1988

Church of England, Board of Education and Board of Mission, *All God's Children? Children's Evangelism in Crisis*, National Society/Church House Publishing, 1992

Church of England, Board of Mission, *Breaking New Ground: Church Planting in the Church of England*, Church House Publishing, 1994

Church of England, Board of Mission, *Setting the Agenda: The Report of the 1999 Church of England Conference on Evangelism*, Church House Publishing, 1999

Church of England, House of Bishops, *On the Way: Towards an Integrated Approach to Christian Education*, Church House Publishing, 1995

Philip Clark and Geoff Pearson, *Kidz Klubs: the Alpha of Children's Evangelism?*, Grove Evangelism Series 45, 1999

Frank Colquhoun, *Harringay Story*, Hodder & Stoughton, 1955

Steven Croft, *Transforming Communities*, Darton, Longman & Todd, 2002

Vincent Donovan, *Christianity Rediscovered: An Epistle from the Masai*, SCM Press, 1982

John Drane, *Cultural Change and Biblical Faith*, Paternoster, 2002

David Evans and Mike Fearon, *From Strangers to Neighbours*, Hodder & Stoughton, 1998

John Finney, *Emerging Evangelism*, Darton, Longman & Todd, 2004

John Finney, *Finding Faith Today*, Bible Society, 1992

Penny Frank, *Every Child a Chance to Choose*, CPAS, 2002

Penny Frank and Geoff Pearson, *Too Little – Too Late! Children's Evangelism Beyond Crisis*, Grove Books Evangelism Series 41, 1998

Charles Freebury, *Alpha or Emmaus? Assessing Today's Top Evangelistic Courses*, private publication, 2002

Michael Frost and Alan Hirsch, 'The Shaping of Things to Come: Innovation and Mission for the Twenty-first Century Church', Hendrickson, 2003

Rob Frost, *The Essence Course*, Kingsway, 2002

Claire Gibb, *Building New Bridges*, National Society/Church House Publishing, 1996

Eddie Gibbs and Ian Coffey, *Church Next: Quantum Changes in Christian Ministry*, IVP, 2001

Michael Green, *After Alpha?*, Kingsway, 1998

Michael Green, *Church Without Walls*, Paternoster, 2002

Nicky Gumbel, *Questions of Life*, Kingsway, 1993; new edn, 2001

Nicky Gumbel, *Searching Issues*, Kingsway, 1994; new edn, 2002

Nicky Gumbel, *Telling Others*, Kingsway, 1994; new edn, 2001

David Hay and Kate Hunt, 'Understanding the Spirituality of People Who Don't Go to Church', University of Nottingham, 2000

David Hay and Rebecca Nye, *The Spirit of the Child*, Harper Collins, 1998

Bob Hopkins (ed.), *Cell Church Stories as Signs of Mission*, Grove Books Evangelism Series 51, 2000

Stephen Hunt, *Anyone for Alpha?*, Darton, Longman & Todd, 2001

Stephen Hunt, *The Alpha Enterprise*, Ashgate, 2004

Bob Jackson, *Hope for the Church*, Church House Publishing, 2002

J. Andrew Kirk, *What Is Mission? Theological Explorations*, Darton, Longman & Todd, 1999

Dun MacLaren, *Mission Implausible*, Paternoster, 2004

Bob Mayo et al., *Ambiguous Evangelism*, SPCK, 2004

Ann Morisy, *Beyond the Good Samaritan: Community Ministry and Mission*, Continuum, 1997

Ann Morisy, *Journeying Out*, Morehouse, 2004

Michael Moynagh, *Changing World, Changing Church*, Monarch, 2001

Michael Moynagh, *emergingchurch.intro*, Monarch, 2004

Ralph Neighbour, *Where do we go from here? A Guidebook for the Cell Church Group*, Touch Publications, 1990

Lesslie Newbigin, *The Gospel in a Pluralist Society*, SPCK, 1989

Martin Percy, '"Join-the-dots" Christianity', review in *Religion and Theology*, 3, 1997

John Pollock, *John Wesley*, Hodder, 1989

Phil Potter, *The Challenge of Cell Church*, BRF, 2001

David Prior, *The Church in the Home*, Marshall Pickering, 1983

Gavin Reid, *To Canterbury with Love*, Kingsway, 2002

Yvonne Richmond et al., *Evangelism in a Spiritual Age*, Church House Publishing, 2005

Philip Richter and Leslie Francis, *Gone But Not Forgotten*, Darton, Longman & Todd, 1998

G. Ritzer, *The McDonaldization of Society: An Investigation into the Changing Character of Contemporary Social Life*, Pine Forge Press, Thousand Oaks, California, 1996

Sara Savage, 'A psychology of conversion – from all angles', in M. Percy (ed.), *Previous Convictions*, SPCK, 2000

Christian Schwarz, *Natural Church Development Handbook*, BCGA, 1998

Christian Schwarz and Christoph Schalk, *NCD Implementation Manual*, BCGA, 1998

Michael Sheard, *The Next Step!*, Diocese of Lichfield, 1999

Lawrence Singlehurst, *Sowing, Reaping and Keeping*, Crossway, 1995

R. Tice and B. Cooper, *Christianity Explored*, Paternoster, 2002

Graham Tomlin, *The Provocative Church*, SPCK, 2002

C. Peter Wagner, *Your Spiritual Gifts Can Help Your Church Grow*, MARC, 1979

Andrew Walker, *Voices from Africa*, Church House Publishing, 2002

Pete Ward, 'Alpha – the McDonaldization of Religion?', *Anvil*, 15/4, 1998

Pete Ward, *Liquid Church*, Paternoster Press, 2002

Robert Warren, *Being Human, Being Church*, Marshall Pickering, 1995

Robert Warren, *The Healthy Churches' Handbook*, Church House Publishing, 2004

Robert Warren, *Signs of Life: How Goes the Decade of Evangelism?*, Church House Publishing, 1996

Robert Warren and Robert Jackson, *There are Answers*, Springboard Resource Paper No. 1

Robert Warren and Janet Hodgson, *Growing Healthy Churches*, Springboard Resource Paper No. 2

Peter Watherston, *A Different Kind of Church*, Marshall Pickering, 1994

Arthur Weiser, *The Psalms*, SCM Press, 1962

Samuel Wells, *Community-led Regeneration and the Local Church*, Grove Books Pastoral Series 94, 2003

John Westerhoff III, *Will Our Children Have Faith?*, Seabury Press, 1976

Derek Williams, *One in a Million*, Word, 1984

John Wimber, *Power Evangelism*, Hodder & Stoughton, 1985

Margaret Withers, *Not Just Sunday: Setting Up and Running Mid-week Clubs for Children*, Church House Publishing, 2003

Margaret Withers and Paul Doherty, *Where are the children? Evangelism beyond Sunday morning*, Barnabas, 2005

Paul Yonggi Cho, *Successful Home Cell Groups*, Logos International, 1981

General index

Resurrection of Jesus: in Alpha course 24, 26, 39
in Christianity Explored 26
in Emmaus course 34, 39
Richter, P. and Francis, L. 38, 182
Ritzer, George 21
Roman Catholicism: courses *see* CaFE
and initiation of adults 38
and use of Alpha 24
Rule of St Benedict (quoted) 12

sacraments: in Alpha course 24, 28, 39
in Emmaus course 34, 39
and occasional worshippers 182-3
St Albans diocese: cathedral 178
church growth and decline 141, 142
and nurture courses 36
survey of process evangelism courses 16
St Thomas Crookes, Sheffield 155
Salvation Army, research 36
Savage, Sara 6
schools, school-based congregations 158
Schwarz, Christian 125, 126-30, 136, 187
Scripture Union, and children's evangelism 120
Searching Issues (Alpha) 28, 32, 40, 59
Senior Alpha 13
servant evangelism 103
Seth, Vikram 6
Sheard, Michael 82, 84
silence, in worship 182
sin: and Alpha course 31
and Christianity Explored 51
and Emmaus course 40
Soul Survivor festival 104
spirituality: authentic 63, 185, 186-7
'bolt-on' 41, 183
and cell church 187
of children 82, 110
and community ministry 187
DIY 175, 178
and Essence course 180-81, 188
and Generation X 175
and Generation Y 177-8
and important issues 175-6
insights from other faiths 184
modern search for 14, 174-87
pick'n'mix approach 175, 183
as route to faith 174-5

and starting where people are 179-80, 181
and suitability of courses 31
and Sunday services 181-3
Springboard 87
and church health 77, 138-9, 140
Start! course 14, 23
and cultural background 52
as preliminary to Emmaus 45, 53
strengths and weaknesses 49
starting where people are 39-40, 50, 53-4, 57, 61, 64, 99, 105-6, 159-60
and home-made courses 55, 57-8
and spirituality 179-80, 181
stewardship: and Alpha course 39
in Emmaus course 39
and spirituality 183
strategy for evangelism 4, 29, 191-2
for children's evangelism 106
long-term 16, 28, 31, 99-100
see also process evangelism
suffering: and Alpha course 59
and Emmaus course 40, 43, 59
and home-made courses 59
and Y Course 53, 59
Sunday school, loss of appeal 63, 120-21, 122
Sylvester, Jeremy 167

Telling Others (Alpha) 17
testimony, personal 30
theology: of the church 167-9
of mission 158-9, 164-6, 167-9
Through Faith Missions 75
Tice, Rico 23, 50-51
Tomlin, Graham 185
transfer growth 85, 151
Trinity: in Alpha course 28, 39
in Emmaus course 38-9

urban priority areas, courses for 23, 46, 52

Vanier, Jean (quoted) 141
videos: in Alpha course 22-3, 29, 30, 31, 44
in CaFE course 54
in Christianity Explored 50, 51
in Emmaus course 39, 40
in Start! course 52
in Y Course 53

Index of biblical references